SINGER
fashion
tailoring

SINGER
fashion tailoring

Jessie Hutton

Book design, art direction and
production supervision
Claire F. Valentine

GOLDEN PRESS • NEW YORK
Western Publishing Company, Inc., Racine, Wisconsin

about
the
author

Jessie Hutton is known to millions of women as the person who takes the mystery out of professional sewing techniques. As Director of Sewing Education for The Singer Company, she has pioneered in the development of new methods of sewing education for the woman who sews at home. And, as an author of the *SINGER Sewing Book* and numerous magazine articles and booklets, she has brought couturier fashion within the reach of the average home sewer.

In this book, Jessie Hutton opens up an exciting world hitherto closed to most home sewers — the world of "fashion tailoring." Through extensive research and experimentation, she has for the first time translated sophisticated tailoring techniques into easy-to-follow instructions. Step by step, she takes the reader from basic principles to the latest advances in methods.

"This book was created," she says, "to enable the sewer with moderate skills to experience the joy of becoming an expert."

introduction

To the home sewer, fashion tailoring brings a greater thrill of accomplishment than any other type of sewing. It also demands greater skill. If you have experience in dressmaking and wish to learn fine, custom tailoring methods, this book is for you. Developed for the Singer Fashion Tailoring course, it contains step-by-step directions illustrated by over 500 drawings.

The book is organized for convenient reference. The first section, pages 1 through 59, deals with basic principles that apply to any tailored garment. It explains how to choose and prepare tailoring fabrics and patterns; how to ensure a perfect fit by working with a muslin duplicate of your pattern; and how to shape a garment with layers of lining, underlining, and interfacing, using the techniques of padding stitches and expert pressing.

The second section, pages 60 through 166, answers specialized questions. For example, if you have a fitting problem, you can refer to the comprehensive section on alterations. If you are making a coat, you will want to refer to the chapter on coats. If you are using a plaid or diagonal fabric, leather, or fur, refer to the chapter devoted to your special fabric. And if your garment includes buttonholes or pockets, consult the chapters on these subjects.

Finally, beginning on page 167, you will find a number of charts, which summarize information that will help you to choose patterns, fabrics, and tailoring equipment.

contents

Chapter I

how to tailor a jacket or coat

preliminaries

The skirt, dress, or pants. If your jacket is part of a suit, finish the skirt, dress, or pants first. Turn and baste the hem in the dress or skirt, but delay final hemming until the hem length can be checked with the jacket over it. If a blouse is part of the outfit, finish it before making the jacket. This procedure enables you to fit the jacket more accurately.

Pattern. Choose a pattern of the brand, type, and size that most nearly fits you to minimize pattern alterations. Do not compromise on your pattern type — that is, Misses, Women's, Half-Size, Miss Petite, or Junior — or on your size within the correct pattern type. Each of these pattern types is drafted to fit entirely different body proportions, and you cannot adequately change one pattern type to conform to another. Since pattern size results merely from grading each pattern type to larger or smaller measurements, the pattern proportions do not change within a pattern type's size range. Always buy the same pattern size that you use for dresses. The extra ease you need for wearing a jacket over a dress or blouse, or a coat over a dress or suit, is already allowed in the pattern.

Styling encompasses all of the considerations that are taken into account by a fashion coordinator when combining a pattern with a fabric for an individual and for a specific fashion season. Ask yourself the following questions:

- Are the pattern and fabric fashion-right?
- Is this pattern style flattering to my size and proportions, and will it suit my personality and activity?
- Do the pattern and fabric complement each other?

Pattern catalogues and pattern envelopes give you a great deal of guidance. The illustrations in the catalogue and on the envelope suggest appropriate fabrics, and the pattern envelope carries the names of both appropriate and inappropriate fabrics.

Fashion fabric. Aside from styling considerations, select for a jacket a good-quality fabric that will shape with pressing and hold its press. Buy worsted rather than plain wool; suit-weight jersey or closely knit double knit; firm, permanent-press cotton or linen; fine tweed; firm, heavy silk: or high-quality fabrics of man-made fibers or blends.

1

Limp, soft fabrics are disappointing in jackets and should not be used.

For coats, select fashion fabrics with loft rather than harshness or weightiness. Pure wool, mohair, blends of wool and hair, cashmere, and camel's hair are traditional choices among wovens.

For durability, a high-quality, heavyweight double knit of all wool or all polyester is a good choice, and polyester can be worn in almost any weather.

For between-season coats and jackets, select cotton or wool tapestry, heavyweight silk, linen, and cotton, or blends of these fibers with polyester or nylon. Pile fabrics, especially corduroy, velveteen, and velour, are currently popular for many fashion looks. Fur-like fabrics are abundant and have their own special place in fashion, but they do require some special techniques in sewing.

Underlining. Most patterns suggest a supple, lightweight underlining for firm fabrics, and a slightly firmer underlining for medium-firm fabrics. An underlining provides a base layer to which the hand padding stitches and other hand stitches are anchored, resulting in less show-through of construction details on the outside. In some situations, the underlining also may act as a color shield, which prevents interfaced sections from showing through as shaded areas. You may need to use more than one weight of underlining; for example, across the upper back and shoulders a firm, shape-retaining fabric is required.

Interfacing. For fine, tailored jackets, use the finest quality hair canvas you can buy. The one that shapes best is an almost-balanced weave, in which warp (lengthwise) and weft (crosswise) yarns are almost the same size and weight. There are many kinds of hair canvas, so be sure to get the best kind for your jacket.

Interfacing for coats may be of a somewhat heavier quality hair canvas that is more rigid in the lengthwise than the crosswise direction.

Interfacing fabrics are sometimes recommended instead of underlining fabrics for underlining an entire coat or jacket since they can serve as a base on which to build shape and silhouette. It is best to follow the recommendations on the pattern envelope in these special fashions.

It is frequently recommended that interfacing of plain canvas or hair canvas be cut so that it supports the entire upper back and both the front and back armhole areas. Again, follow the pattern recommendations.

Lining. Jackets may be unlined, partially lined, or fully lined. The lining fabric for a jacket should be opaque, supple, smooth surfaced, and light in weight. It should be sufficiently porous to breathe so that it will be comfortable to wear. It should be dry-cleanable because most suit jackets will be dry-cleaned owing to their multiple-layer construction. However, if you plan to launder your jacket, the lining, as well as all other fabrics and notions, should be washable and preshrunk or shrunk by you. The fiber content should be such that pressing temperatures for the fashion fabric, lining, underlining, and interfacing are the same.

The lining fabric for a coat may be somewhat heavier than for a jacket. Traditionally, all-silk or synthetic satin fabrics are chosen because of their durability and because they enable you to slip into the coat easily. However, wool crepe, fur-like fabrics, and wool jersey or double knits are frequently used for aesthetic reasons as well as for added warmth.

fitting before cutting

A coat or jacket must fit impeccably; and to achieve this goal, you must consider your fitting needs before you cut the garment. There are two ways to proceed: 1) to fit by measuring and adjusting the paper pattern; 2) to make only the obvious pattern alterations, and then cut and fit a muslin shell. Experienced sewers who have made suits and coats, and who require only minor pattern alterations, may safely proceed the first way; all others should work with a muslin shell.

Pattern Alterations

Pattern alterations are the same for coats and jackets as for dresses; but the way you determine what to alter and how much to alter is different. More minimum basic ease is built into jacket patterns than dress patterns, and the amount varies in different pattern types and brands. The same is true of coat patterns, in which the amount of basic ease is even greater than in jacket patterns. Length measurements vary less than width or girth measurements; therefore, changes in the length of a coat or jacket pattern are easy to make accurately.

Remember that any changes you make in the garment pattern must also be made in the corresponding pattern pieces for facing, interfacing, and lining.

A reference chapter, "How to Alter Patterns," pages 143 to 166, and Your Measurements Chart, pages 168 and 169, provide additional detailed information.

Muslin Shell

If you have many figure differences to accommodate, or if you are making a coat or jacket for the first time, the most dependable way to fit is with a shell made from heavy-quality unbleached muslin. Or, for a coat of heavy fabric, or of leather-like or fur-like fabric, make the "muslin" shell of nonwoven interfacing fabric.

Alter your pattern before cutting the muslin shell, making only the large and obvious alterations. Later, when you fit the shell, make the small or subtle changes that are difficult to identify by a comparison of measurements alone.

Alter Pattern

The first step in altering your pattern before cutting the muslin is to compare standard body measurements given on your pattern envelope

with your measurements, using the chart below. Make a plus (+) notation if your measurement is larger and a minus (−) notation if your measurement is smaller than the pattern envelope measurement.

Pattern Size _____	Your Measurement	Pattern Envelope Measurement	Your + or − Difference
Bust (#2†)			
Waist (#11a†)			
Hip (#12 a or b†)			
Finished back length (#15†)			
Back waist length (#7†)			

† Measurement numbers on Your Measurements Chart, pages 168 and 169.

This first step enables you to adjust your pattern for the most important girth measurements (bust, waist, and hip) and length measurements when your proportions differ from the standard proportions that the pattern was designed to fit.

If your bust, waist, or hip measurement is *2 inches or less larger* than the *pattern envelope* measurement, do not alter your pattern, but do add 1 inch to each underarm and sleeve seam allowance when you cut the muslin, and mark the pattern seam lines on the muslin. Baste on the original seam lines for the muslin fitting.

If your bust, waist, or hip measurement is *2 inches or less smaller* than the pattern envelope measurement, do not change the pattern or the width of the seam allowances.

If your bust, waist, or hip measurement *is more than 2 inches larger or smaller* than the *pattern envelope* measurement, alter your pattern before you cut the muslin.

3

If your back waist length is 1 inch or more longer or shorter than the pattern envelope measurement, alter the pattern to the correct length before you cut the muslin. (You will alter the front in the second step, below.)

If the finished back length of a coat pattern is more than 2 inches shorter than your measurement after the back waist length has been corrected, add length at the lower edge of the front and back patterns before cutting the muslin. If the finished back length of a coat pattern is longer than your measurement, do not change the pattern now, but correct the length when fitting the muslin shell.

Refer to "How to Alter Patterns," pages 101 to 130, for making the above pattern alterations.

The second step *in altering your pattern* before cutting the muslin is to compare some actual pattern measurements with your body measurements plus ease allowances.

Use the group of measurements charted below to correct your pattern for the bust dart location and the front shoulder-to-waist length. Also correct your pattern for sleeve width, length, and elbow location.

Complete the chart below in the following sequence.
1. Transfer your measurements (actual body) from the chart on page 141, to column 1.
2. Add the standard ease allowance to your measurement and write it in column 3.
3. Measure your pattern in the same place each body measurement was taken. Do not include seam or dart allowances. Remember to use an accurate tape measure. Record measurements in column 4.

4. Ask the question, "Is the pattern measurement more (+) or less (−) than the total (column 3) measurement?" Record the difference in column 5 with the appropriate sign.

Alter your pattern to take care of any significant differences, following the appropriate instructions in "How to Alter Patterns."

The third step in altering your pattern before cutting the muslin is to consider any other major pattern changes that you always need to make in a dress pattern to take care of your figure characteristics. Remember, coats and jackets do not fit the body as closely as dresses; therefore, not all of the pattern alterations you apply to a dress pattern will be necessary for a coat or jacket. Do not over-alter your pattern, but do make as many pattern changes as you know are necessary. When you are in doubt about a pattern alteration, do not make it.

Cut and Mark Muslin Shell

Select only the major pattern sections for the muslin shell. These pattern sections include the front, back, sleeve, and under collar. Do not include upper collar and facing patterns or lining and interfacing patterns.

Lay out and cut the selected pattern sections on the muslin as carefully as you would on the fashion fabric. Observe pattern and fabric grain lines; cut extended notches; and carefully cut on the cutting lines of the pattern or on the new cutting lines if you have enlarged the pattern by adding to seam allowances.

Right-side markings. Using a tracing wheel and brightly colored tracing paper, mark all lengthwise grain lines, extending them the full length of the garment section. Mark center back and

Where to Measure	1. Your Measurement	2. + Standard Ease Allowance Suits	Coats	3. = Total	4. Pattern Measurement	5. + or − Difference
Front—Shoulder to apex of bust (#8†)		¼"	½"			
Front—Shoulder to waist, over apex (#9†)		½"	¾"			
Upper arm (biceps) (#13a†)		2¾"	4"			
Lower arm (forearm) (#13b†)		2½"	3½"			
Sleeve length (entire) (#14a†)		1"	1"			
Shoulder to elbow (#14b†)		½"	½"			

†Measurement number on Your Measurements Chart, pages 168 and 169.

4

Right Side Markings for Muslin Shell

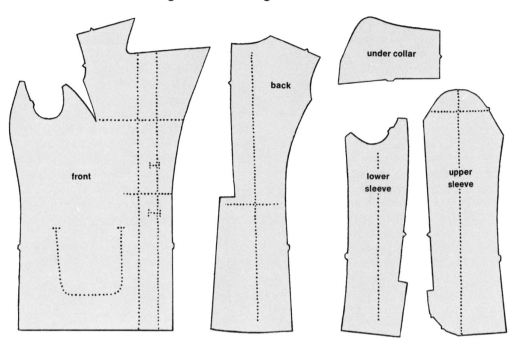

center front lines. Mark horizontal lines, perpendicular to the lengthwise grain line, at the bust, waist, and hip levels. On the sleeve, mark a lengthwise grain line, parallel to the pattern grain line, from the symbol at the top of the sleeve cap to the bottom edge of the sleeve. Also, mark a crosswise line, perpendicular to the sleeve grain line, at the level of the front armhole/sleeve notch. Mark buttonhole and pocket locations.

Wrong-side markings. Mark all seam lines and construction symbols, including the collar and lapel roll lines, with a second color of tracing paper. If construction symbols are of different kinds that might be easily confused, use more than one color of tracing paper. Mark all symbols that appear on seam lines and that must be matched with corresponding symbols for distributing ease correctly.

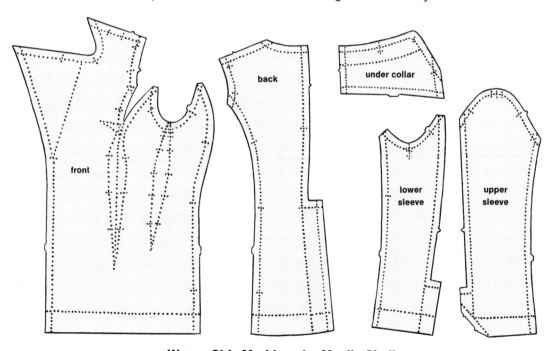

Wrong Side Markings for Muslin Shell

Assemble Muslin Shell

With 12 stitch length, stay-stitch the back neckline 1/8 inch outside seam line from center back to shoulder and the front from shoulder to lapel symbol; overlap stay stitching at center back. Slash back neckline seam allowance at 1/2-inch intervals to the stay stitching.

With right sides together and matching seam lines and symbols, pin all darts and sectional seams. Machine-baste, using a 6 stitch length and the Even Feed foot. Press darts and seams as you proceed. Pin and baste shoulder and underarm seams. Control the ease in the sleeve cap; pin and hand-baste sleeve to armhole.

Pin the under collar to the garment, overlapping the seam allowances, seam lines coinciding. Hand-baste on the seam lines from center back to lapel symbol, overlapping basting at center back. Tie threads at lapel symbol.

Press and pin sleeve and garment hems, and press the entire muslin garment neatly for the fitting step.

Do not topstitch or form welt seams in the muslin shell if they are shown in the pattern. Do not make buttonholes, apply pockets, or attach facings or interfacings.

Evaluate Fit

For trying on your shell, dress as you will when wearing the finished jacket or coat, keeping the thickness of your clothing similar. Shoes influence your posture, so wear the correct heel height. Shoulder shapes or pads must be used for this fitting if you intend to use them in your finished garment because they influence the fit of the entire garment.

Since tailored garments must be fitted precisely to body contours, you will find it helpful to have a knowledgeable friend work with you as you evaluate and correct the fit of your muslin shell. However, it is possible — though more time consuming — to evaluate the fit yourself and make corrections by the trial-and-error method.

Try on the muslin shell. Overlap the fronts, center front markings coinciding; and pin at each buttonhole mark.

Evaluate how the garment fits by observing the ten fitting check points listed below. Make no fitting changes until you have observed every point.

Ten fitting checkpoints

1. Center front and center back basting lines and side seams should be perpendicular to the floor. [A] and [B]
2. The amount of ease at the bust, waist, and hip should be adequate but not excessive, considering the additional fabric layers that will be added.
3. The front and back waistline markings should coincide with your waistline.

4. The shoulder seam line should be in the proper position and of adequate length. Observe both neckline and armhole ends.
5. The neckline should be neither too large nor too small, too high nor too low. Observe both back and front.
6. The collar and lapel roll lines should be in the correct position, and the collar at center back should be of a comfortable and appropriate height for your figure.
7. Buttonholes should be located to provide for normal arm movement without gaping.
8. Darts should be directed toward body curves but should not extend quite to the apex or fullest part of the curve.
9. Pockets should be positioned for function and design balance.
10. Sleeves should hang so that the lengthwise grain line is perpendicular to the floor and the crosswise grain line is horizontal to it. [C] on opposite page. Observe the sleeve cap for distribution of ease; observe also the sleeve width at upper arm, forearm, and wrist; and, sleeve length from shoulder to elbow, and elbow to wrist.

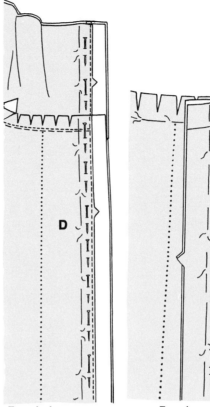

Correct the Fit

General procedures. You have a choice of four procedures to follow when correcting the fit of a muslin shell.

1. *Release the seam basting* and pin a new seam line outside the original seam line to make it larger, or inside the original seam line to make it smaller. The seam lines of both sides of a seam can be changed equally, keeping the seam in the same position [D] and [E], or unequally, repositioning the seam in relation to the body [F] and [G].

To release a short line of machine basting, clip every fifth stitch with pointed scissors and lift out each segment of thread; for a long line of basting, clip stitches on one side and pull the unclipped thread from the other side of the seam in one long piece.

To make larger, adding an equal width along each seam line.

To make smaller, removing an equal width along each seam line.

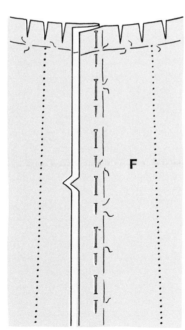
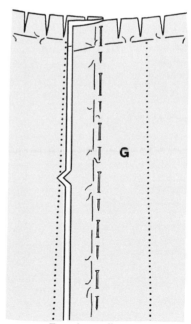

To make larger, adding unequal widths along each seam line.

To make smaller, removing unequal widths along each seam line.

2. *Without releasing the seam basting,* establish a new seam line by pinning a dart or tuck either centered on the basted seam, taking up equal amounts from each side [A] or near one side of

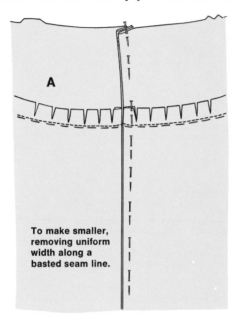

A

To make smaller, removing uniform width along a basted seam line.

the basted seam. [B] Later, remove the shell and redraw the seam line to take out an amount equal to the dart. The dart will then be eliminated.

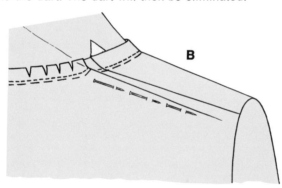

B

3. *Pin a dart or tuck within* a garment section rather than on a seam line to reshape and reduce the size of the garment section. [C] Later, alter the pattern by applying the appropriate pattern alteration as described in the chapter "How to Alter Patterns."

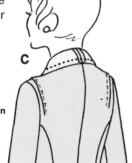

C

To make smaller within a garment section. (Later, alter the pattern to eliminate the fitting dart.)

4. *Slash and spread* the muslin; then add fabric under the slash. Let the slash spread an equal amount along the entire length [D] or an unequal

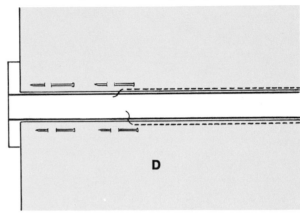

D

amount. [E] Pin and stitch the added fabric ¼ inch from the edges of the slash to form a wedge. Remember, the fabric section must lie flat when the alteration has been completed, and seam lines that join must be of equal length.

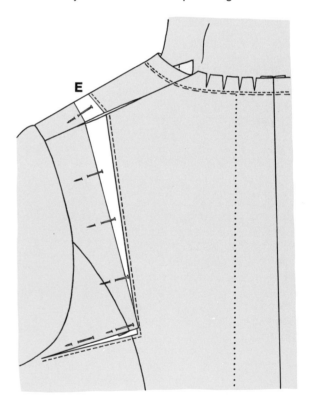

E

Fitting corrections will be different for each person, and the sequence in which the corrections are made will also be different. No one will require all fitting changes suggested. Make only those changes that you require. Decide which fitting corrections should be made on the basis of the fit of the muslin; for example, if the muslin is too small at the bust, a fitting correction will be needed in that area.

Too-small bust, waist, or hip

If the muslin clings to the figure or if it has too little ease at the bust, waist, or hip level, remove the basting from the underarm seams to allow the garment to hang freely. Refit, pinning new seam lines. Seam allowances may extend to the outside or inside, whichever is most convenient. Plan to re-evaluate the fit at these points after other above-the-bustline fitting changes have been made.

Too-wide back neckline

If the muslin is too wide across the back neckline, the shoulder seams will locate too far front near the neckline, or the neckline seam and collar will stand away from the neck at the back. Also,

the garment will not balance properly on the shoulders. It will at times pull to the front, causing the entire center back seam of the coat or jacket to pitch outward.

Before attempting to correct the fit, examine the back width from the neckline to the waistline and decide whether the entire upper back of the muslin is also too wide or whether only the neckline is too wide.

If the entire upper back of the muslin is too wide, correct the fit at the center back seam. Pin a dart, centered on the center back seam, starting at the waistline and continuing through the neckline and under collar.

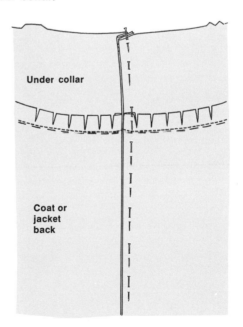

Under collar

Coat or jacket back

Take off the muslin shell, mark new seam lines on the back and under collar, rebaste, and try on again. Transfer alteration by redrawing seam lines on pattern sections for back, back facing, lining, under collar, and upper collar.

Take off muslin shell. Remove bastings at back neckline and shoulder seams. Measure the width of the dart; redraw each back shoulder seam line, removing a tapered amount like the dart. Also, re-draw the under-collar center back seam lines, removing the amount taken from the back shoulder seam. Machine-baste on new seam lines and try on again.

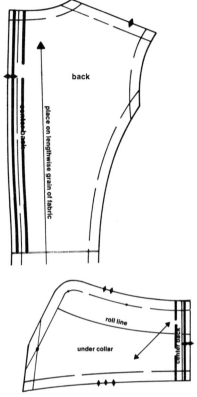

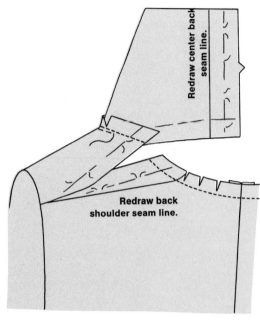

Transfer the alterations to the back and under collar. Also alter the back facing, upper-collar, and lining pattern sections.

If only the neckline is too wide, pin a dart near the back shoulder seam line on right and left sides.

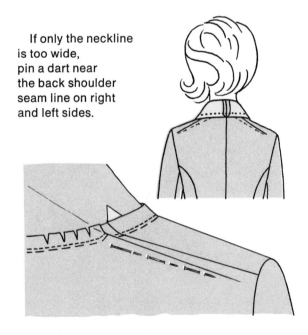

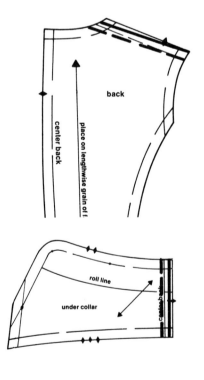

Too-narrow back neckline

Patterns are sometimes too narrow across the back neckline for women who have a large bone structure. When too narrow, the shoulder seams near the neckline will pull to the back and the back neckline seam may pull up, resting on the neck, where the body is narrower, rather than at the proper level.

If the entire upper back of the muslin is too narrow, correct the fit at the center back seam. Take off the muslin, remove the basting from the center back seams of the collar and garment to the waistline. Try on again and, with seam allowances extending to the outside, pin new seam lines outside the old. If the seam allowances are not wide enough for the increase needed, stitch a narrow strip of muslin to each edge and then pin the new seam lines.

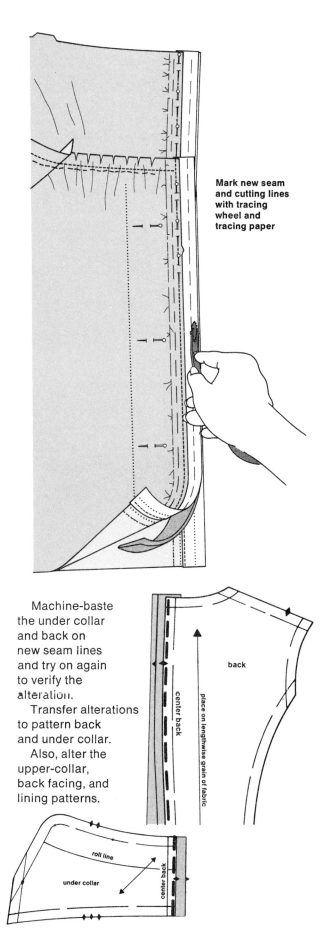

Mark new seam and cutting lines with tracing wheel and tracing paper

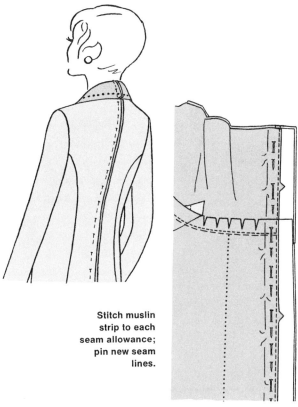

Stitch muslin strip to each seam allowance; pin new seam lines.

Take off the muslin shell, true the pins along the seam line, and mark new seam and cutting lines. Mark on the right side along and between the pins. Mark the position of the new cutting line $5/8$ inch outside the new seam line. Pin the muslin layers together an inch or more inside the new seam line to keep the seam layers from slipping, remove the pins along the seam line, and insert folded tracing paper. Using a tracing wheel, trace the new seam and cutting lines to back seam layers on the inside of the muslin. Cut excess fabric from new seam allowances on new cutting lines.

Machine-baste the under collar and back on new seam lines and try on again to verify the alteration.

Transfer alterations to pattern back and under collar.

Also, alter the upper-collar, back facing, and lining patterns.

back

center back

place on lengthwise grain of fabric

roll line

under collar

center back

If only the neckline is too narrow, take off muslin shell and remove basting from back neckline, center back of under collar, and shoulder seams almost to armhole. Baste a muslin strip to the back shoulder seam allowance. Try on again and pin a new back shoulder seam line by letting the folded front seam line overlap the back seam allowance. [A] Do not pin collar yet.

Take off muslin shell. Mark a new back shoulder seam line on each shoulder. Rebaste seams. To each side of under collar at center back seam line, add the same amount as at the shoulder. Rebaste center back seam of the under collar and the neckline seam. Try the shell on again to observe fit.

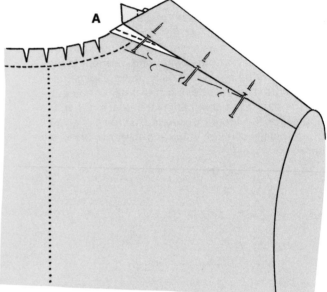

A

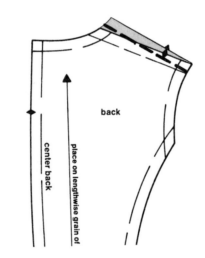

back

place on lengthwise grain of

center back

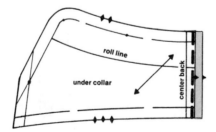

roll line

under collar

center back

Transfer alterations to back and under-collar patterns. Also alter the back facing, upper-collar and lining pattern sections.

Too-long back above top-of-armhole level

When a fold forms across the back at the level of the top of the armhole, and the armhole fits correctly at the underarm, the muslin shell is too long. This common fitting problem occurs with an erect posture where the head is held high, chin in, and back of neck perpendicular.

To fit the muslin, pin a horizontal dart starting with the deepest part at the center back and taper the dart to nothing at the junction of the shoulder and armhole seams. Keep the lower line of the dart on the crosswise grain line of the muslin. Repeat for a second side.

Take off the muslin shell; measure the entire width of the dart at the center back. Remove pins along dart. Mark a true crosswise line from center back to top of armhole on each side. At the center back seam line, measure from this line upward for the width of the dart and mark a point. Draw a line from that point to the end of the true crosswise line. Remove the center back seam basting across the dart. Slash the muslin on the true crosswise line and overlap the slash, bringing the cut edge to the line above. Machine-baste near the edge to hold the adjustment permanently in place. [B]

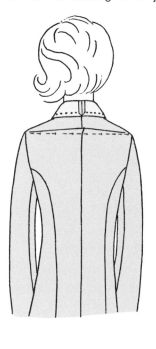

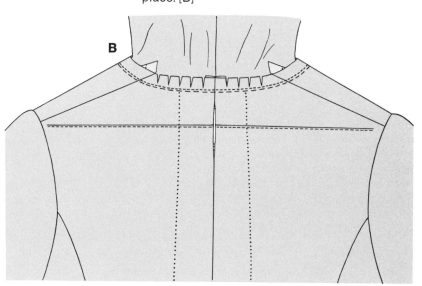

B

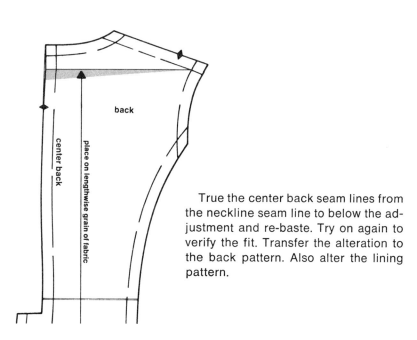

back

center back

place on lengthwise grain of fabric

True the center back seam lines from the neckline seam line to below the adjustment and re-baste. Try on again to verify the fit. Transfer the alteration to the back pattern. Also alter the lining pattern.

Too-short back above top-of-armhole level

When the neckline seam line is too low at the back but the shoulder seam is straight and the armhole fits correctly, the muslin is too short at the center back above the top-of-armhole level.

This fitting problem
occurs on women
who hold their head
at a forward tilt
thus enlarging
the prominent vertebra.

To fit the muslin, slash from center back along a horizontal line at the top-of-armhole level almost to the armhole. Let the slash spread until the neckline seam line is properly positioned. Prepare two muslin strips; pin ends together at the center. Place the strips under the opening, pinned seam at center; and pin along all edges. [A]

Take off the muslin shell. Mark the muslin strip along the edges of the slash, but do not un-pin. From the center back seam, remove pins and basting. True the adjustment, flattening the muslin on the table. Machine-baste near all edges and re-baste center back seam, allowing the slight curve that has been caused by the adjustment to remain in the seam. [B]

Transfer the
adjustment to the
back pattern.
Also alter lining
pattern sections.

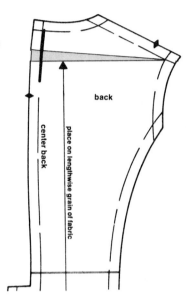

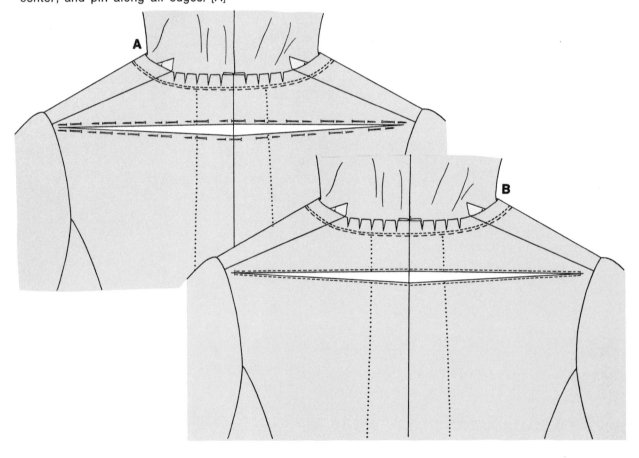

Too-long shoulder seam

The length of the shoulder seam varies with fashion, so study the fashion drawing on the pattern envelope before making fitting changes. Remember also to fit over shoulder pads if you plan to include them. When the shoulder seam is too long, pin a dart about 2 inches from the armhole, deepest part on shoulder seam line and tapering to nothing at the armhole notch level, on both front and back. Keep right and left sides the same unless your shoulders differ greatly in length.

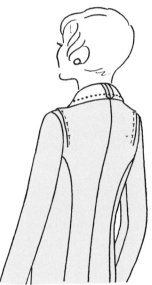

Take off muslin shell, mark along the pins and the fold of the dart. Remove pins and part of shoulder seam basting. Compare right and left sides and equalize the adjustments unless your shoulders vary greatly. Measure the width of decrease at the shoulder seam line. [C]

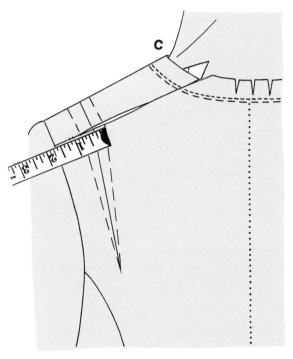

Refer to pages 158 to 160, for narrow-shoulder alterations. Work now with the patterns and apply the decrease as described to both front and back patterns. If you plan to cut your fashion fabric from the muslin, apply the same alteration to the muslin. Do the same if you feel the need to verify the alteration. Also alter interfacing and lining pattern sections.

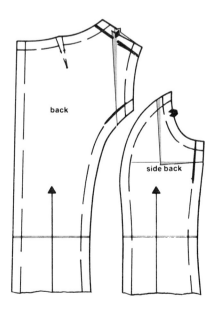

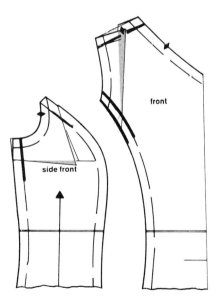

Too-short shoulder seam

When the shoulder seam is too short, refer to pages 116 to 118 for broad-shoulder alterations. Take off the muslin and slash through the shoulder seam about 2 inches from the armhole. On most styles, slash vertically both front and back and right and left sides to the armhole notch level; then, slash horizontally almost to the armhole seam line. On modified princess style, illustrated, extend vertical slash into side section and slash horizontally at the underarm level. Remove the shoulder seam basting for 2 inches on each side

of the slashes. To form underlays to accommodate the alteration, use four separate muslin strips. Pin and baste a strip under each slashed edge nearest the center. Anchor the outside section to the strip with pins. Try on the muslin shell, and let the slashes spread to elongate the shoulder seam properly; then pin the outer edges of the slashes to the underlays.

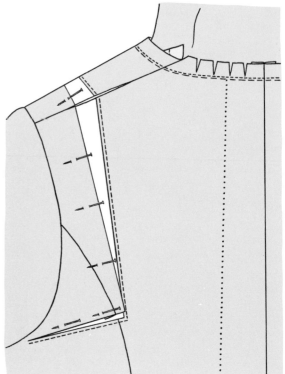

Take off the muslin shell; true the alterations, making them flat. Machine-baste near the edges of the slashes. Redraw the shoulder seam lines to straighten them. Rebaste shoulder seams and try on again to verify fit.

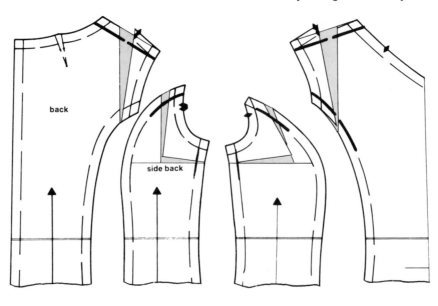

back

side back

Transfer alterations to front and back pattern sections. Also alter the interfacing and lining patterns.

Too-square shoulders

Horizontal folds will form at the underarm, tapering to nothing near the center of the garment, and the sleeve cap and shoulder seam will stand above the shoulder.

1. To correct, pin new shoulder seam lines front and back, decreasing equally from the basted seam line, tapering from nothing near the neckline to the needed depth at the armhole. The armhole will feel too tight and too high temporarily, but the horizontal folds should disappear.

2. Take off the muslin. Measure and note the width of the decrease at the point where the armhole and shoulder seam lines intersect. Remove pins and also remove shoulder seam and part of side seam, also armhole and neckline bastings.

3. Refer to pages 161 to 163 for sloping-shoulder alterations and proceed to alter the muslin in the same way, except for using fabric instead of paper to support the alteration and basting instead of taping. With tracing wheel and tracing paper, mark seam lines and symbols on the right side of the muslin. Alter the front and back, and right and left garment sections.

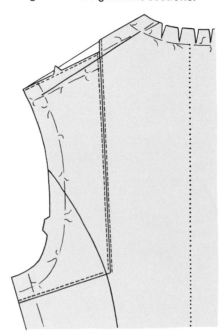

4. Baste shoulder, underarm, and collar seams and try on again to verify the alteration.

5. Alter the front and back garment sections. Alter, also, the facing, interfacing, and lining patterns.

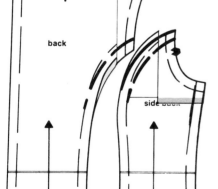

back

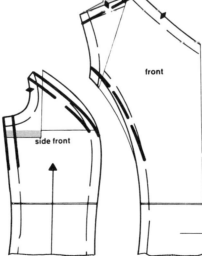

side front

front

Too-sloping shoulders

When diagonal folds radiate from the tips of the shoulders toward the center back, the shoulder seam is too slanted for a square-shouldered figure.

2. Try on the muslin and re-pin the shoulder seam, raising the seam lines at the armhole end. The diagonal folds should disappear but the arm-hole will be too low at the underarm.

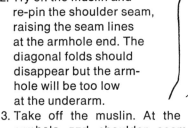

3. Take off the muslin. At the point where the armhole and shoulder seam lines intersect, measure from the original to the new seam line. Record this measurement; it is the amount of increase for this alteration.

Unpin shoulder seam, remove muslin strip and underarm seam basting for several inches. Also, remove under collar so that you can work on the garment more easily.

1. To correct, take off the muslin shell, remove the sleeves and the shoulder seam basting, and clip neckline basting at shoulder seam. Baste a strip of muslin to the edges of the front and back shoulder seam allowances temporarily for the next fitting step.

4. Refer to pages 161 to 163 for square-shoulder alterations and proceed to alter the muslin in the same way, except for using fabric instead of paper to support the alteration and basting instead of taping. With tracing paper and tracing wheel, mark seam lines and symbols on the right side of the muslin. Alter the front and back, and right and left garment sections.

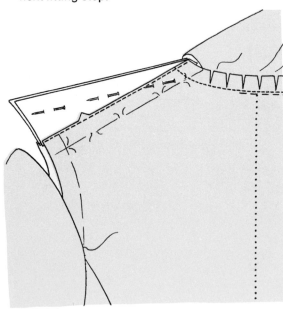

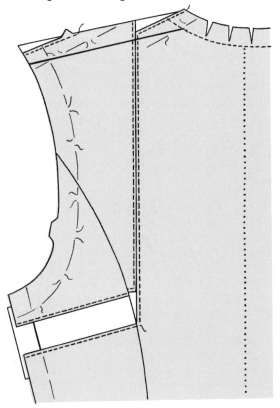

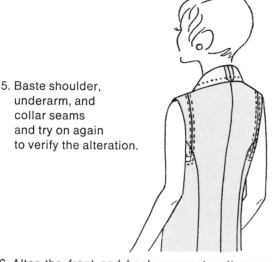

5. Baste shoulder,
   underarm, and
   collar seams
   and try on again
   to verify the alteration.

6. Alter the front and back garment pattern sections. Also lining, interfacing, and facing sections.

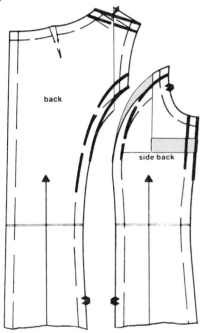

back

side back

Too-short back at shoulder-blade level

When the muslin shows strain over rounded shoulders, and the back armhole stands away from the body, the back of the muslin is too short over the shoulder blades. Refer to pages 143 to 145 for round-shoulder alterations.

1. To alter, cut the muslin horizontally on the crosswise grain at the fullest part of the back from center almost to each armhole, and let the slash spread. If the spread is 1/2 inch or less and the garment has a center back seam, remove the center seam basting and let the opened seam spread also. [A] If the spread is greater than 1/2 inch or if there is no center back seam, slash upward from the shoulder blades to the center of the shoulder seam. [B] Insert an underlay of muslin and temporarily pin along all edges, keeping the lower edge on the straight grain of the muslin underlay.

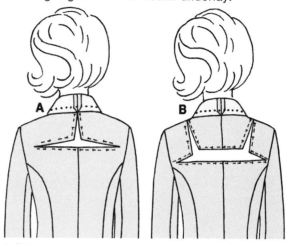

2. Take off the muslin, measure, and make a note of the width of each spread.
3. Next, work with the pattern to perfect and flatten the alteration. Mark and cut the pattern on a horizonal line perpendicular to the lengthwise grain line from center almost to the armhole at the same level the muslin was altered. Place tissue under the slash and tape the lower edge of the slash, keeping it perpendicular to the grain lines. Spread the upper edge of the slash the amount of the increase and pin it temporarily. [C]

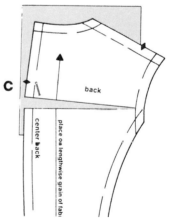

back

center back

place on lengthwise grain of fabric

You have three alternatives for completing the alteration:

The first alternative is to straighten the back grain line or center back fold line by creating a neckline dart. Mark a vertical line, centered on the pattern neckline, and cut from the neckline to horizontal slash. Tape the center part of the upper pattern section to the tissue underlay, keeping the grain or the back center fold line continuous and the increase equal to the measurement noted. The vertical slash will spread at the neckline. Remove the increase at the neckline seam line by marking a short dart. [D] Neckline darts will be stitched in the garment.

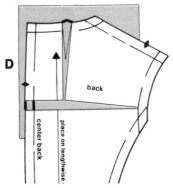

The second alternative should be used when the increase is less than ¹/₂ inch and the pattern has a center back seam. Tape the upper edge of the slash, draw the seam and cutting lines across the increase, and redraw the grain line above the slash, using the lower portion of the grain line for direction. [E]

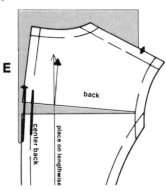

The third alternative should be used when the increase is more than ¹/₂ inch. Mark and slash the pattern from the center of the shoulder line to the largest part of the shoulder blade. (This slash can, instead, be made from the neckline end of the shoulder line parallel to the lengthwise grain for a straight-grain dart.) Keeping the center back fold or grain line straight and the increase equal to the

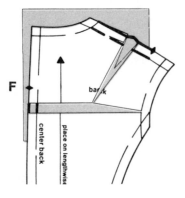

measurement noted, tape the center section at the upper edge of the horizontal slash to the tissue. Also tape the upper edge of the horizontal slash near the armhole. The vertical slash from the shoulder will spread, widest at the shoulder to nothing at the horizontal slash. Draw a short dart to remove the excess shoulder length. [F] Shoulder darts will be stitched in the garment.

Transfer the alteration chosen to the muslin, using the pattern as a guide. Reassemble the muslin garment for a fitting to verify the alteration.

Alter the back and lining pattern sections. Alter, also, the back reinforcement or interfacing pattern if there is one.

Note: For a figure with an extreme spinal curvature, carry the increase through the armhole and into the back sleeve cap. Refer also to the notation on opposite page for altering the front for a muslin that has a too-long front at upper chest level.

Too-long back at shoulder-blade level

The reverse of the round-shoulder alteration is sometimes necessary when the back is concave and the posture is very erect. Instead of slashing and spreading, fold and tuck in the same locations.

Too-long front at upper chest level

Refer to page 157 for hollow-chest alterations.

It is sometimes difficult to decide whether the muslin front should be shortened at the upper chest or at the bustline. Shorten at the upper chest when the grain line at the bust is level but the excess fabric is between the front neckline and the bustline. A person with a hollow chest, thin bone structure from front to back, or who carries her head at a forward tilt is likely to need this alteration. Many round-shouldered figures require this alteration.

1. To determine the width of the decrease, pin a tuck across the front, above the modified princess seam and below the neckline. Place the pins on the crosswise grain line and let the tuck fold slant, deepest at center front to nothing at the armhole seam line. Do not carry the tuck into the lapel.

2. Now work with the paper pattern [A] to perfect the alteration.

To position the horizontal tuck (a), draw a horizontal line perpendicular to the center front grain line at the same position as the tuck. Measure the width of the tuck in the muslin at the center front from pins to fold. Using this measurement, mark the pattern above the horizontal line. Draw a slanted line above the horizontal line to indicate the tuck fold line.

To prepare for separating the lapel at the center front line, draw another horizontal line from front edge to center front at the symbol at the bottom of the roll line. Cut the pattern horizontally on this line and upward on the center front line through the neckline edge, separating the lapel from the front.

To complete the alteration, fold and tape the horizontal tuck. Add tissue to the center front; tape. Redraw the center front line from tuck to neckline seam line.

Reposition the lapel section, matching neckline seam lines and abutting the cut edge against the new center front line. Let the bottom edge of the lapel section fall under the horizontal slash of the garment section; tape.

Redraw the seam and cutting lines of the lapel near the overlap. Redraw the roll line, following the original line on the garment section, and intersect the roll-line symbol on the garment where the tissue overlaps.

Alter the lapel facing [B], the under collar [C], and the upper collar [D] or refer to page 157 of "How to Alter Patterns" for way to restore the neckline to its original size. Alter, also, the interfacing and lining patterns to match the garment sections.

3. Transfer the alterations to the muslin to verify the fit.

Note: For a figure with an extreme spinal curvature, this alteration must be extended into the armhole and sleeve cap, which will shorten the front armhole and sleeve cap to accommodate the posture difference.

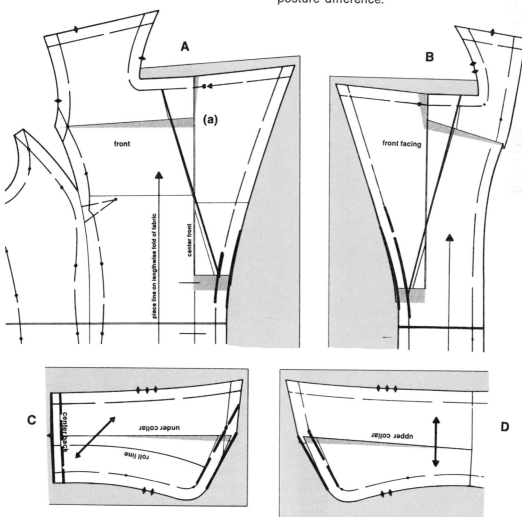

Too-narrow front at bust level

The altered muslin will indicate how much increase (or decrease) is needed at the bust level, but the final alteration must be perfected on the paper pattern.

Bust fitting may involve changing the width only, or it may involve changing the width and the front length. Observe the location of the waistline marking at the front.

When only the bust width must be increased, on a garment styled with darts, mark the crown (or apex) of the bust, and slash the muslin upward almost to the center of the shoulder and downward almost to the waistline. Let the slash spread and pin the edges to an underlay of muslin to hold the adjustment temporarily. [A]

For princess styling, open the seam and re-pin, making the increase entirely on the seam line of the side section if the original seam locates properly over the apex of the bust; or increase equally on both seam lines if the seam location is too far to the center.

For modified princess styling, open the seam to within an inch of the armhole and almost to the waistline; repin, making the increase entirely on the seam line of the side section. Add muslin to the seam edges of the princess or modified princess seams if the seam allowances are not wide enough to accommodate the increase temporarily.

When both bust width and front length must be increased on a garment styled with darts, mark the crown (or apex) of the bust. Slash upward

from the mark almost to the center of the shoulder and downward almost to the waistline. Also slash from the apex mark horizontally to the front edge and, following the underarm dart, slash just above the stitching line. Pin all edges of the slashes to strips of muslin to hold the increases temporarily. [B]

For princess or modified princess styling, a length change may be made in the same position as for darted styling.

Take off the muslin shell, measure and make notations of the increases, then perfect the alteration on your pattern, using the muslin only as a guide for the amount of increase.

Refer to pages 143 to 145 for large-bust alterations.

When your pattern has been altered, apply the same alterations to the muslin and fit again to verify the changes. In some situations where alterations are extensive, it is wise to cut a new front by the altered pattern.

Transfer the pattern alterations to all additional pattern sections affected, such as the facing, interfacing, and lining.

Too-wide front at bust level

Refer to pages 147 to 149 for small-bust alterations.

When the bust development is smaller than average, decrease the muslin in width and, when necessary, in front length by pinning tucks, instead of slashing and spreading, at the locations described above for a muslin that is too narrow at the bust level.

For princess [C] or modified princess [D] styling, decrease at seam lines equally when the seam lines locate too far from the center front, and unequally, on side section only, when they locate properly.

Alter pattern sections by redrawing seam and cutting lines, adding tissue where necessary.

Repeat the refined pattern alteration on the muslin, and baste and fit again.

Transfer the verified alterations to other pattern sections affected by the alteration, such as the facing, interfacing, and lining.

Too-narrow waist and hip

Increase the muslin to accommodate a larger-than-average waist and hip by increasing either equally or unequally at seam lines to position the seams perpendicular on the figure. [E]

Where there are no seams, slash and spread, adding muslin. [F] Alter only the back, only the front, or both back and front as required to keep the underarm seams properly located to bisect the body width and to be perpendicular to the floor. Alter, keeping center front and center back lines perpendicular, which may require increasing seams on one side more than the other. When differences in right and left sides occur on seam lines, alter the pattern to accommodate the larger side, and mark the seam lines for the smaller side from the muslin after the garment is cut. In extreme cases, cut right and left sides separately, using the muslin as a pattern, or make a duplicate section of the paper pattern and alter each side as needed.

Make the alteration on all pattern sections affected, usually the garment and lining patterns. Refer to pages 150 to 152 for alterations to increase waist and hip.

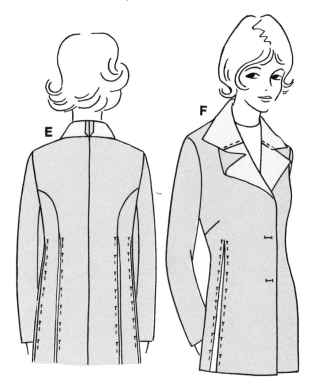

Too-wide waist and hip

Decrease the muslin at the waist and hip levels to accommodate smaller-than-average proportions by decreasing on seam lines or by pinning a tuck where there is no seam. Refer to the description above for too-narrow waist and hip and to "How to Alter Patterns," pages 150 to 152.

Sleeve grain-line position

The lengthwise grain line of a set-in sleeve should be perpendicular to the floor when the arm is dropped in a relaxed position, and it should extend from the natural shoulder seam to the lower edge of the sleeve.

The crosswise grain line should be perpendicular to the lengthwise grain line at the sleeve cap, front notch level.

When the crosswise grain line rises at the center, the sleeve cap is too short; and when it drops, the sleeve cap is too long.

Sleeve fitting should be done after all other fitting has been done above the waistline. If changes in armhole size have been made, the sleeve must be altered to accommodate the changes.

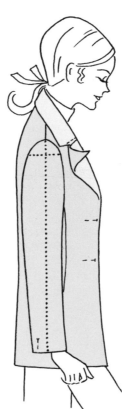

When fitting a muslin, if you anticipate alterations that might change the armhole, cut and fit the sleeve after the body of the garment has been fitted.

Too-short sleeve cap

When the sleeve cap is too short, slash the muslin on the crosswise grain line. Pin a muslin underlay to the lower edge of the slash, keeping fabric grains straight.

Try on the muslin, let the slash spread, and pin along the upper edge of the slash to hold the increase.

Take off the muslin, and measure the width of the increase at the center of the sleeve cap.

Working with the sleeve pattern, add tissue to the top of the sleeve cap, mark the width of the increase above the shoulder-line symbol, and redraw the sleeve-cap seam and cutting lines, tapering to nothing at the crosswise grain-line mark. Redraw the lengthwise seam and cutting lines of both upper and under sleeve patterns to remove most of the increased seam-line length.

Some of the additional length can be handled as increased ease in the sleeve cap. (To determine how much length has been added, stand a tape measure on its edge to measure the new and original seam lines.) Alter a one-piece sleeve by slashing and overlapping the slashes at the same positions as the seams in a two-piece sleeve.

Alter the sleeve lining pattern, also, if there is one. Cut fashion fabric and lining from paper patterns rather than from the muslin.

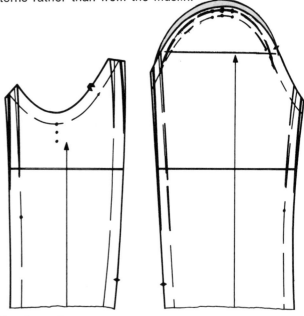

Too-long sleeve cap

To shorten the sleeve cap, pin a dart along the crosswise grain line, making the dart deepest at center and tapering it to nothing at the armhole seam lines. Measure the width of the dart at the center.

Working with the sleeve pattern, apply the decrease to the sleeve cap by measuring and marking below the pattern lines at the shoulder symbol. Redraw the sleeve-cap seam and cutting lines, tapering to nothing at the crosswise grain

line. Increase the lengthwise sleeve seam and cutting lines on both upper and under sleeve patterns to restore the sleeve-cap seam length as described above for the too-short sleeve cap.

Too-wide sleeve

When the sleeve is too wide, draped folds may form. To alter, pin a tuck along the lengthwise grain-line marking, carrying it as far down the sleeve as necessary. Measure the width of the tuck at the crosswise grain line.

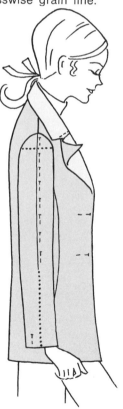

Working with the sleeve pattern, make the alteration for a thin arm, page 165.

Alter both the sleeve and lining patterns if there is a separate sleeve lining pattern.

It is also wise to examine the size of the armhole carefully to determine whether it is also too large, because this is frequently the case when the arm is thinner than average.

Too-narrow sleeve

Women who have large arms often need added length and width at the sleeve cap and more width in the entire sleeve.

To alter, slash the muslin on both lengthwise and crosswise grain lines. Pin a muslin underlay, which has been marked with corresponding lengthwise and crosswise grain lines, to coincide with the sleeve grain-line markings. Anchor the underlay at the top of the lengthwise slash.

Try on the muslin and let the slashes spread, adjusting the marked insert so that the lines fall in the center of the spreads. Pin along the edges to hold the adjustment temporarily. Take off the muslin and measure the width of the spreads.

Working with the paper pattern, make pattern alterations described on page 164 for large upper arm, or page 165 for a large arm (two-piece sleeve).

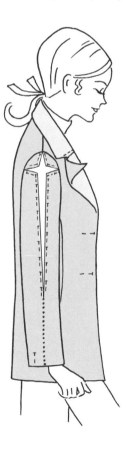

Alter garment and lining sleeve patterns. Do not try to cut from the altered muslin unless you have duplicated the pattern alteration in muslin, making the muslin flat.

Other sleeve alterations

Lengthening and shortening alterations may be needed to position the dart or elbow ease. Use the slashing and spreading technique to lengthen, and the folding and tucking technique to shorten the sleeve above or below the elbow as needed.

Elbow curve: When not enough ease has been provided in the sleeve at the elbow, the sleeve will bind at the forearm.

For a one-piece sleeve, to correct, open the sleeve seam below the elbow and slash at the elbow from the back sleeve seam edge on a horizontal line toward the front. Allow the slash to spread an estimated amount by pinning to an underlay. Form one large or three small darts at the elbow and rebaste the sleeve seam. Try on

to test the amount of increase and repeat, adding or subtracting, until the correct amount is determined.

For a two-piece sleeve, open the back sleeve seam from lower edge to elbow, slash at the elbow of the upper and under sleeve sections almost to the front seam. Pin edges of slashes to muslin underlays, letting the slashes on each sleeve section spread an equal estimated amount. Rebaste seam and try on. Repeat until the increase has been determined. The grain-line position will change within the lower sleeve sections.

Transfer the alteration to the sleeve pattern sections and redraw grain lines. Use the paper pattern sections for cutting the fashion fabric.

Collar roll line, stand and fall

The collar roll line separates the under collar into two parts, the stand and the fall. The stand is the portion between the roll line and the neckline that stands up against the neck. This is the section that is made rigid with small padding stitches taken through the interfacing and under-collar fabric.

The fall is the portion between the roll line and outside edge of the under collar. When the garment is worn, the collar turns on the roll line and the fall portion extends downward beyond the neckline seam.

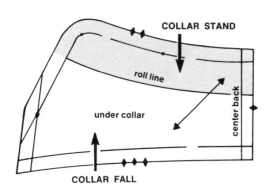

The correct height of a collar is governed by both fashion and figure proportions. A person with a short neck will be uncomfortable with a collar that stands too high at the center back, and her neck will look even shorter than it is. A person with a long neck will be equally uncomfortable with a collar that stands too low and her neck will look even longer than it is. Change the collar height at the roll line before the garment is cut.

Too-high collar

When the muslin collar stands too high at the back of the neck, place pins across the back through both the stand and the fall to indicate where the new roll line should be.

Take off the muslin and measure at the center back from pin to roll line. This measurement is the amount of decrease for the stand. Apply the same decrease to the fall.

Working first with the under-collar pattern, cut the pattern apart on the roll line. At the center back seam line, mark the position of the new roll line (amount of decrease) with a $1/2$-inch-long line, on both the stand and the fall pattern pieces.

Working next with the upper-collar pattern, place the stand section of the under collar over the upper collar pattern, matching all neckline symbols, and draw a roll line on the upper-collar pattern. Set aside the upper-collar pattern until you have completed the alteration in the under collar.

Lay tissue under the entire under-collar pattern, and work over a surface you can pin to, such as the ironing board or a piece of cardboard. Anchor the two under-collar pieces with pins, abutting the edges of the roll-line slash at the front seam line. The pins become pivot points.

At the center back seam line, lap the stand over the fall, new roll-line marks coinciding. Anchor with pins. The overlap will be widest at the center back, tapering to nothing at the front seam line, and the center back seam line will be slightly offset. Tape the overlap along the roll-line slash, and mark the new roll line in the center of the overlap.

Redraw the center back seam and cutting lines, using the neckline seam line [A] and the outside edge seam line [B] as points for determining a straight seam line. Redraw the grain-line arrow, extending the line of the fall section.

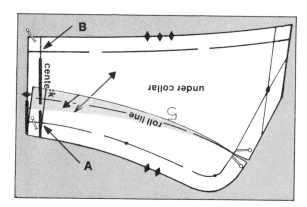

To alter the upper-collar pattern on which you have marked the roll line, cut the pattern apart at the roll line and at the center back, if the pattern is a whole collar rather than a half. Mark the decreases at the center back on the stand and fall pieces. Work as you did on the under collar. All seam lines (except center back seam, fold or slashed line) must abut so that they remain identical to the original pattern; the cutting lines may change slightly.

Draw a line on the tissue underlay to represent center back temporarily. Anchor the stand portions first, placing a pin at each neckline seam line [C]. Center the back on the drawn line of the tissue. Next anchor the outer edge seam lines of the fall pieces at the drawn line [D], allowing the roll-line slash to overlap, new roll-line marks coinciding. Do not pin at the overlap yet. The four pins now serve as pivot points, and enable you to move the stand and fall pieces to a position where all seam lines abut and the roll-line slash overlaps at the center back, tapering to nothing at the front. Tape the edges of the overlap, and redraw the center back line, using the outside and neckline seam lines as points for determining the straight line.

To verify the pattern alteration, cut a new muslin under collar; mark, assemble, and attach it to your muslin shell for another fitting.

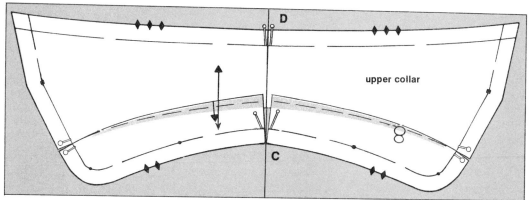

Too-low collar

Estimate the amount of increase by letting the collar roll above the marked roll line. Pin through both layers at center back and on each side of center. The fall portion will not extend over the neckline seam at this time.

Take off the muslin and measure from the roll-line mark to the new roll-line fold to determine the amount of increase.

Work with the under- and upper-collar patterns, as described for the too-high collar, but slash and spread the pattern pieces, adding the amount of increase to both the stand and fall pieces. Abut the outer seam lines, keeping them the same length as the original pattern.

Cut a new under collar of muslin from the altered pattern, and reassemble the collar on the muslin shell for a fitting to verify the alteration.

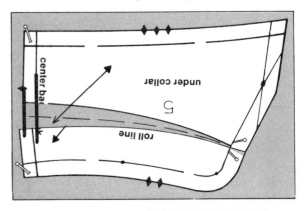

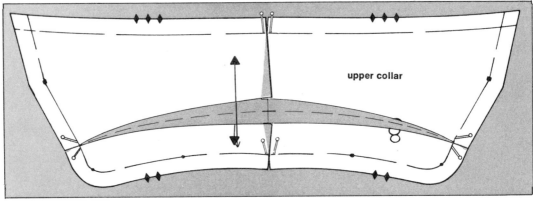

Too-long or short hemline

Make length corrections on the muslin, considering fashion, your proportions, and the proportions of the garment. Consider, also, adequate hem-width allowance for your fabric. Alter at the hemline in most situations, or slash and spread to lengthen, or fold and tuck to shorten within the muslin and pattern whenever design features are served best by using this method. Be guided by the lengthening/shortening lines on your pattern.

Other fitting considerations

Consider buttonhole and pocket markings as one of the final fitting steps, and reposition them if doing so will make them more fashionable or practical.

As you fit your muslin shell, you may find fitting variations that are not covered in the corrections described. No listing can cover every possible situation. However, those described will provide a foundation for fitting a muslin garment.

pattern preparation before cutting

You can cut a jacket or coat from the muslin shell or from the altered pattern sections; or you may, instead, cut from some muslin pieces and some pattern pieces. Whichever you choose as your pattern for cutting, all sections must be pressed to remove folds, all altered sections must lie flat, and all markings and symbols must be distinct. Use your pattern guide to select the pattern sections for cutting the fashion fabric and, as you prepare to cut each other kind of fabric, such as underlining, interfacing and lining, review again which sections should be cut.

There are three additional decisions that you must make about your pattern. The first concerns seam allowances on the collar and lapel interfacing. The second involves the lapel and collar allowances for shaping and concealing the seams along the outside edges. The third relates to the optional back reinforcement.

Seam allowances; collar and lapel interfacing

Look closely at the pattern sections for the collar and lapel interfacings. Do they include seam allowances on the outside edges? Usually the collar interfacing is cut from the same pattern as the under collar and it will include seam allowances. If a separate collar interfacing pattern is included that does not have seam allowances, add tissue and mark new cutting lines $5/8$ inch from the edges or seam lines.

For a garment with set-in sleeves, the lapel and front interfacing pattern should extend the entire length of the shoulder seam and either part way or all around the front armhole; and it should include seam allowances at the shoulder and armhole. It should also include a $5/8$-inch seam allowance on the lapel edge beyond the lapel roll line. It need not include seam allowances at the neckline, along the outside front edge below the roll line, or on any inside edges.

Whenever the necessary seam allowances are lacking, add tissue and mark new cutting lines $5/8$ inch outside the lines given.

Garments with raglan sleeves call for interfacing that does not extend to the sleeve seam, but all other needed seam allowances are the same as on garments with set-in sleeves.

Lapel and collar allowances for shaping

Compare the facing and garment front pattern pieces by laying the facing pattern on top of the front pattern, matching end-of-neckline seam markings and the other symbols along the front seam line, especially the one nearest the roll line.

Notice that the lapel facing seam between the marking at the end of the neckline seam and the lapel point is both longer and higher ($1/8$ to $1/4$ inch more) than the corresponding seam on the garment front. Notice also that the lapel facing seam line begins to angle outward from the garment seam line at the pattern symbol nearest the roll line and continues to angle away more at the lapel point. The lapel facing pattern is, therefore, both longer and wider than the garment lapel pattern.

On most patterns, you will see the words "stretch seam" printed along the seam line of the smaller side of the lapel. The added length and width provide ease across the lapel point so that, after the seam is completed, it will position slightly to the underside and will not be seen when you wear the jacket.

You will also notice that the roll line is not marked on the facing because its position will vary, depending on the fabric thickness.

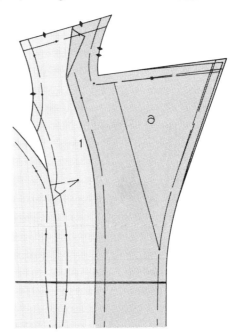

Now compare the collar pattern pieces by laying the under-collar pattern over the upper-collar pattern. The upper collar is both longer and wider than the under collar for three reasons:

1) to provide extra width across collar point, allowing the completed seam to be positioned out of sight;

2) to provide extra length to accommodate the roll at the collar back;

3) to provide enough ease for the collar to encircle the neck.

The under collar is cut bias to allow the seam edges on each side of the corners to be stretched when they are seamed to the upper collar.

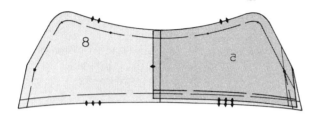

If your pattern does not include these allowances for shaping, add tissue to the lapel facing and upper-collar outside edges, and redraw seam and cutting lines outside the pattern lines. Or, if your fabric is more bulky than the pattern was made to accommodate and you want to increase the amount allowed, add to the edges in the same way.

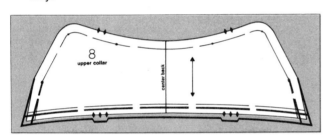

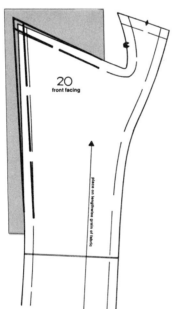

Optional back reinforcement

If you do not underline your entire jacket, and if your pattern does not call for interfacing to encircle the armholes, you may want to reinforce the back shoulder section to give permanent shaping

and better fit. Or, if you have chosen a supple underlining for the entire jacket, you may want to increase the firmness across the back shoulder section with a firm reinforcement.

Tweed, knit, or lightweight woven fabrics often need the additional body of this reinforcement.

Some patterns include a pattern piece for hair-canvas interfacing to be used across the back.

If no pattern is provided, cut one, using the jacket pattern as a guide. If the back has a straight-grain center seam, pin the pattern pieces together with the seam lines coinciding, cut the reinforcement pattern in one piece (6 to 10 inches deep at the center), and shape it to fit around the armholes. If the jacket pattern has seams that curve to produce roundness, cut the back reinforcement pattern according to the pattern. Plan to make plain, pressed-open seams, trimmed to half-width; catch-stitch along the edges to keep them open. If there are shoulder or neckline darts, plan to slash through the center; lap one edge over the other with the seam lines meeting in the center and stitch, using the multi-stitch zig-zag stitch. Press over a rounded press mitt or tailor's ham, and trim excess from edges.

When you attach the reinforcement to the back, place it over the wrong side of the assembled back section, matching center lines and seam edges. Pin, and then baste the reinforcement in place about 1 inch from the edges. Hair-canvas reinforcements may be treated the same as the interfacing at shoulder, underarm, and neckline seams; other fabric reinforcements should be included in the seam-line stitching the same as underlining.

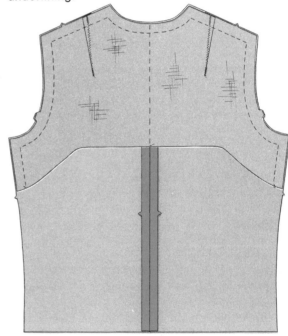

fabric preparations before cutting

Before you begin cutting your tailored garment, be sure to straighten the fabric for each layer — that is, the fashion fabric, underlining, interfacing, interlining, and lining. In addition, you may need to shrink and press each layer. And you will surely need to shrink and press all findings, such as tapes, bindings, and zippers.

Straightening. There are three methods for straightening the crosswise ends: to tear, to pull threads and cut along the drawn thread, and to square along table edges.

The tear method is appropriate only for firmly woven fabrics of even weave. The pull-thread method is the one most often used, but it cannot be applied to knit, bonded, nonwoven, or permanent-press fabrics. The method of squaring the fabric along table edges is appropriate for polyester double-knit, single-knit, bonded, nonwoven, and permanent-press fabrics.

To find out whether the crosswise yarns are on grain, fold the fabric lengthwise and place the selvage edge along the table edge. If on grain, the crosswise edges will be together and will follow the edge of the table. If off grain, the crosswise edges running from the fold to the selvages will slant away from each other.

To straighten most woven fabrics that do not have a permanent-press finish and some wool knits, pull the fabric in a diagonal direction to readjust the yarns. A damp steam pressing will sometimes relax the yarns enough to allow for straightening. Always re-check your straightening efforts by testing the fabric along the table edge.

Woven fabrics with a permanent-press finish and many wool knits cannot be straightened. These fabrics must be cut square along the crosswise ends.

Shrinking. Not all fabrics need to be shrunk. Those labeled Sanforized, guaranteed preshrunk, or ready to sew have been stabilized against further shrinkage by the manufacturer. All others should be shrunk by you. (And don't forget to shrink the findings as well.) If you omit this important step, the differences in fabric shrinkage will begin to show up as puckers during the pressing and shaping steps. And later, after the garment has been worn and dry-cleaned, it will be unsightly.

If you are doubtful of the need for shrinking a washable fabric, cut a 4-inch square on grain. Then draw a square the same size on plain paper. Immerse the square of fabric and, when it is almost dry, press lightly. Compare the two squares and, if the swatch shows shrinkage, shrink the entire yardage.

If shrinking is necessary, fold the fabric lengthwise, bringing selvages together, and match crosswise ends. Hand-baste along the two ends and the selvage edge. Snip selvages at 6-inch intervals.

There are four methods for shrinking fabrics, depending on whether the fabric care recommended is machine washing, hand washing, or dry cleaning.

Machine-washable fabrics: Place straightened and basted length of fabric in the washing machine and put it through the same cycle and water temperature you would use for the finished garment. Either dry the fabric in a dryer until almost dry, or hang to dry over a rust-proof shower rod.

Hand-washable fabrics: Immerse prepared fabric in a basin of warm water; squeeze out as much water as possible, but do not wring. Hang to dry over a shower rod. Remember to shrink interfacing, zipper, tape and seam binding at the same time. Also shrink underlining and lining if they are hand washable.

Dry-cleanable fabrics: You may choose either steaming or London shrinking. For steaming, take the prepared fabric to the dry cleaner. This is the best method for wools and worsteds.

For London-shrinking, saturate a sheet in warm water. Wring out excess water. Lay the wool cloth on the wet sheet. Check to see that each layer is smooth and free of wrinkles.

Fold the edges of the sheet over the ends and sides of the wool cloth. Begin at one end and roll loosely, avoiding wrinkles. Cover the roll with plastic or Turkish toweling to retain moisture. Lightweight wools become thoroughly damp in a few hours, but heavier fabrics require more time. Unroll the cloth, dry the fabric on a flat surface, and check grain lines.

Pressing. After shrinking, press the fabric if necessary. Press lightly and avoid creasing the fold.

layout, cutting and marking

Fabric layout. Plan to cut the fashion fabric first. Circle the pattern guide-sheet layout for the pattern view and fabric width. Use a with-nap layout so that the sheen and color of the fabric will be uniform throughout.

Place the fabric on a large table, folded or flat, the same way the guide-sheet layout suggests. Lay it with the lengthwise grain straight and the crosswise grain perpendicular. Make folds at one end of the fabric so that it does not hang off the table. Be sure that the pattern and fabric are wrinkle-free and flat.

Lay out all pattern pieces as shown on the guide sheet. Heed lengthwise grain lines, fold lines, and pattern pieces to be cut on a single thickness. Place pattern pieces as close together as practical. Anchor each piece at the top and bottom of the grain lines. Measure from selvage to each end of the grain line and adjust the position of the pattern so that both measurements are alike. Then pin pattern edges, 3 to 4 inches apart, at right angles to the cutting edges. Pins must not extend across the cutting lines. On curves or on slippery fabrics, place pins 2 inches apart.

If you are working with a special fabric, such as a plaid or diagonal, fur or fur-like, or leather or leather-like refer to the appropriate chapter for additional suggestions.

After all pattern pieces have been pinned or planned for, re-check for the correct number of pattern pieces and for the placement of the pattern grain lines on the fabric.

Cutting the fashion fabric. Use bent-handle shears and long, even strokes on straight edges and shorter strokes on curves. Cut notches outward, and cut double or triple notches in groups. Rest the lower blade of the shears on the table. Hold the pinned pattern down with your free hand, and do not lift the fabric to cut. Cut the entire garment and leave the pattern pinned on until the pattern markings have been transferred to the fabric pieces. Handle the sections carefully and as little as possible, keeping them flat and wrinkle-free.

Marking the fashion fabric. Pattern markings must be transferred to the cut fabric so that you can assemble and construct the garment accurately.

If you underline the entire garment, almost all pattern markings can be transferred to the underlining rather than to the fashion fabric. The exception is the under collar, where pattern symbols on the underlining are covered by the interfacing. If you do not underline the entire garment, transfer all pattern markings to the fashion fabric.

Marking methods. There are five ways to transfer pattern markings to fabrics: tailor's tacks, simplified tailor's tacks, tracing wheel and tracing paper, chalk (clay or wax types) and hand basting.

Tailor's tacks, the custom method of marking, will not rub off, press off, or mar the fabric. Tailor's tacks are recommended for marking all internal pattern symbols on the fashion fabric. [A]

Simplified tailor's tacks have the same advantages as regular tailor's tacks and are preferred for marking pattern lines as opposed to symbols on the fashion fabric. Use them for marking collar and lapel roll lines, pleat or fold lines, or lines for important stitching details. [B]

Tracing wheel and tracing paper are ideal for marking the underlining and interfacing. They may sometimes be used for marking the lining, but the color of the tracing paper must be light enough not to show on the outside of the lining fabric. Test on a scrap before using on the lining. If unacceptable, use tailor's tacks. [C]

Chalk, clay or wax type, is ideal for marking when construction is to be done immediately. Clay brushes off most fabrics. Wax chalk leaves a residue that may appear as a grease spot, but it can be removed with cleaning fluid. [D] and [E]

Hand basting is ideal for marking straight lines on the fashion fabric. Mark center front and center back lines with hand basting. Also, when the garment is to be fully underlined, use hand basting to trace stitching lines, dart folds, pocket folds, and center back or center front garment lines through both the underlining and fashion fabric. [F] See page 34.

Cutting and marking the underlining and interfacing. After you have marked the fashion fabric, remove the pattern and lay out the appropriate pieces on the underlining. Follow the pattern

(continued on page 34)

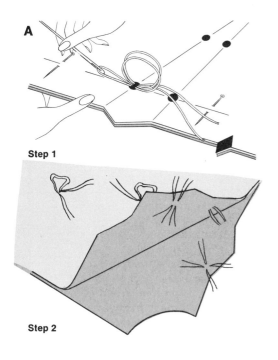

A

Step 1

Step 2

A. Tailor's Tacks
Step 1. With double thread, make two short stitches through pattern and both fabric layers, leaving a 3/4-inch loop in between. Lift pattern off fabric.
Step 2. Separate fabric layers, cutting threads as you go.

B. Simplified Tailor's Tacks
Step 1. With double thread, baste through pattern and both fabric layers. Make small stitches, 2 inches apart, leaving loops between stitches. Cut loops. Lift pattern off fabric.

Step 2. Separate fabric layers, cutting threads between layers as you go. Trace lines with long basting stitches for permanence.

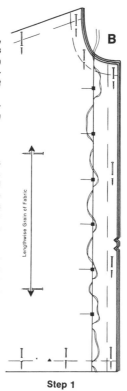

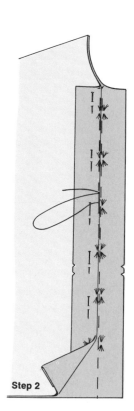

B

Step 1

Step 2

C. Tracing Wheel and Tracing Paper
Place right sides of tracing paper against wrong sides of fabric layers, one piece under the pattern, the second piece under the lower layer of fabric. Use a ruler to keep lines straight while you mark with tracing wheel.

D. Chalked Pins
Plunge pins through pattern and fabric layers. Lift pattern off fabric. Reposition pins as illustrated. Mark with tailor's chalk over the pins on one side. Turn fabric and mark over the pins on the other side. Always mark on the wrong side of the fabric. Remove pins.

D

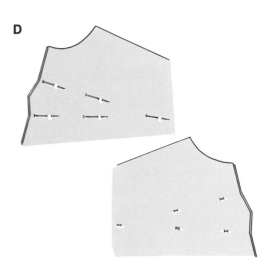

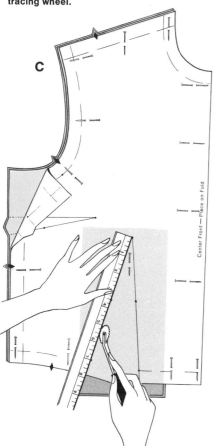

C

Center Front — Place on Fold

E. Chalked Thread
Using a needle threaded with a double strand of thread, wrap the thread around a square of tailor's chalk several times and pull until its entire length is covered with chalk.
Take a stitch through both fabric layers at each pattern marking, pulling the thread through entirely. Re-chalk thread frequently. Baste construction details immediately or trace marking with basting for permanence.

E

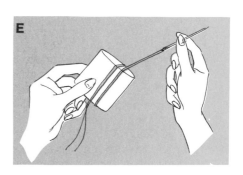

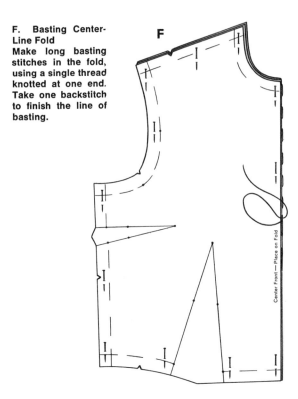

F

Center Front — Place on Fold

guide-sheet diagram for the fabric width. Remember that the underlining and fashion fabric are put together with the wrong sides of the fabrics facing together and that tracing marks are put on the right side of the underlining fabric. When you are cutting a pattern that has separate right and left sections that are cut singly, place the pattern pieces with the opposite side up from the way they faced on the fashion fabric.

Cut the underlining carefully and, with tracing wheel and tracing paper, transfer all pattern lines and symbols to the right side of the underlining.

Cut the interfacing, checking the pattern guide sheet for the proper selection of pattern pieces.

When cutting a one-piece collar that has a fold rather than a seam at the outer edge, cut the interfacing from the under-collar portion so that it will extend ½ inch beyond the fold. When cutting the front interfacing for a garment that has an attached facing, cut the interfacing to extend ½ inch beyond the facing fold line.

The lining and interlining may be cut now or later, depending on convenience. Neither will be required until the garment itself is entirely assembled.

first steps for constructing the garment

Prepare for First Fitting

Preparation steps vary, depending on whether you use a full or a partial underlining and whether you have fitted a muslin shell before cutting the garment. However, in all situations, fitting the garment at this stage is recommended to verify the fit of the fashion fabric.

For a fully underlined garment, pin each underlining to the corresponding fashion-fabric section, wrong sides together. If the garment section is small or if it contains a great deal of construction such as darts and shaped seaming, hand-baste, with the underlining side up, along the roll lines, seam lines, stitching lines, and dart center lines.

If the garment section is large and has only a few internal seams and darts, baste from the right side of the fashion fabric, using diagonal basting. This hand stitch is made with a single length of thread knotted at one end. Small horizontal stitches are taken parallel to each other at inter-

vals to form diagonal floats. Diagonal-baste down the center of the garment piece and near the cut edge to secure the underlining to the fabric.

Transfer symbols, previously marked on the underlining only, to both layers, fashion fabric and underlining, with thread tacks. Also, transfer important stitching lines with hand basting. Sometimes tracing lines disappear after steam pressing and before you want them to.

For a partially underlined garment or one that has no underlining, the above step may be omitted entirely, but make sure that all pattern symbols and important construction lines have been transferred to the fabric with tailor's tacks, simplified tailor's tacks, or basting.

Stay-stitch the back neckline from center to shoulder seam and the front neckline from shoulder seam to end of neckline symbols. Use a regular stitch length, but place stitching ½ inch from the seam edge (¹⁄₈ inch outside the seam line). If the garment has curved sectional seams, stay-stitch them also to preserve their shape while you work on the garment.

Assemble each section. When you have fitted a muslin shell, you may machine-stitch darts, sectional seams, under-collar center back seam, and sleeve seams; otherwise, hand-baste these seams. Whether basted or machine-stitched do not press, clip or trim these constructions until after the fitting has been done.

Baste sections together. Hand-baste side and shoulder seams; baste under collar to neckline. Do not attach set-in sleeves.

First Fitting
Try on the garment over the skirt, pants, dress, or blouse that will be worn with it, or over one of similar weight if the companion garment has not been made. Use shoulder pads if you plan to use them in the finished garment.

Lap the fronts so that the center lines coincide, and pin at the buttonhole markings. Check the fit, as outlined on page 6.

Make all fitting corrections on seam or dart lines only. When fitting the fashion fabric do not follow the same procedures as diagramed in the "Fitting Before Cutting" section.

Pin-mark all adjustments. Remove the garment, make the adjustments with basting and try on again.

Pull the sleeves up over the arm. Bring the armhole seam of the sleeve to overlap the armhole seam of the garment at the shoulder line. Match construction markings. Do not be concerned about the distribution of fullness in the sleeve cap, but check the sleeve for width, length, and elbow location.

After First Fitting
Trace all new seam-line locations with basting. Transfer all fitting changes to the partial underlining, the interfacing, the lining, and the interlining if these sections are affected.

Remove bastings from neckline, shoulder, and side seams to separate garment into sections. If darts and sectional seams have been permanently stitched and not changed by fitting, press and shape them, clipping as needed. If darts and sectional seams have only been basted, permanently stitch, clip, and press them.

Buttonholes
Make bound or corded buttonholes before applying the hair-canvas interfacing to the front. Make them through a stay of crisp, firm fabric or use a strip of press-on nonwoven interfacing if the strip will not show through to the right side of your fashion fabric. If you are using a firmly woven underlining, the stay may be omitted because the underlining will act as a stay.

Refer to "How to Make Buttonholes," page 117.

hair canvas interfacing methods

There are three methods of attaching hair canvas interfacing to the lapels and under collar of a jacket. All methods use padding stitches but to a different extent.

Padding Stitches
To make padding stitches, use a sharp, fine needle and a single length of thread that matches the fashion fabric. When making padding stitches in the stand of the under collar or on the lapel, pass the needle through the interfacing from right to left, catching the underlining and only a single thread of the fashion fabric; when working within the body of a garment, pass the needle through the underlining only. Rows made in alternating directions without turning the garment produce a chevron effect. Rows made in the same direction produce stitches that slant in a parallel fashion. Padding stitches may be long or short. Generally, use long padding stitches to keep

layers together as one, and short padding stitches to increase firmness, as in the under collar and the lapel.

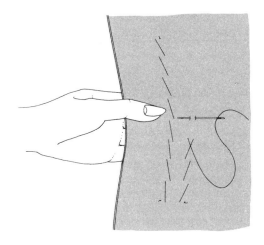

Method 1

For underlined jackets, the hair canvas is anchored with padding stitches to both the underlining and the fashion fabric within the collar stand and the lapel, and to only the underlining elsewhere. The front seams and the lapel and under-collar roll lines may or may not be taped.

The Under Collar is usually cut bias and seamed at the center back. On the fashion fabric, cut extended notches and mark symbols for shoulder-seam location, end of neckline seam, and any other important symbols with tailor's tacks. Mark roll line, if pattern indicates one, with simplified tailor's tacks. Cut extended notches on the underlining but not on hair-canvas interfacing.

Prior to the first fitting, pin, baste, and stitch the center back seam, including the underlining in the seam. Steam-press the seam open, and trim seam allowances to half width. [A]

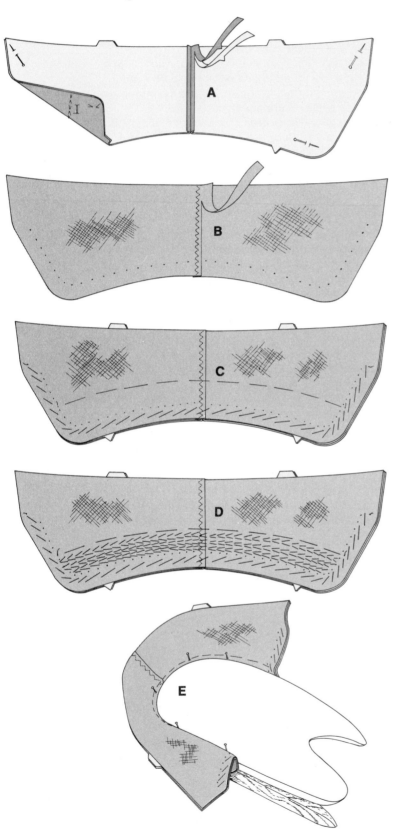

Prepare the hair canvas by marking ⅝-inch seam allowances along the neckline edge as far as the symbol and on the center back seam. Overlap seam allowances, matching seam lines at the center back, and stitch with the multi-stitch zig-zag stitch on the seam line. Trim the seam allowances near the stitching and press. [B]

Baste interfacing to under collar with diagonal basting within neckline seam allowance, leaving collar ends and outside edges free. Baste along the roll line, with even basting stitches through all layers, using the simplified tailor's tacks in the fashion fabric as a guide. After basting, remove the simplified tailor's tacks. [C]

1. Make closely spaced rows of short padding stitches through the under collar, the hair-canvas interfacing, and underlining, catching only a thread of the fashion fabric. Make the first row parallel to, and near, the roll line. Fill the entire area from roll line to neckline seam line with rows of padding stitches, working toward you on the first row and away from you on the second row, continuing to alternate the direction of each row. [D] Steam-press the stitched area, and allow it to dry before taking the next step.

2. With the interfacing uppermost, pin the interfaced under collar to the rounded end of a sleeve board, press board, press mitt, or tailor's ham. Keep the neckline seam edge down and the roll line along the top edge of the padded surface. [E]

Make a soft, *thin* roll of your wool pressing cloth, [F] and roll the collar over it. Use your steam iron

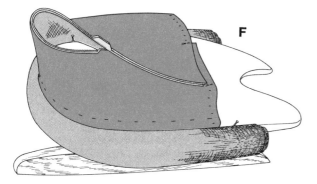

lightly to put steam into the rolled portion of the collar, but do not press a crease at the roll line. [G]

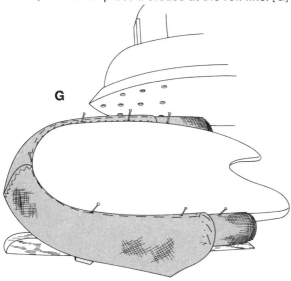

The fashion fabric will extend beyond the interfacing at the collar edge because of the roll. The extended amount will be greater if the fashion fabric is thick than if it is thin. Place pins parallel to the collar ends and lower edge about ¾ inch from the cut edges and through all fabric layers. Remove collar from the press board, but do not remove the row of pins. [H]

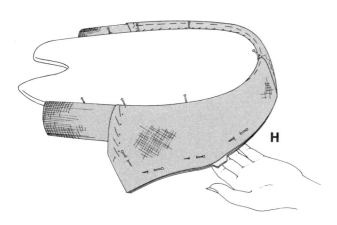

3. Now that the collar is shaped, you must preserve the shaping by working with it rolled at the roll line rather than in a flat position. Baste with diagonal basting within the seam allowance and through all layers along all of the remaining unbasted edges. Then measure ⅝ inch from the fashion fabric edge, and mark the seam line on the interfacing with pencil dots. [I] Make two rows of padding stitches close to, and parallel to, the seam line, and make a few single rows of padding stitches, following the grain line of the interfacing from the roll line to collar edge, stopping at the rows of padding stitches.

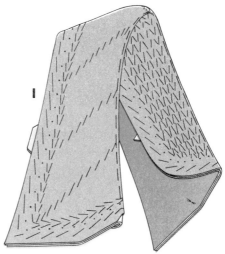

Cut off interfacing seam allowances, including pencil marks. Cut off outside corners of the interfacing diagonally ⅛ inch inside seam line to reduce bulk. [J] By cutting off pencil marks, you can machine-stitch near to, but not through, the interfacing when you join the under collar to the garment and the under collar to the upper collar.

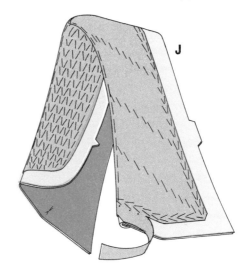

The Jacket Front

Mark the lapel roll line, all seam and dart lines, and all construction symbols on the underlining with tracing paper and tracing wheel, except for the seam line along the edge of the lapel beyond the roll line. Mark center front line with hand basting on the fashion fabric. Mark the roll line on the interfacing. Pin underlining to underside of jacket front, matching all edges very carefully.

Hand-baste through the underlining and fashion fabric, and make thread tacks on all symbols.

These bastings hold the two layers together accurately, and the thread tacks preserve the marked lines and symbols, which tend to fade when steam-pressed. Do not skimp in this step; however, you may use long basting stitches along long, straight lines, but always use short basting stitches on curves. Leave thread ends long so that they can be removed easily. [A]

1. From interfacing, cut off the 5/8-inch seam allowance at the front edge below the roll line and also at the neckline and shoulder seam. Some interfacing patterns are made to eliminate seam allowances in these places. Do not cut off the seam allowance beyond the roll line along the lapel edge, and if the interfacing pattern does not include a seam allowance in this area, you should have added one when you cut.

Pin the interfacing to the basted front section.

Match the lapel roll lines and pin. Bring the edges of the interfacing just to the basted seam and dart lines and pin. Baste along the lapel roll line through all layers; then baste ¼ inch from the interfacing edges, except for the lapel edge beyond the roll line, which should remain unbasted. Make short padding stitches along the neckline, shoulder, and armhole edges through the interfacing and underlining only.

Make long padding stitches over the entire interfacing area, except for the portion between the lapel roll line and the lapel edges. Stitch through the interfacing and underlining only. Make the first row of short padding stitches, starting just below the roll line and very near the front edge, working downward. Make the second row of long padding stitches, working upward and stopping at the roll line. Continue making rows of large padding stitches until the interfacing is covered except for the lapel. Steam-press the stitched area. [B]

2. Lay the jacket front right side up on a flat surface. Place a seam roll, or a wool pressing cloth that has been rolled firmly, along the lapel roll line, and turn the lapel back over the seam roll, keeping the basting line visible along the edge of the roll. Use your steam iron to put steam into the lapel near the roll. Then place pins parallel to the seam edges, allowing the fabric layers to adjust for the roll. The edge of the fashion fabric will extend slightly beyond the interfacing edge. If the fashion fabric is thick and bulky, the offset will be greater than if it is thin. [C]

Working with the lapel turned back over the seam roll, hand-baste the three layers together with diagonal basting within the seam allowance, and remove the pins. Then measure ⅝ inch from the edge of the fashion fabric, and mark the seam line with pencil on the interfacing.

Make short padding stitches through all fabric layers, starting near the lapel roll line and working in parallel rows, made in alternating directions, until the lapel is filled almost to the marked seam line. Make the padding stitches while the lapel remains rolled back over the seam roll. [D]

Remove the diagonal basting, and trim off the interfacing seam allowance, cutting away the pencil marks and cutting the lapel point diagonally.

Steam-press over the roll first; then, using your press mitt under the lapel, press the entire lapel.

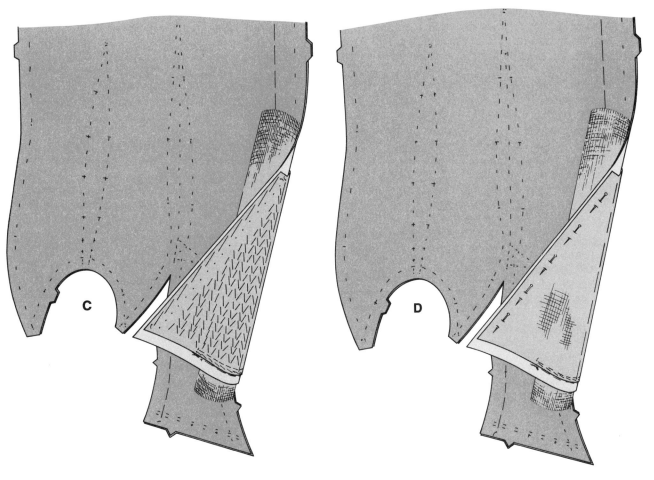

Method 2

For partially underlined jackets, the hair canvas is machine-stitched to organza or another thin crisp underlining fabric with multi-stitch zig-zag stitching. Then the hair canvas is cut off just inside the seam line to allow only the underlining fabric to be included in the permanent machine stitching, which attaches the upper collar and facing to the garment. Padding stitches attach the interfacing to the lapel from the roll line to the edge. The front seams and the roll lines may or may not be taped.

The Under Collar

Seam the fashion-fabric under collar and the firm, sheer underlining, such as silk organza, separately at the center back; press seams open; and cut seam allowances to half width.

Prepare the hair-canvas interfacing by marking $5/8$-inch seam allowances along neckline edge, collar ends, and along center back seam. Mark roll line. Overlap center back seam allowances, matching seam-line marks, and stitch with a multi-stitch zig-zag stitch. Trim seam allowances near stitching and press.

1. Baste hair-canvas interfacing to underlining with straight, even basting 1 inch from all edges. Set sewing machine for multi-stitch zig-zag stitch, 5 stitch width, and 20 stitch length. Stitch all edges, placing the outermost points of the stitch slightly more than $5/8$ inch from edge. Press.

2. Pin the interfaced underlining unit over fashion-fabric under collar, with inside of under collar next to underlining. Baste with straight, uneven basting on the roll line and along inside edges of the multi-stitch zig-zag stitching, along the neckline edge and the collar ends, leaving the outside collar edge unbasted.

3. Using the multi-stitch zig-zag stitch, machine-stitch through all layers along the roll line, and make additional parallel rows of stitching until the space between the roll line and the neckline is filled. (Instead of machine stitching, hand padding stitches may be used.) Tie thread ends. Press and shape collar at the roll line as in step 2 of Method 1, pages 36 and 37. Place pins through all layers, parallel to the ends and outer edges of collar.

Measure and mark the new seam line on the outside edge, then cut off the hair canvas including the pencil marks. With diagonal basting, baste the underlining and under collar together within the seam allowance.

With multi-stitch zig-zag, stitch the three layers together in three or more places along the fabric grain between the roll line and outer edge of collar to hold all layers together securely.

Trim remaining interfacing seam allowances to slightly more than $5/8$ inch so that the facing and undercollar units can be machine-stitched together on the seamline. [A]

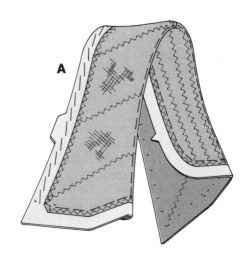

The Jacket Front

Using the jacket front pattern, cut a section of firm, sheer underlining, such as silk organza, so that it extends into the armhole seam and as far into the jacket as the first side front seam or long dart. It may be extended to the side seam if there are no sectional seams or long darts in the jacket front. Mark any darts that fall within this section with tracing wheel and tracing paper, cut extended notches, and mark roll lines. Mark all other construction details on the fashion-fabric section with tailor's tacks or basting lines.

Pin, baste, and stitch all darts separately in the fashion fabric and the underlining.

Cut hair-canvas interfacing by the interfacing pattern, allowing a full $5/8$-inch seam allowance on the lapel section opposite the roll line, if the pattern does not include it.

1. Baste interfacing to underlining and stitch with the multi-stitch zig-zag stitch, placing the outermost point of the stitching slightly more than $5/8$ inch from the edge. Press. Cut off the interfacing seam allowances slightly more than $5/8$ inch on all edges except the lapel edge opposite the roll line and the armhole seam allowance.

Pin the interfaced underlining unit over the fashion-fabric front section, with inside of jacket next to underlining. Baste with uneven basting along the roll line and along all edges, except the lapel edge opposite the roll line, placing the basting just inside the multi-stitch zig-zag stitching.

With catch stitching, join the underlining to the sectional seam allowance that has been pressed toward the center front. Make one row of padding stitches inside the roll line. [B]

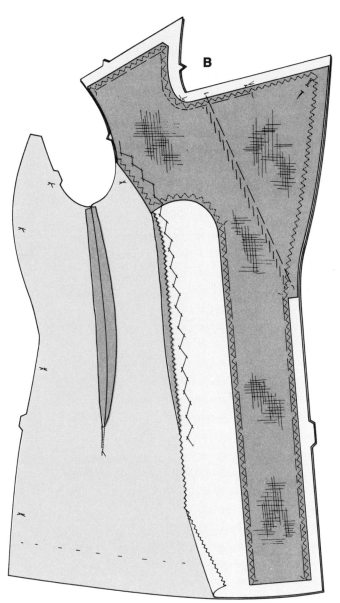

B

2. Shape the lapel roll as in Method 1, step 2, page 39, and pin, mark, and baste the interfacing seam allowance along the lapel edge. Make padding stitches within the lapel area, and cut off the interfacing seam allowance. Subsequent machine stitching will be placed outside the interfacing edge. [C]

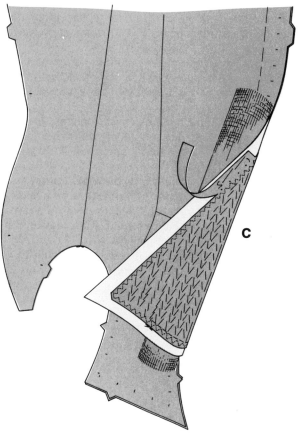

C

Method 3

For jackets without underlining, the hair canvas is cut off just inside the seam line and is anchored by hand with catch stitching. Padding stitches attach the interfacing to the lapel from the roll line to the edge. The front seams and the roll lines may or many not be taped.

The Under Collar

Seam the fashion-fabric under collar at center back; press seam open, and cut seam allowances to half width.

Prepare the hair-canvas interfacing by marking ⅝-inch seam allowances along neckline edge, collar ends, and along center back seam. Mark roll line.

Overlap center back seam allowances, matching seam line marks, and stitch with multi-stitch zig-zag stitch. Trim center back seam allowances near stitching line.

1. Pin the interfacing over the inside of the under collar. Baste along roll line with even basting, and long collar ends and neckline with diagonal basting, placed 1 inch from seam edge, leaving the outside collar edge unbasted.

2. Pin the top edge of preshrunk ¼-inch twill tape along roll line, and let the lower edge extend toward the neck edge. Stitch the tape in place with short padding stitches on both edges. Fill remaining area between tape and neckline seam line with rows of padding stitches. Trim interfacing seam allowances, trimming off seam-line markings. Catch-stitch over the interfacing edge slightly beyond the seam line.

Press and shape collar at roll line as in step 2 of Method 1, pages 36 and 37. Place pins through both layers parallel to the ends and other edge of collar.

Measure and mark the new seam line on the outside collar edge. Baste with diagonal basting 1 inch from collar edge. Trim off interfacing seam

allowance, cutting off marks and ⅛ inch at collar points.

Catch-stitch over the interfacing edge, slightly beyond the seam line. [A] To add firmness to the fall of the collar, make a few single rows of padding stitches from the roll line to the collar edge, as shown on page 37.

The Jacket Front

Stitch and press jacket front darts and seams. Baste the interfacing to the underside of the jacket front with straight basting along roll line, and with diagonal basting 1 inch from seam edges on all sides except beyond lapel roll line.

1. Catch-stitch over interfacing edges slightly beyond seam line. Keep catch stitches loose, and catch only a thread of the fashion fabric. Catch-

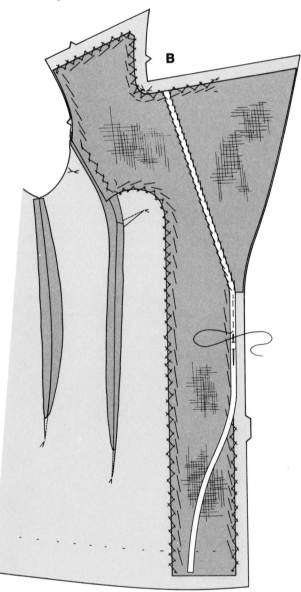

A

B

stitch the inside edge to the seam allowance that presses toward center front if there is one.

Pin twill tape, one edge along roll line, the other edge extending toward the body of the jacket. Make short padding stitches along both edges. Extend twill tape down front seam line, and baste with tape centered over the edge of the interfacing. Subsequently, when joining facing to jacket, the permanent stitching will fall alongside this basting and through the twill tape, but not the interfacing. [B] Taping is optional and is used on fabrics that require added firmness to prevent stretching. This procedure for taping may be used with Methods 1 and 2 if this added support is needed. Cardigan and V-neckline garments should be taped around the entire neckline. Garments with applied collars that button to the neckline should be taped up to the neckline seam line.

2. Shape the lapel roll as in Method 1, step 2, page 39, and pin, mark, and diagonally baste the interfacing seam allowance along the lapel edge. Then cover the lapel with short padding stitches to within ¾ inch of the seam line. Trim the interfacing seam allowance beyond seam-line markings. Catch-stitch over the interfacing edge slightly beyond the seam line. [C]

The lapel seam edges usually do not need to be taped and should not be taped at this stage of assembling the garment because the lapel front and top edges are usually stretched slightly to match the larger lapel facing.

Subsequently, when the facing is joined to the jacket front, the stitching will come between the interfacing edge and the catch stitches.

Staying Seams with Tape

In the seam. In Method 3, ¼-inch twill tape is centered over the seam line and is included in the permanently stitched seam. Use this in-the-seam taping method for shoulder, armhole, side, and neckline seams where stretch must be prevented. Fabrics with a great deal of stretch such as tweed, loosely woven novelty fabrics, and most coating fabrics respond best to this taping method. Substitute woven-edge seam binding for ¼-inch twill tape on lightweight silk or synthetic fabrics.

Adjacent to the seam. The ¼-inch tape may be applied adjacent to the seam line on the interfaced front of a garment. Some prefer to apply the tape before the facing is permanently stitched to the garment; others, afterward.

When the tape is applied first, the garment is less bulky to handle, but hand stitching may show on the outside.

When it is applied after the permanent stitching, the hand stitching is less likely to show, but the facing adds bulk to the garment being worked on.

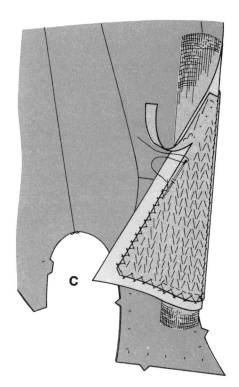

Furthermore, if your pattern indicates that the under collar and lapel seams should be stretched to match corresponding seams of the upper collar or facing, apply the tape *after* the seam has been permanently stitched.

Where there are no stretched areas in the under collar or front facing seams, apply the tape *before* the permanent stitching is done. Cardigan necklines, buttoned-to-neckline styling, and collarless necklines are examples of such styling.

Position the tape with one edge along the seam line and the other edge overlapping the interfacing. Pin, baste, and hand-stitch one edge to the seam line and the other edge to only the interfacing, using a flat hemming stitch or a catch stitch. [D]

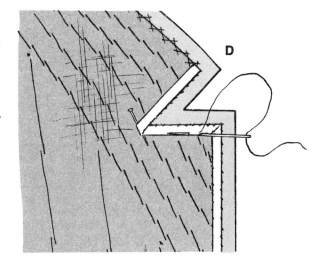

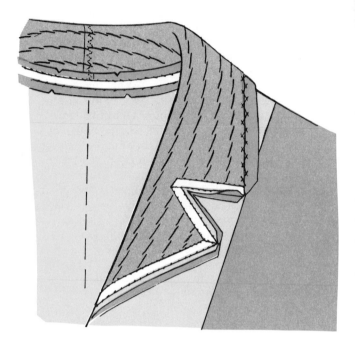

Over the seam. The back neckline seam, where the under collar joins the garment, is usually pressed open to minimize seam bulk, but it also should be taped to prevent stretching. Center ¼-inch twill tape over the seam line, and stitch each edge of the tape to a seam allowance with flat hemming stitches or catch stitches. Then trim the seam allowances to half width.

To shape twill tape. Twill tape may be pressed to conform to a curve before it is applied. Dampen the tape first. Then, using a steam iron, begin pressing at one end of the tape while you hold the other end taut and draw the tape into a curve as you move the iron. Narrow tape, ¼ inch wide, will curve more easily than ½-inch-wide tape.

Pin and baste the curved tape along the outside edge, letting it extend slightly beyond the seam line. Let the inside edge overlap the interfacing.

Whip the inside edge to the interfacing in lightweight fabrics.

Steam-press the basted tape, to make it conform smoothly to the curve.

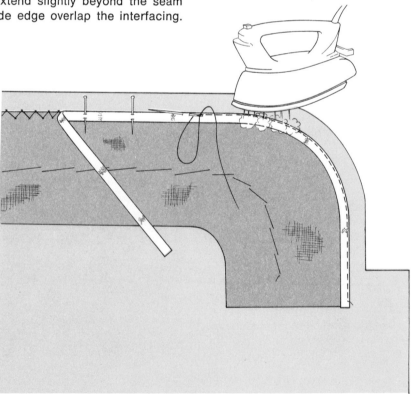

assembling the jacket

Shoulder Seams

There are two methods for handling shoulder seams.

In one method, include in the shoulder seam only the fashion fabric and the underlining. Press this seam open, and then extend the back reinforcement over the pressed-open seam. Overlap the front interfacing over the back, and catch-stitch the layers to the seam allowances. This method supports the shoulder seam more firmly than the second method.

In the second method, the back reinforcement and the front interfacing come only to the shoulder seam line and are held with catch stitches. Stitch the shoulder seams to include only the fashion fabric and the lightweight underlining. Press the shoulder seam allowances open, and secure edges with catch stitching.

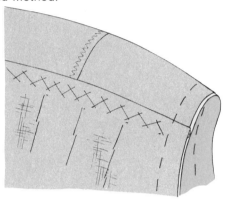

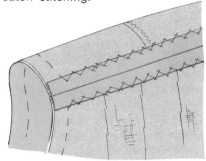

Shoulder seams made by either method may be taped, using the in-the-seam method or the over-the-seam method.

Attaching the Under Collar

When the shoulder seams have been completed, attach the under collar to the jacket before stitching the underarm seams. This allows you to work with the jacket in a flat position.

Important pattern symbols to heed are those that mark the exact seam-ending points on both the collar and front neckline, the center back, and the shoulder-line position. Work with the outside of the garment uppermost, and place the under collar on the garment, right sides together. Pin at center, at the ends, and at shoulder-line markings. Continue to pin at short intervals and clip into the neckline seam allowance almost to the stay stitching to relieve strain on the neckline seam allowance. Hand-baste with short, even stitches.

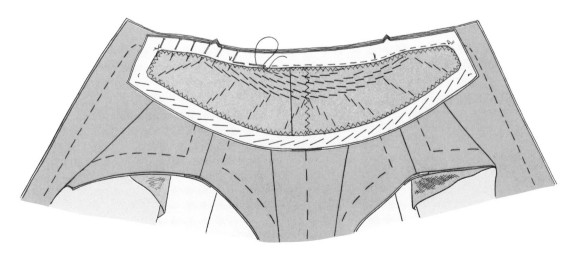

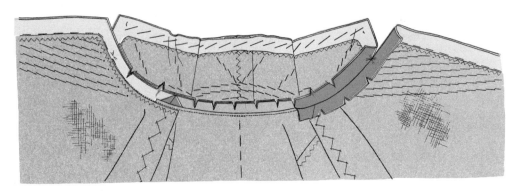

Machine-stitch exactly on the seam line, collar side uppermost, starting at the center back and stitching precisely to the end marking. Backstitch two or three stitches, draw threads through, and tie. Stitch second side, collar side up; overlap stitching at center back, and backstitch as before. The seam allowances will extend to the right of the presser foot for one side and to the left for the other.

Slash into the seam allowances at evenly spaced intervals so that they will lie flat when pressed open. Press the seam open.

Buttonholes in interfacing. The buttonhole seam edges should be brought through the hair canvas interfacing before the next step is taken. Hand-baste through the interfacing and garment layers around each buttonhole beyond the seam edges. Carefully slash through the center of the buttonhole, and from the interfacing trim a rectangular opening just large enough to fit around the stitching lines of the buttonhole. Draw the buttonhole seam edges through the opening in the interfacing, and handstitch them to the interfacing.

Joining facings and upper collar. Join front and back facings at the shoulders, and press seam allowances open.

Note: If your pattern does not include a back

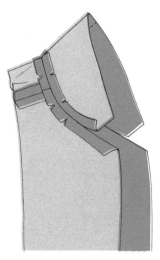

facing, cut one 3½ inches deep from the back pattern. To provide seam allowances on the facing and lining, remember to cut off the back lining only 2⅜ inches.

Inspect the facing and upper collar for important markings: center back, shoulder line, and end markings for the neckline seam.

Stay-stitch the facing neckline between the end markings.

Pin upper collar to facing, matching end markings, center back, and shoulder line. Baste with short, even stitches. Machine-stitch, following the same procedure as for joining the under collar to the jacket. Pull threads through to one side and tie. Press the seam allowances open.

Attaching the Facing and Upper Collar

The exactness with which you handle the seams that attach the facing and upper collar to the jacket unit has more to do with the professional look of your jacket than any other seaming step. When you understand what has been designed into the lapel and collar pattern pieces, you will be able to do this seaming expertly.

Review "Lapel and Collar Allowances for Shaping," pages 29 and 30.

Basting collar and lapel seams. Pin facing and upper collar unit to the jacket and under collar unit, matching all markings exactly. Lift neckline seam allowances so they are not caught in the basting, and stretch the seams where indicated on both the lapel and collar. Baste slightly inside the seam line so that the machine stitching can be placed just outside the basting, rather than through it. Use short even stitches and silk thread.

Stitching collar and lapel seams. To stitch the collar seam, start at the center back and place the under collar uppermost, letting the seam allowance extend to the right or left of the needle as it will, depending on which side you are stitching. Stitch just outside the basting on the seam line. Blunt the collar point by taking two or three stitches across the point rather than making a sharp point. Continue stitching only to the neckline seam, and backstitch two stitches. Remove from machine, and tie threads. Stitch the remaining side, overlapping stitching at center back, and tying thread ends.

To stitch the lapel seam, start at the roll-line marking and place the garment side uppermost, letting the seam allowance extend to either the right or left of the needle. Blunt the lapel point just as you did the collar point, and continue to stitch, stopping exactly at the neckline seam; then make two backstitches. Draw thread ends through to the facing side. Insert a hand needle at the junction of the neckline and facing seams; thread hand needle, and make two hand backstitches to reinforce the seam. This gives added strength at the notch of the collar.

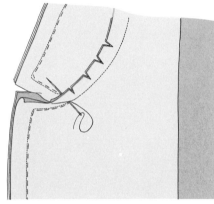

Stitch front seams below the lapel downward, facing side uppermost, and overlap stitching at roll line. Tie threads of overlapping stitching. These stitching directions are based on sound sewing machine principles.

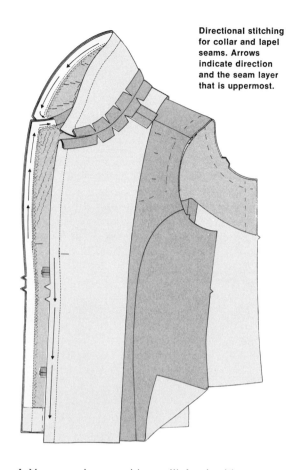

Directional stitching for collar and lapel seams. Arrows indicate direction and the seam layer that is uppermost.

1. Your sewing machine will feed with greater accuracy when you stitch toward, or into, a crossing seam than when you attempt to start stitching at the crossing seam.

2. A seam layer that is eased to another should always be against the feed.

Pressing, Trimming and Shaping the Collar and Lapels

There are 12 steps for completing the collar and lapels. Two steps (3 and 5) are optional, and two steps (8 and 9) offer the alternative to do one or the other.

1. To embed stitching, steam-press only the collar, lapel, and front facing seams; do not press the entire lapel or collar. Press seams from both sides. Do not lift garment from ironing board until it is dry.

2. Trim seam allowances to uneven widths, keeping the widest allowance next to the side that will be uppermost when the garment is worn, and trim collar and lapel corners diagonally to reduce bulk. Trim to the following widths:

Collar, under collar to 1/8 inch for thin fabrics, to 3/16 inch for thick fabrics. Upper collar to 1/4 inch for thin fabrics, to 3/8 inch for thick fabrics.

Lapel, above roll line — Garment to 1/8 inch for thin fabrics, to 3/16 inch for thick fabrics. Facing to 1/4 inch for thin fabrics, to 3/8 inch for thick fabrics.

Front, below roll line — Facing to 1/8 inch for thin fabrics, to 3/16 inch for thick fabrics. Garment to 1/4 inch for thin fabrics, to 3/8 inch for thick fabrics.

In garments without lapels and collars, trim seam allowance the same as the *front, below the roll line.* In garments with collars but no roll line, trim seam allowances the same as the *front, below the roll line.*

3. (Optional) If you have chosen to tape the collar and front seams adjacent to the seam line after the collar and facing seams are stitched, **do it now.**

4. Trim under collar and neckline seam allowances to ³/₈ inch, and catch-stitch the opened seam edges one to the under collar and the other to the front.

5. (Optional) Hand-stitch twill tape over the back neckline seam, which joins the under collar to the garment.

6. Press all collar, lapel, and front seam allowances open over a seam board, and protect the fabric with a press cloth. For polyester and wool fabric, you will need more steam than comes from a steam iron; so, to provide additional moisture, use a dampened cheesecloth, and control iron temperature according to your fabric. Silk fabrics usually can be pressed with the steam that comes from the iron. Press the seam thoroughly, but do not over-press or fuse the fibers.

7. Turn facing and collar to right side, and baste near the edges as you carefully position the seams to slightly favor the side that will be uppermost when the garment is worn. Silk-thread basting will not mar the fabric when you press over it, but almost all other kinds of thread will leave an im-print. Use straight basting near the seam edge if you plan to whip seam allowances in place from the inside, as in Step 9. Use diagonal basting, if you plan to hand-understitch the edges. Steam-press the seam edges from the underside, and protect the fabric with a press cloth.

8. Hand-understitch the seam allowances to the underside, reversing sides at the roll line of the lapel. (Steps 8 and 9 are alternative methods, depending on personal preference.)

To hand-understitch an enclosed seam, use fine, matching thread such as silk, and work from the underside within ⅛ to ¼ inch of the lapel or collar edge. Make two backstitches at the start rather than tying a knot. Pass the needle through all layers, except the outer layer that shows when garment is worn, making the stitch about ¼ inch long before bringing the point up through the underside of the collar, lapel, or front. Return the needle into the layers, making this stitch cross just one yarn of the fabric and continue. Remember to work always from the side that will be underneath when the garment is worn.

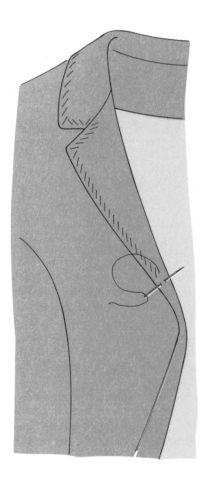

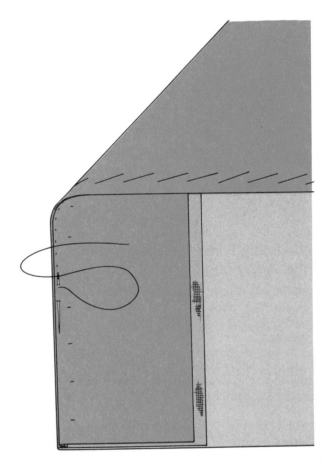

To hand-understitch a seam that is exposed, remove the diagonal basting that held facings for pressing. Work from the inside along the seam edge. Hand-stitch through the seam allowances and the under layer, keeping inside stitches about ¼ inch long and outside stitches only long enough to extend over one fabric yarn. Replace outside diagonal basting along lapel front and collar edges.

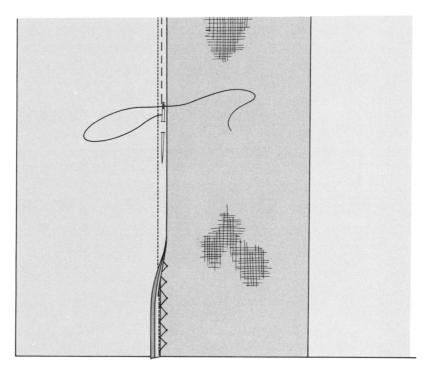

9. (An alternative method for Step 8 and one that requires straight basting in Step 7.) Roll the facing and upper collar back to expose the trimmed seam allowances. Loosely whip the seam edges to the interfacing while the outside basting holds them in position.

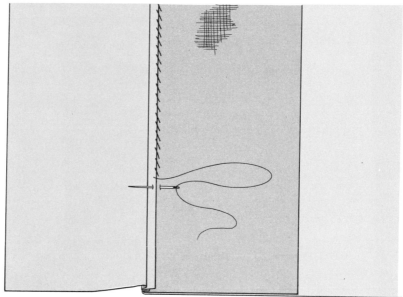

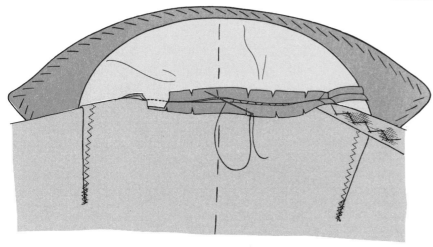

10. Slip-stitch the seam allowances of the back facing and the garment back together at the neckline, matching shoulder seams.

11. Steam collar and lapels to shape the roll. Lay the garment front right side up. Lightly roll a wool press cloth to fit under the collar and lapel along the roll line. Hold the collar around a seam-pressing board. Do not touch the iron to the collar, but put only steam into the collar and lapel roll. Let fabric dry before moving it. [A]

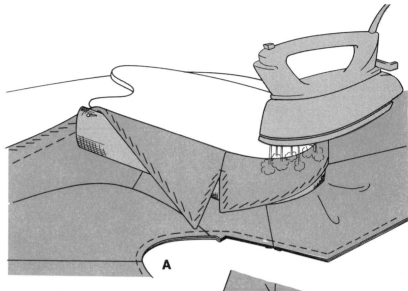

A

Remove the press cloth, and pin from the outside through all layers under the lapel and near the inside facing edge to hold the facing in place. Then baste from the inside with silk thread and remove pins. [B]

12. This step is done after sleeves have been completed, shoulder shapes or pads positioned, and the jacket hem completed. In jackets, catch-stitch the upper portion of the facing to the interfacing, and use a running stitch ½ inch from the edges to hold the lower portion of the facing and interfacing together. [C]

In coats or jackets where a wide facing is used, slipstitch the facing to the interfacing an inch or two inside the roll line working with the facing turned back to expose the interfacing and underside of the facing. Make these stitches through only the interfacing and a thread of the facing. Do the same down the front in the center of the facing. Then control the facing edges as described above. [D]

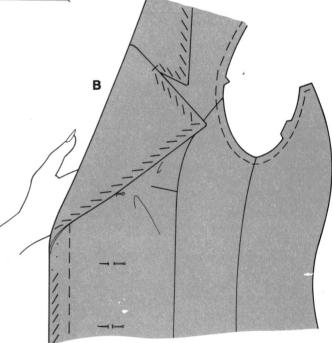

B

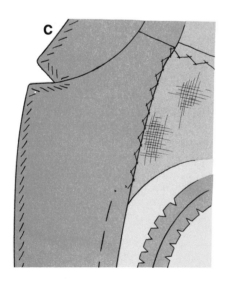

C

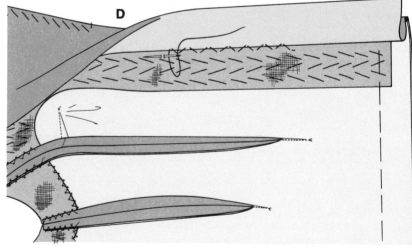

D

Side Seams

Pin and baste side seams along the seam lines established at the first fitting. Try on the jacket over an appropriate blouse or dress and with shoulder pads pinned in place. Match center front markings and the buttonholes to button locations. Evaluate the fit around the body and at the armholes. Make changes in side seams if necessary. Consider the seam line at the armhole rather than the seam edge, and remember that while the lining will add to the girth, it will also prevent the fashion fabric from clinging to your dress or blouse and, thereby, improve the hang of the jacket.

Stitch, press, and slash into the seam allowances at the waistline.

Setting and Shaping Sleeves

Many patterns indicate hair canvas interfacing around the entire armhole; others indicate interfacing only at the front, extending for 2½ to 3 inches from the shoulder. When the entire armhole is interfaced, the hair canvas should be included in the stitching of the armhole seam. But, when only a part of the armhole is interfaced, none of the hair canvas should be included in the armhole seam.

Prepare the sleeves.
Stitch and press elbow darts or control ease at elbow. Press darts downward. Baste, stitch, and press sleeve seams.

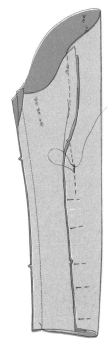

Prepare the sleeve cap.
Place one row of ease stitching from single notch (or symbol on sleeve where ease begins, if it is not at the notch) to the marking at the top of the sleeve cap, and another row from the double notch to top of sleeve cap. Stitch length should be only slightly longer than for seaming, and the needle-thread tension may be set at one number lower than for a balanced stitch. Place the ease stitching just outside the ⅝-inch seam line, holding the right side of the sleeve against the presser foot and keeping the seam allowance even.

Gently pull the bobbin threads to start the ease in both sides of the sleeve cap.

Baste sleeve to armhole. With the garment inside out and the sleeve right side out, place the sleeve into the armhole, matching and pinning underarm seams or markings, notches, sleeve-top markings, and intermediate markings indicated with pattern symbols (dots) along armhole and sleeve cap seam lines. These intermediate markings aid in properly distributing the ease. Place pins perpendicular to the seam line nipping into the seam layers at the seam line. Draw the bobbin thread ends more if needed. With your fingers, distribute the sleeve cap ease as evenly as you can between each pinned section, but do not put ease within ½-inch of the sleeve-top marking. Place additional pins at ½-inch intervals, and hand baste with short, even stitches just inside the ease stitching. Remove pins, and try on jacket with shoulder pads in place. Turn seam allowances toward the sleeve.

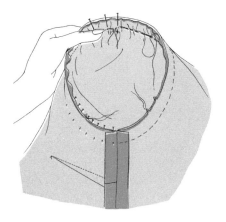

Evaluate fit. Observe the distribution of ease in the sleeve cap, the grain-line balance within the sleeve cap, and the fit around the arm at three levels: upper arm, forearm, and lower edge. Turn up the sleeve end for length. Long sleeves should end just below the wristbone. Remember, the armhole may feel a little snug at the underarm because the full seam allowances have not yet been cut to half-width. Make all final fitting corrections.

Remove garment. If ease appears to be well controlled, as it should in knits and other soft, pliable fabrics, you need not take the next step. However, worsted and rigid fabrics require a pressing and shaping step.

Shrink ease from sleeve cap. To press and shape the sleeve cap, tie threads at ends of the ease stitching, and take out the basting to remove the sleeve from the garment. Using a sleeve board with a press mitt on the small end, steam-press along the ease stitching with the tip of the iron and a press cloth covered with a moist cheesecloth to shrink the fullness. Do not press the entire sleeve cap, and do not shift the ease; merely shrink it. Pin and baste the sleeve into the armhole as before.

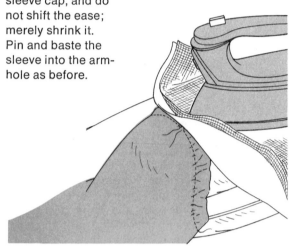

Stitch armhole seam. To stitch the sleeve into the armhole, reset your needle-thread tension and stitch length to normal, and put on the *straight stitch* presser foot. Work from the inside of the garment and, with the sleeve turned as for basting, place the armhole seam under the presser foot, sleeve side up, seam allowance to your right. Start at the underarm seam, and stitch around the armhole just far enough inside the basting to avoid stitching through it. Overlap stitching at the ends. Remove both basting and ease stitching in segments.

Finish armhole seam. A second row of stitching will be placed within the seam allowance ¼ inch from the armhole seam. Hand-baste the seam allowances together over the sleeve cap area where

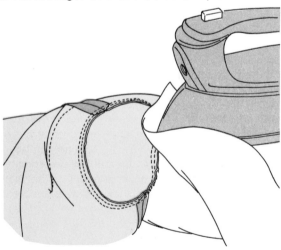

the sleeve seam allowance is fuller than the armhole seam allowance. Press this seam allowance to reduce the fullness. Then, stitch around the entire armhole, using the straight stitch presser foot edge as a width guide, and trim seam allowances close to the second stitching. Press only to embed stitching, but do not press into sleeve cap. Turn seam allowance toward the sleeve at the cap, but allow it to extend upward at the underarm.

Pad sleeve cap. To support the roll of the sleeve cap, use lamb's wool, polyester fleece, or, for lightweight fabrics, one or two layers of polyester all-bias, nonwoven interfacing. You may apply padding in one of two ways, depending on personal preference.

Cut a rectangle 6 inches long and 1¼ inches wide, fold in center, pin with folded edge along seam line on the sleeve side at the top of armhole. Hand-stitch to seam allowance with loose running stitches.

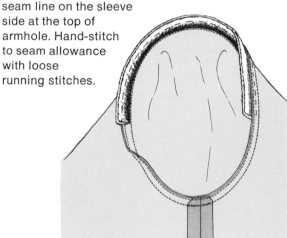

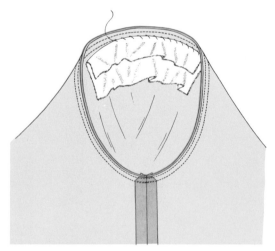

Or cut a rectangle 6 inches long and 3 inches wide. Fold back an inch along one long edge. Hand-stitch fold to armhole seam line at top of sleeve, keeping the widest part of strip against sleeve.

finishing steps

Shoulder Pads or Shapes

Lined jackets with set-in sleeves usually need shoulder shapes or pads to give them a sharp, tailored look, and most figures are improved by this built-in shaping. Shoulder shapes are thin, and are made with two layers of heavy, nonwoven interfacing; shoulder pads, which have padding added between layers of nonwoven interfacing, may be as thick as fashion decrees. Shoulder pads, when popular, can be purchased, but those you make yourself are more likely to suit your needs and the pattern styling.

To make a pattern for shoulder shapes or pads, use the jacket front and back pattern pieces. Pin darts and seams that extend into the shoulder seam or upper armhole. Cut a back and front pattern of the shoulder portion, starting 1 inch from the neckline and extending to the edge of the armhole seam allowance. Cut the armhole seam to extend down 3 to 3½ inches on the back, and 3½ to 4 inches on the front. Large sizes need the larger measurements. Shape the back edge on a slight curve, running diagonally from the armhole to neck; the front should be rounded for figures with a high bustline, and squared for those with a hollow chest or low bustline.

Shoulder shapes. For a pair of shoulder shapes, cut four front and back sections from heavy, nonwoven interfacing. Mark shoulder seam lines. Lap one back section over a front section matching seam lines, and stitch with multi-stitch zig-zag stitching on the seam line. Make four units. Place one on top of another, forming one pair, each of two layers, and stitch as illustrated. Cut off ¼ inch from the outer edge of the layer that will be placed away from the jacket.

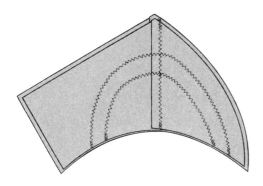

Shoulder pads. For a pair of shoulder pads, cut four front and back sections from heavy, nonwoven interfacing. Mark shoulder seam lines on two front and back sections. Lap one back section over a front section, matching seam lines, and stitch with multi-stitch zig-zag stitching on the seam line. Make only two units to form an upper right and upper left layer.

On the remaining two front and back sections, which will form the bottom layers, trim the shoulder seam edges ¼ inch or more at the armhole, tapering to nothing at the neck edge. Mark the new shoulder seam lines ⅝ inch from the edges, overlap back over front, and stitch as before. Make one for the right and one for the left. This trimming step will allow space between the bottom and top layers for padding.

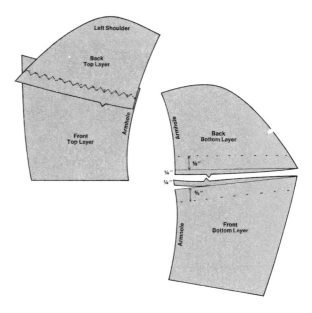

Using one each of the assembled top and bottom sections as a pattern, cut two top sections and two bottom sections from polyester nonwoven fleece.

Starting with a bottom interfacing section, place, pin, and baste with long stitches, a bottom fleece, a top fleece, and a top interfacing over a bottom interfacing, in that order. Keep edges even and allow the layers to shape like your shoulder. Smaller, rounded sections may be added between the padding layers to increase the depth at the top of the pad. Trim outside edges, except armhole, to make padding layers end ¼ inch or more apart. Stitch as illustrated.

garment facing. Hand-stitch the pads or shapes along shoulder line with loose running stitches, working between the pad and the inside of the jacket, and then hand-stitch them to the armhole seam allowance, working from the underside of the seam allowance. [A]

To attach pads or shapes to garment, turn garment right side out. Position pads or shapes with shoulder seams matching, and with armhole seam allowance extending ⅝ inch beyond armhole seam line. Pin in place from top side of jacket. Neck edge of shoulder pad or shape may extend under the

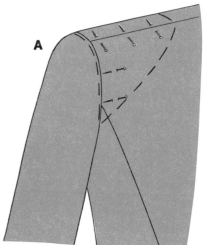

A

Jacket and Sleeve Hems

Hems may be constructed with either a sharp or a soft folded edge, depending upon the location of the interfacing and how the hem is pressed. Your pattern guide and prevailing fashion determine which method to use.

Preparatory steps common to both hemming methods are: 1) Compare edges to be sure that they are equal. 2) Try on the jacket to be sure the length is becoming and even. 3) Mark hem fold with long basting stitches. 4) Press hem area before turning. 5) Trim seam allowances within the hem, from fold to edge, to half-width. 6) Remove bastings enough to extend the front facings, and press the facing seam allowance open for an inch or so above the hem fold. The front interfacing should extend to the hem fold for the sharp-fold hem, and ⅝ inch below the hem fold for the soft-fold hem. 7) Trim front facing hem allowance ½ inch below interfacing. [B]

Sharp-fold hem. Cut bias strip of interfacing ½ to 1 inch wider than hem and as long as the measurement around the bottom of the jacket. Piece if necessary.

Position interfacing edge on the fold line, and catch-stitch lower edge to underlining, or carefully catch-stitch to jacket fabric if there is no underlining. Allow the end to overlap the front facing ½ inch, and catch-stitch to the interfacing. Catch-stitch the top edge to the underlining, or tack only at seams if there is no underlining. Press lightly to shape interfacing.

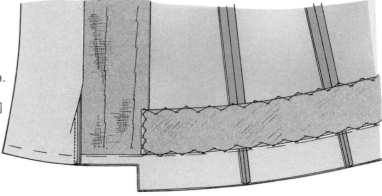

B

Turn and pin the hem on the fold line; then baste ¼ inch from hem edge with silk thread, carrying this step across the opened facing, and easing the hem downward at seams to achieve a straight edge. Steam-press the hem fold.

Catch-stitch top of hem to interfacing only and to cross seams, easing fullness between stitches and matching seams. Slip-stitch bottom seam allowances together across the facing between the layers rather than at the fold edges. Catch-stitch facing edge across hem with small stitches. Steam-press entire hem. [C] The sleeve hem is done the same as the jacket hem. [D]

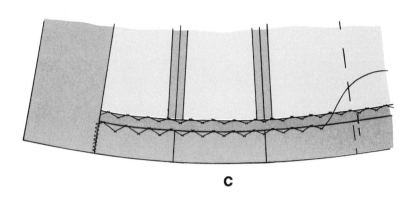

C

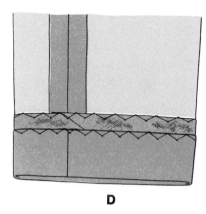

D

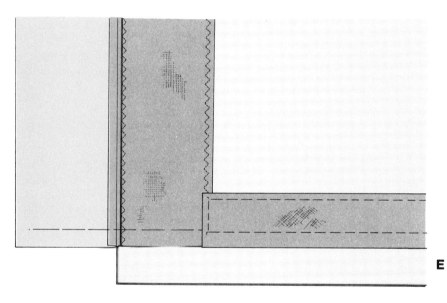

E

Soft-fold hem. *For underlined jackets,* cut bias interfacing the same width as the hem. Position lower edge of bias interfacing ⅝ inch below the hem fold line, and stitch through only the interfacing and underlining along the hem fold line with running stitches. Stitch top edge and ends, which overlap the front facing ½ inch, with running stitches. [E]

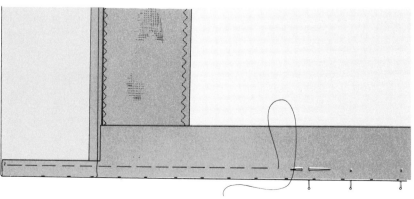

F

Turn hem on fold line, pin, and baste through all layers ½ inch from fold with silk thread. [F]

Turn hem back on basting, exposing the lower edge of the bias interfacing, and catch-stitch the edge to the interfacing. [A]

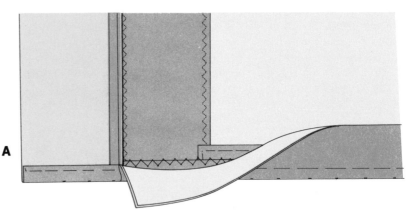

A

Straighten hem. Steam-press, but do not let the weight of the iron rest on the hem. Tap lightly with pounding block or ruler to remove steam and to flatten, but not crease, hem edge. Catch-stitch top hem edge to underlining. Blindstitch lower edges of facing, and catch-stitch facing edge across hem with small stitches. [B]

Finish the sleeve hems the same way as the jacket hem.

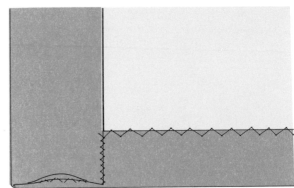

B

For jackets not underlined, cut bias interfacing 1¼ inches wider than the hem. Position the lower edge of the bias interfacing ⅝ inch below the hem fold line. Hand-baste on the fold line. Catch-stitch securely to crossing seam allowances and to the overlap at the facing edge. Catch-stitch the top edge of bias interfacing loosely to the inside of jacket, keeping stitches invisible from the outside. Fold and pin hem on fold line. Baste ½ inch from fold through all layers with silk thread. Turn hem to expose lower edge of bias interfacing, and catch-stitch edge to interfacing.

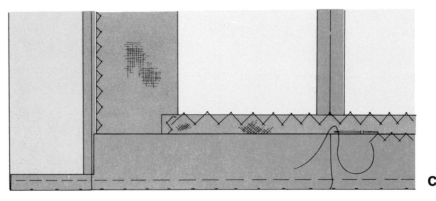

C

Straighten hem. Steam-press, but do not let the weight of the iron rest on the hem. Tap hem edge lightly with pounding block or ruler. Catch-stitch top of hem to bias interfacing. [C] Blindstitch lower edges of facing, and catch-stitch facing edge across hem with small stitches. Remove basting, and give final steam press.

Finish the sleeve hems the same way as the jacket hem.

lining the jacket

Preliminary Steps

Making and putting in the lining is an easy process, provided you make all changes in the lining that you have made both in altering the jacket pattern and in fitting the jacket, and provided you are meticulous in maintaining exact seam widths in constructing the lining. Lining patterns allow about 2 inches at the center back for a 1-inch release pleat. Baste and press this pleat, and do not remove the basting until the lining application is completed. Stay-stitch the back neckline of the lining across the release pleat, and catch-stitch the pleat from the neckline downward for about 2 inches. Stitch sectional seams and darts in the lining. Catch-stitch release pleats or darts in the front lining. [D]

Joining Lining to Jacket

Place the lining inside the jacket, wrong sides together, matching center backs and all seams. Pin at center back, back sectional seams, side seams, and around armholes in that order. Lining at armhole will extend beyond trimmed armhole seam allowance, so match seam lines.

Fold back the lining front, and pin the front seam allowances of the lining and jacket together, matching notches. Stitch with long running stitches, starting below the armhole and ending 3 inches above the hem. [E] Fasten thread ends, and do not pull this stitching taut. Trim off extending notches.

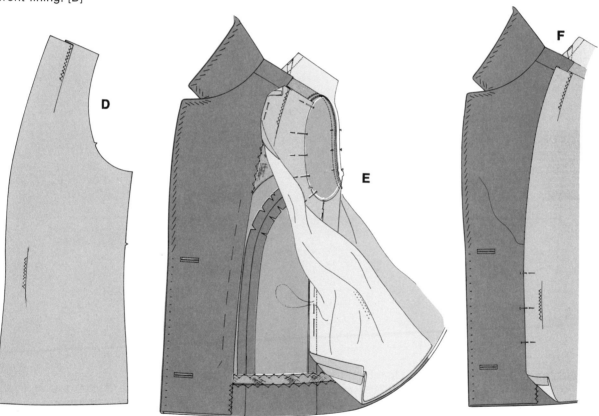

Stitch underarm seams, and press them open. Do not stitch shoulder seams; they will be hand-stitched later. Stitch sleeve seams, and prepare sleeve cap with ease stitching and the underarm portion with stay stitching. Press jacket lining thoroughly. Cut off all extending notches except on the armhole and from underarm seam allowances.

Turn under and baste the seam allowance along the front edge of the lining. Pin lining over edge of the facing, keeping lining even at hem, and allowing a full seam allowance to extend beyond the shoulder seam. Slightly ease front edge of lining near bustline if necessary. Slip-stitch in place. [F]

If your jacket has shoulder pads, do not turn the jacket inside out as illustrated. Instead, work from the inside with the jacket right side out on the table. With shoulder pads, the lining will overlap at the shoulder seams slightly more than the normal seam width. This is why the shoulder seam is stitched by hand instead of by machine. Baste through the lining and shoulder pad or interfacing along the shoulder seam line.

Pin and baste around the armhole through all layers, slightly outside the armhole seam line. [A]

Clip the seam allowance of the lining back neckline, turn it under on the seam line, and baste. Then, pin it to the back neckline facing.

Fold under the back shoulder seam allowances to follow the front shoulder line basting, and pin.

Slip-stitch the back shoulder seam, catching through the front lining and the underneath layer of shoulder pad or interfacing. Slip-stitch the back neckline. [B]

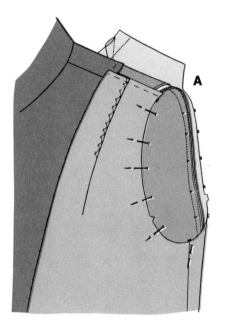

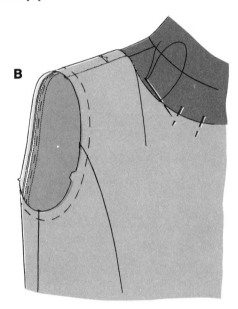

Attaching lining at hem. Try on jacket, and have someone pin through jacket and lining about 3 inches from hem. If you are alone, put the jacket on a dress form or hang the jacket on a hanger and place the pins. Remove the jacket, and turn up the the lining hem to the inside, allowing the turn to come about ½ to 1 inch above the jacket hemline. Pin the lining to the jacket hem, matching seams. Baste it in place ½ inch or more above the lining fold, catching the top edge of the lining hem and the jacket hem. Lift the bottom fold of the lining, and slip-stitch the lining hem to the jacket hem, catching only the under layer of the lining. Remove

basting. Press the fold lightly to shape it rather than to crease it. The loose fold allows vertical ease and prevents the lining from pulling at the hemline as you move.

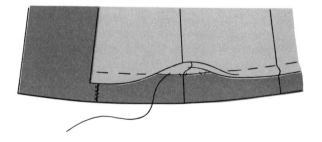

Lining sleeves. Turn both jacket and lining sleeves inside out and pin, matching the sleeve seam allowances. Match the allowances that press toward the upper sleeve of both seams of a two-piece sleeve. Stitch with long running stitches, beginning about 3 inches from armhole and stopping about 3 inches above hem. [C] Fasten ends securely, but do not draw stitches taut.

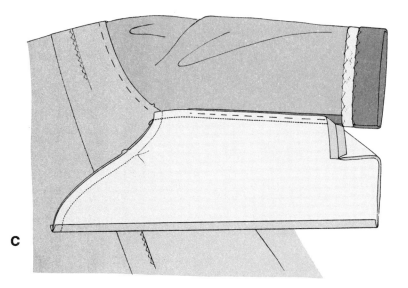

C

Turn the lining sleeve to the right side over the jacket sleeve. Draw the ease stitching at the lining sleeve cap to fit the armhole. Turn under the seam allowances around the entire sleeve, slashing to the stay-stitching at the underarm. Overlap the armhole seam allowance, and pin the sleeve lining in place at the shoulder, notches, and underarm seam, and at intervals between. Slip-stitch in place. [D]

If your jacket has shoulder pads, do not turn the jacket inside out, but work from the inside with the jacket right side out.

Finish sleeve lining the same way as the jacket lining at the hem.

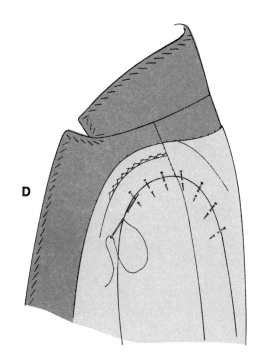

D

Chain Weights

To add weight at the hem to give the jacket a better hang, use chain weights that are available specifically for this purpose. The chain weights come in two weights and may be shortened by removing links, or lengthened by joining two chains together.

Place the chain on the inside of the jacket hem, extending either from one facing edge to opposite facing edge, or only across the back from side seam to side seam.

Overcast the chain flat against the jacket at the ends and about every two inches in between. Make the stitches through hem and interfacing so they will not be visible on the right side. The chain should be removed for dry cleaning.

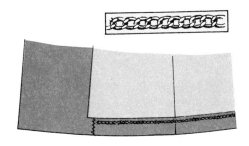

tailoring a coat

Making a coat is no more difficult than making a jacket. In fact, it is often easier since a coat usually does not require such exact fitting. The steps are almost the same, with the exceptions of the hem and the sleeve lining. The coat and lining are hemmed separately, and the sleeve lining is usually machine-stitched to the lining.

preliminaries

Coat patterns incorporate all the necessary ease for fitting over other garments, and it is important to buy the same pattern type and size that you use for dresses. Do not be misled by ready-to-wear size designations because they have no relation to pattern sizes.

Alter the coat pattern to take care of your major figure variations from standard pattern proportions. If you normally need extensive pattern changes, fit a muslin shell before cutting your coat fabric. Fit over the weight of clothing you plan to wear under your coat and allow for the

thickness of a lining—and an interlining, if you plan to use one. If you plan for a pile or fur fabric lining and your pattern does not specify one, you will need considerably more width in the body of the coat and in the sleeves. You can safely add up to ¾ inch on side and sleeve seams to accommodate the thickness of a pile or fur fabric lining. Any additions you make in the pattern must also be added to the lining pattern as well as the coat.

Fabrics suitable for coats extend far beyond traditional wool coating fabrics. Today, velour tapestry, furlike fabrics, leather, synthetic leather, canvas and firm heavy knits are popular for coats. Depending on the season and climate, coats can be made of almost any fabric with reasonable body.

Your choice of interfacing, underlining, interlining, and lining fabrics depends on the fashion fabric, the pattern styling, and the season or climate. Read the recommendations for fabrics on the back of the pattern envelope for guidance.

Interface all coat fabrics in the collar and along the fronts and lapels. For traditional coating fabrics use hair canvas of a weight consistent with your fashion fabric and styling. Interfacing canvas may be used in tapestry, leather, leatherlike and vinyl fabrics. Where loft is desirable, as in leatherlike and vinyl fabrics, add to the canvas a layer of thin all-polyester all-bias interfacing. Or, instead of interfacing canvas, use a thick layer of all-polyester, multipurpose fleece.

Underline most fabrics for a more professional result and for better body and shape. The weight of the underlining that is best for your coat will depend on how much body and shape your fabric and styling need. You may choose a thin underlining, such as cotton batiste, or one as heavy and crisp as tailor's canvas. Evaluate the fashion and underlining fabrics together since they will be sewn together and treated as one during construction.

Interline for added warmth. Woven interlining of cotton flannel, woven cotton and wool blend, woven or knitted lamb's wool, and nonwoven multipurpose fleece are popular types of interlining fabric. The interlining may be constructed and appled as a separate layer between the inside of the coat and the lining, or it may be stitched as one with the lining.

Traditional lining fabrics are crepe, brocade, or satin of silk, rayon, or synthetic fibers. These make the coat easy to slip into. However, many other fabrics are also used, such as the long-pile or fur fabrics; wool in woven plaid, crepe, jersey or double knit; or all-polyester in crepe or satin. A special lining fabric with a satin face and fleece back serves as both lining and interlining. Other fabrics have a chemical coating on the underside for warmth.

Shrink all fabrics that are not specifically labeled as not requiring shrinking.

Use shoulder pads or shapes if pattern suggests them and use them for your first fitting and at all subsequent fittings.

When you cut, it is usually wise to cut the fashion fabric with all pattern pieces running in the same direction. There are almost always subtle differences in shading that will show in the finished garment if sections are cut in different directons. Normally, the fabric nap or pile should run down from top to bottom for longer wear. But in luxury garments of velvet, veleveteen, velour, and corduroy, the pile may run up for richer shading. Tapestry often has a one-way pattern, which should be matched at seams. Leather, leatherlike and vinyl fabrics are exceptions; they may be cut with sections running in different directions. Follow this rule: when in doubt, cut the sections running in only one direction, even though it takes more yardage.

After cutting the fashion fabric, cut underlining the same way except for facings. Then cut interfacing sections. Finally, cut the lining and interlining by the same pattern sections.

Mark the fashion fabric with basting and tailor's tacks. Use tracing wheel and tracing paper or chalk on the other layers.

Initial Steps for Constructing a Coat

The initial steps for constructing a coat follow the same sequence as for constructing a jacket. Prepare for the first fitting by attaching the underlining to the fashion fabric, transferring pattern markings, and basting darts and seams. Fit and make corrections. Then, separate sections in order to make buttonholes, inset pockets, and attach interfacing. Facing seams and roll lines are usually taped in heavy coatings, as are back neckline, shoulder, underarm, and armhole seams.

Machine-Stitching Coating Fabrics

Traditional coating fabrics are usually somewhat thicker and more spongy than dress and suit fabrics. They may also be more dense and harsh than the fabrics you regularly sew on. These characteristics make hand basting essential for good seaming. For permanent stitching, select strong,

matching thread such as all-polyester, polyester core, silk, or nylon twist threads in the all-purpose weights. Equip your sewing machine with a size 14 needle for dense coatings. Set the stitch length at 10 for inside seams. Set the presser-foot pressure at normal or slightly above normal for spongy coatings and at maximum or heavy for dense coatings. Test tension by stitching a test seam. The needle-thread tension will probably need to be set at a higher reading to balance the stitch. When you start a seam, bring the needle into the fabric $\frac{1}{2}$ inch from the end of the seam; then lower the presser foot and hold thread ends. Make a stitch or two forward, then backstitch not quite to the end, before stitching forward along the seam line. This technique prevents tangled threads and poor starts in heavy fabrics and with synthetic threads. Backstitch at the end of the seam. Observe pattern seam allowances precisely. The natural tendency is to take wider seams because the fabric is thick, but doing so will destroy the fit.

Even feeding of seam layers has always been a challenge in stitching coating fabrics as well as multiple layers of fabrics of different textures. A special accessory that introduces top-feeding action is available for your SINGER sewing machine. This Even Feed foot actually has a movable feed that acts with the feed of the machine, keeping the seam layers together without easing or stretching either of them. Perfect for inside seaming as well as topstitching, this accessory adds a new dimension to accurate stitching. For stitching fabrics that adhere, such as leather, leatherlike, vinyl, and plastic-coated fabrics the Even-Feed foot is invaluable. It functions for forward and backstitching as well as for straight and zig-zag stitching.

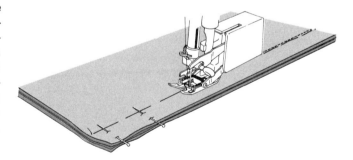

Special sewing machine needles with a wedge point should be used for stitching leather, leatherlike, vinyl and plastic-coated fabrics. Packaged in units of three (sizes 11, 14 and 16), these SINGER needles are catalogue 2032, style 15 x 2. Ball-point needles for stitching knits are catalogue 2021 for most machines and catalogue 2045 for Models 640 (series), 750 (series), 417, and 418.

assembling a coat

After attaching and shaping interfacings, you are ready to assemble the back and front units at the shoulder seams. Tape shoulder seams following the in-the-seam technique, page 43. Follow your pattern directions for sequence of assembling the coat units, but generally you will find conventionally styled coats easier to manage when you complete the front facing and collar before stitching side seams. Then, set in the sleeves. Tape armhole seam at underarm, following the in-the-seam method.

Pressing at every step is essential. Use all of the helpful equipment, such as a seam board, sleeveboard, treated press cloth, press mitt, cheesecloth, brown paper strips for insertion under seams to prevent marking on right side, needleboard for steaming napped and pile fabrics, wool pressing pad for softening the pressing surface, wool press cloth to prevent shine, a tailor's ham for shaping curved surfaces, and a pounding block for tapping out steam and flattening.

finishing steps for a coat

Coat Hem

The coat and lining hems are made separately to hang free. Finish the coat hem edge with binding, or stitching and pinking, or machine overedging. Extend the full hem width through the entire front facing. On a coat without underlining interface, as illustrated or according to the directions for soft- or sharp-fold suit hems on pages 54 and 55.

Hong Kong binding finish. Use a 1½ inch wide bias-cut strip of soft underlining fabric. With right

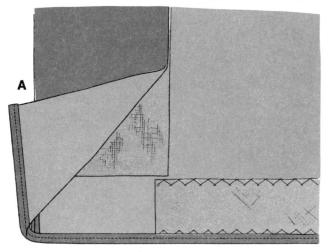

sides together, stitch bias strip to hem ¼ inch from the edge. Turn bias strip over the seam allowances and pin or baste. Stitch from the outside in the crevice of the first stitching. [A] Trim the unfinished edge of bias strip to ¼ inch.

Use a blind catch stitch or blind hemming stitch to secure the hem. [B] Do not use a flat hemming method that carries the stitches over the edge. Flat hemming always causes a ridge at the top of the hem on the face of the fabric. Use two rows of blind hemming for extra heavy or loosely woven fabrics; place the first row midway between the hem fold and top edge, the second row ¼ inch from the top edge between the hem and garment.

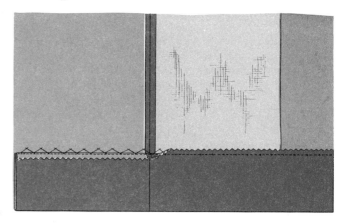

Lining and Interlining

Cut the lining and interlining by the same pattern pieces, but make the interlining shorter by cutting it only to the lining hem fold at the bottom of the coat and sleeves.

Place each lining section over a matching interlining section, wrong sides together. Pin and baste together near the edges, and place several rows of diagonal basting within each large section. If no interlining is used, omit this step and continue with the lining only. Treat darts and release pleats the same as on the jacket lining, page 57. Stitch sectional, underarm, and shoulder seams, handling the lining and interlining as one. Press seams open. Assemble and set in the sleeves, using two lines of stitching ¼ inch apart and trimming seam allowances to half width.

Hand-baste neckline and front edges together ½ inch from edge. Stay-stitch back neckline.

To join the lining to the coat, start by attaching the sleeve seam allowances. To do this, turn both coat and lining inside out. Match sleeve al-lowance of coat and lining. Pin and baste them together, and stitch with long running stitches, starting 3 inches from armhole and ending 3 inches above hem. Follow the same procedure for both sleeves. Then turn sleeve lining over coat sleeve. Turn sleeves right side out. Place lining inside coat, wrong sides together. Pin it in place at the center back, shoulder, armhole, and underarm seams. Stitch lining and coat seam allowances together at the underarm, armhole, and shoulders. Remove any pins necessary to do this. Clip lining neckline seam allowance to stay stitching, turn edge under beyond stay stitching, and pin it to overlap facing edge. Continue pinning down fronts and then slip-stitch in position. [C]

Turn sleeves lining side out, and finish sleeve ends as described for jackets, pages 55 and 56.

French tacks about 1 inch long [D] and at facing with French tacks ¼ inch long. [E]

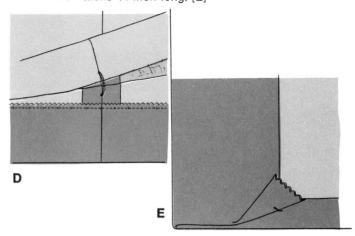

To handle interlining separately, construct the interlining with lapped seams stitched on the seam line with the multi-stitch zig-zag stitch. [F]

Use plain seam for stitching sleeves to armhole and trim seam allowances to ¼ inch. Press open, and edge-stitch 1/16 inch from seam line on each side of stitching. Clip seam allowance at underarm where necessary. Attach interlining to coat, as described for attaching lining, but do not turn neckline or front edges. Instead, trim off seam allowance and hand-stitch to overlap facing edge ½ inch. Hem edges are not finished. Follow lining instructions for attaching lining.

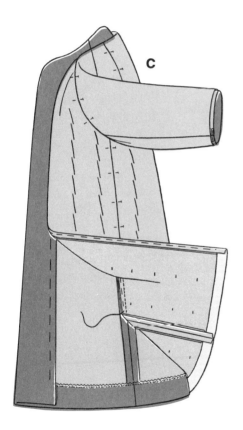

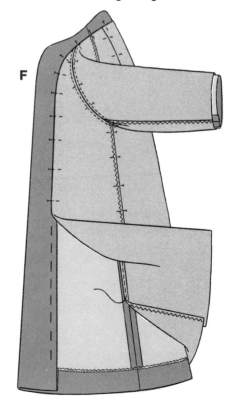

To hem lining, turn the hem to 1 inch above the coat hem fold or turn it so that it overlaps the coat hem 1 inch. Trim the interlining at the lining hem fold and bring the lining hem over it. Pin, baste ½ inch above fold, and press. Turn free edge of lining hem under ½ inch and pin. Finish by hand, using a flat hemming stitch. Anchor lining at seams with

Even plaid

Plaid uneven lengthwise

Plaid uneven crosswise

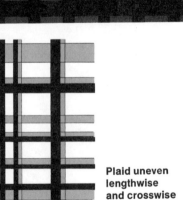

Plaid uneven lengthwise and crosswise

plaids and diagonals

Plaids, stripes and diagonal-weave fabrics lend fashion interest to a suit or coat, but they are a challenge to sew. When handled well, they are especially attractive; when done poorly, they are disturbing. Plaids must be given special attention at several stages: in selecting an appropriate pattern, in planning the way the design is to fall on the figure, in laying out the pattern to make designs match, and in constructing seams.

kinds of plaids

Plaid fabrics have woven or printed lines, spaces, and colors running in both lengthwise and crosswise directions. A plaid design may be even or uneven.

An even plaid repeats the same size, color, and sequence of lines and spaces in the crosswise direction from both the right and the left sides and in the lengthwise direction from both the top and the bottom.

An uneven plaid fails to repeat in one or both directions. A plaid may be uneven in only the crosswise direction, in only the lengthwise direction, or in both.

64

Variations of Plaids

Checks are simple, even plaids. Checks ¼ inch or larger require matching. Houndstooth checks should be treated as uneven plaids.

Plain check

Houndstooth check

Striped fabrics must be handled much like plaids, except that you need to consider the even or uneven aspects in only one direction.

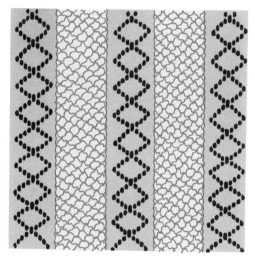

Even stripe

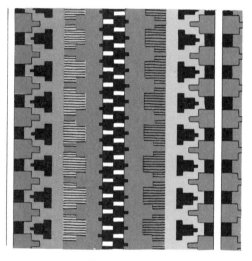

Uneven stripe

selection

Fabric Choice

Plaids differ in design characteristics, and some require more special attention than others. The simplest type is the small, even plaid or check; the most complex is the large, bold plaid that is uneven in both directions. With the simplest plaid, the pattern must be placed on the fabric so that the plaids match on seam lines at strategic points, as described on page 69. With more complex plaids, in addition to matching along seam lines, you must plan for the dominant lines of the plaid to fall attractively on the figure, as described on pages 67 and 68.

Plaids, checks, and stripes offer opportunities for emphasizing one or more sections of the garment by using the fabric grain differently from the way you would if the fabric were plain. For example, you can use plaids on the bias or use stripes crosswise. (If you plan to cut on the bias, be sure to choose an even plaid.) A word of caution: choose no more than one or two points of emphasis—for example, the collar and cuffs or pockets, or the sleeves and yoke, or the bodice, or the skirt. Do not confuse the eye by directing it to several points.

Pattern Choice

Naturally, you must avoid patterns marked "not suitable for plaids." The safest course is to choose a pattern that is illustrated in plaid either in the pattern catalogue or on the pattern envelope. However, you will find many other patterns that are also suitable for plaids.

When evaluating a pattern, look first at the seams. Usually, the fewer seams, the better: Ex-amine all pattern seams, darts, and eased or gathered details in the light of how much they will preserve the continuity of the plaid and how much they will interrupt it. Keep these points in mind: Straight-grain darts [A] will interrupt the plaid less than diagonal darts. [B] Patterns with underarm seams allow for continuous horizontal lines; those with underarm darts (like the pattern illustrated in the tailoring section) do not. Set-in sleeves allow for better planning of dominant lines than raglan. However, raglan sleeves, cut on the bias, are often used for even plaids, and raglan sleeves can be effective for coats of large bold plaids. Princess [C] or modified princess [D] styling distorts bold plaids and interrupts their continuity in both lengthwise and crosswise directions. Straight-grain, slim, or pleated skirts have a fairly straight hemline and distort the plaid less than flared or circular skirts.

Usually, you will need more yardage of a plaid than of a plain fabric. The larger the plaid, the more additional yardage is needed. Uneven plaids take more yardage than even plaids, and still more if they are uneven in both directions. Except for very small, even plaids, add at least ½ yard to pattern recommendations for "with nap" or "one-way" cutting. Add more for plaids that are large or uneven or both.

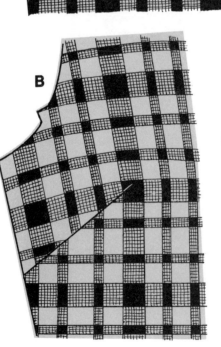

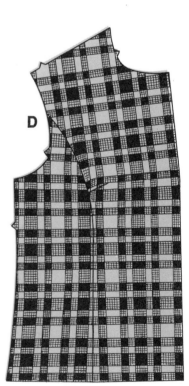

planning

After you have purchased your fabric and pattern, spend some time on specific planning. Decide whether the plaid is small enough so that you need not concern yourself with positioning dominant lines on the figure. Usually, a plaid that repeats itself at intervals of less than two inches does not require positioning.

Classifying Plaid

Classify the plaid as being even, uneven lengthwise, uneven crosswise, or uneven both ways. An *even plaid* has no up-and-down direction that requires all pattern pieces to be placed with the tops in the same direction; but, because of the nap or sheen of suit or coat fabrics, it is best to observe one-way cutting.

A plaid that is *uneven* in the *lengthwise* direction only must be cut with the tops of all pattern pieces facing in the same direction. The plaid in the right and left sides of the garment wil be identical if regular matching procedures are followed.

A plaid that is *uneven* in the *crosswise* direction only sometimes can be cut so that the sequence of the design is the same on the right and left sections of the garment. This is done by laying the pattern sections on a single layer of fabric, placing the tops of the right-hand pattern pieces in one direction and the tops of the left-hand pattern pieces in the other direction. However, to do this, two requirements must be met:

1. The fabric weave or nap must look the same in both lengthwise directions.

2. The pattern must have center front and center back seams, or you must be able to create center seams.

Otherwise, a plaid that is uneven in the crosswise direction must be cut with the tops of all pattern pieces in the same direction. In this case, the plaid design moves in sequence around the figure. This is an acceptable application of plaid.

A plaid that is *uneven* in both *lengthwise and crosswise* directions must be cut with the tops of all pattern pieces facing in the same direction. The plaid design will move in sequence around the figure. It is not possible to achieve identical right and left sides unless the fabric is reversible, so that the fabric can face up on the right-hand side of the garment and face down on the other side. Few coating and suiting fabrics meet this test.

Positioning the Dominant Lines

With a plaid that is either large or uneven, or both, you must plan to create an illusion of balance by directing the eye to an area of emphasis. To do this, you must first identify the dominant lines of the plaid and then place them in your garment where they will produce the most attractive optical illusion.

Dominant lines

The dominant lines of the plaid are the two lines —one vertical and one horizontal—you see at the greatest distance. They are the part of the design that is advancing in contrast to receding.

To identify the dominant lines, drape the yardage over a dress form or a chair and stand as far away as you can. With your eyes squinting, decide which lines (vertical and horizontal) you see just before you close out all vision. These are the dominant lines.

Optical illusion

To achieve the best influence from optical illusion, find the best positions for the dominant horizontal and vertical lines in the body of the garment. Then consider the hemline and plan the sleeves.

Body of garment. The dominant horizontal line of the plaid should fall across the figure below the shoulder seam but high enough to broaden the apparent shoulder width. [E] When you emphasize shoulder width, you minimize bust, waist, and hip width. Normally, the dominant horizontal should not fall precisely at the bust, waist, or hip.

E

Standing in front of full-length mirror, drape your fabric over your figure, moving it up and down to change the position of the dominant horizontal lines of the plaid until you achieve the most favorable illusion for your figure. [A] A dress form proportioned the same as your figure is a valuable aid for accomplishing this task.

To plan the position for the dominant vertical line, remember that a single center line will carry the eye upward and give the illusion of more height. [B] Two lines spaced a narrow distance from center will also carry the eye upward and give the illusion of height. [C] However, two vertical lines widely spaced will carry the eye across from line to line and give the illusion of increased width. [D]

The best test, again, is to drape the fabric and evaluate the different illusions you create by trying the dominant lines in different positions.

Hemline. Ideally, the hemline of a jacket, coat, or dress should fall on a dominant horizontal line of the plaid. This seems to hold the design together and give a base or foundation to the costume. However, if placing a dominant horizontal at the hemline would prevent the best placement of dominant lines in the body of the garment, disregard this rule. When you can follow the rule, remember that most hemlines are not precisely straight-grain folds; therefore, the variation caused by the curved hem fold should locate within the prominent portion of the plaid.

Sleeves. Usually, the dominant vertical line of the plaid on a sleeve should center on a new grain line drawn on the sleeve pattern through the symbol at the top of the sleeve cap and parallel to the printed grain line. [E] Sometimes the illusion of a wider shoulder can be emphasized by placing the dominant vertical line of the plaid in the front of center on the sleeve so that it is visible from a front view of the garment. [F] In most instances, it is best to avoid locating the dominant vertical line of the plaid so that it intersects the sleeve front notch because this gives an illusion of narrow shoulders.

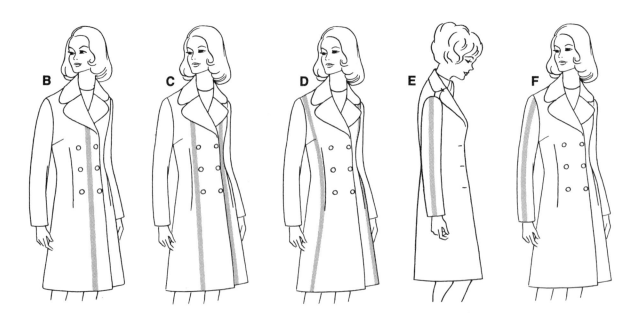

Matching Plaids at Seam Lines

Although plaids cannot be matched on every seam line, they should match along as many seam lines as possible. When working with the pattern, be sure to do the matching at the seam line, not at the cutting line or seam edge.

Remember, when working with a small, even plaid or check, you need only be concerned with seam-line matching. But, when working with large or uneven plaid, you must also decide where the dominant lines of the plaid should fall on the figure.

Lengthwise matching points in a jacket or coat

1. Back [A] and front [B] center lines should fall on the center of the plaid unless, for reasons of optical illusion, you have planned them otherwise.

2. On the upper collar, the center back line [C] should fall on the same plaid as the center back of the jacket. [A]

3. If a jacket has a tailored collar and lapel, the lengthwise line of the plaid on the lapel facing [D] should match that on the collar at the seam-line symbol that indicates the end of the upper collar and neckline facing seam. (In this instance, the lengthwise line of the plaid of the lapel facing need not match the lengthwise line of the plaid in the jacket front.)

4. On sleeves, the lengthwise line of the plaid that intersects the front sleeve-cap notch at the

seam line should match the lengthwise line of the plaid in the jacket front at the corresponding notch seam line, if possible. This should not be a dominant line.

Crosswise matching points in jacket or coat

1. The front and back garment sections should be matched at the first notch below the bust dart on the underarm seam. [E]

2. On the sleeve, a crosswise line drawn on the pattern perpendicular to the lengthwise grain line, through the front sleeve notch, should match the crosswise design of the plaid at the corresponding armhole notch of the garment front. [F] Because of the ease on the sleeve cap, the sleeve and back sections will not match at the back armhole notch.

3. If a jacket has a tailored collar and lapel, the crosswise design of the plaid on the front facing should match that of the garment front section at the notches.

Lengthwise matching points in a suit or ensemble

1. When pants or a skirt or dress are to be worn with a jacket, the back and front center lines should fall on the same part of the plaid in both garments

2. All other lengthwise matching points listed for a jacket or coat should be matched within an

(continued on page 70)

accompanying dress, but they need not be on the same part of the plaid design as the jacket.

Crosswise matching points in a suit or ensemble

1. The crosswise line of the plaid should be identical at the center front waistline in the jacket and the skirt, pants, or dress.

When the crosswise lines are matched at waistline center front, all other crosswise lines below the waistline of both the jacket and the accompanying garment should coincide. As an added precaution, check the way the plaids match at the side seams of both garments from waistline to hemline.

How to Prepare Pattern

For straight-cut garments, you can save time and avoid confusion by adding a few lines to your pattern before you begin to lay it on the fabric. Using a T square and ruler and colored pencil or crayon, trace on the pattern pieces the positions at which you have decided the key dominant lines should fall. [A] and [B]

Also, draw lengthwise and crosswise lines to intersect notch seam-line positions at each point where the design of the plaids should match in corresponding pattern sections. [C] and [D] Draw lengthwise lines parallel to pattern grain lines and crosswise lines perpendicular to grain lines.

Added dominant lines are used as guides when pattern pieces are layed on fabric.

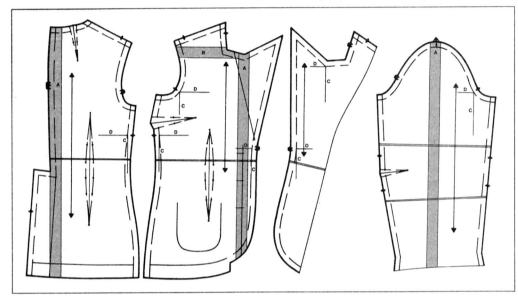

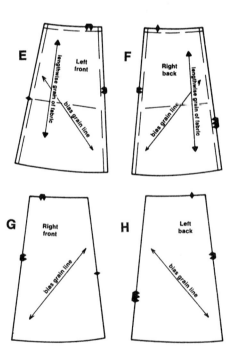

For bias-cut garments or sections, when the pattern does not include a grain-line arrow for cutting on the bias, mark a new lengthwise grain line:

1. Draw a crosswise grain line perpendicular to the lengthwise grain line.

2. Measure about 4 inches up from the point at which the lengthwise and crosswise grain lines intersect and mark a point on the lengthwise line.

3. Measure from the intersecting point the same distance and mark a point on the crosswise grain line.

4. Draw a diagonal line on the pattern through the two points This line becomes the new lengthwise grain line for cutting the section on the bias. [E] and [F]

Duplicate a half pattern section in tissue or on the non-woven product, Trace-a-Pattern by Stacy, marking one pattern for the right side and the other for the left side. [G] and [H]

Remember that an even plaid is the best choice for a bias-cut design and that cutting from a single layer of fabric is more accurate.

laying out pattern and cutting

Shrink the fabric according to the process appropriate for the fiber content.

Straighten and square the ends of the yardage, letting the crosswise design of the plaid take precedence over the crosswise yarn if they differ, as they do in some printed plaids.

If you plan to cut two layers at once, pin the fabric at short intervals, matching the plaid precisely throughout.

Two-layer cutting can be done on an even plaid and on a plaid that is uneven in the lengthwise direction only, with the fabric folded lengthwise on the center of the plaid design. Remember to cut these uneven plaids with all pattern pieces in the same direction.

Two-layer cutting can be done on a plaid that is uneven in the crosswise direction only, by making a crosswise fold at the center of the yardage, matching and pinning the plaid design precisely throughout. Remember, your pattern must have center front and center back seams rather than fold lines, and all pattern pieces must be laid in the same direction.

All other plaid designs must be cut singly, making sure you cut a right and left section by turning the pattern over, printed side up for one and down for the other.

Take plenty of time to place the pattern on the fabric. Plan tentatively where all pieces will be placed before you cut a single piece, even though you cannot always pin each pattern piece precisely in position initially. At this step, you will appreciate the extra yardage you have purchased to enable you to match the plaid designs. Differentiate between placement of dominant lines and the matching points for the lines of the plaid in pieces that join.

Lay out the front first; it is the one pattern section that is marked with both lengthwise [A], and crosswise [B], dominant-line positions. Next, lay out the back on a dominant vertical line at the center back [C], and match the horizontal line to the front at the corresponding underarm notches. [D] Lay the center back of the upper collar [E], on a dominant vertical line (to match the back section), keeping the horizontal plaid lines the same at [F] on the collar and back. Then match the vertical lines of the plaid of the lapel facing and collar at the end of the neckline symbol [G], and the horizontal lines. [H] Match the sleeve to the garment front, positioning the dominant vertical line [I] and matching horizontal lines at corresponding armhole notches. [J]

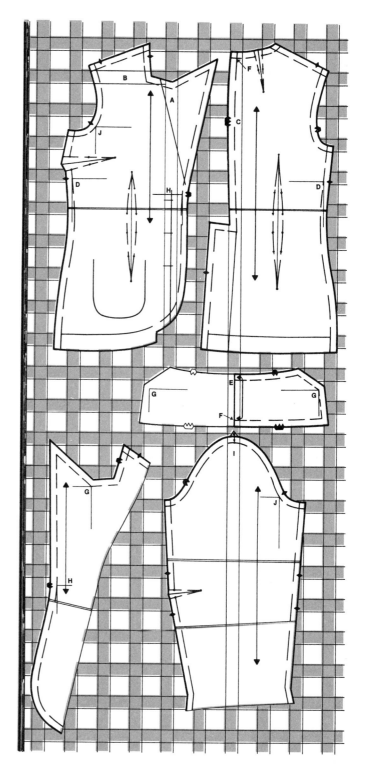

After you have cut one piece, lay it next to the adjoining piece, checking the placement of dominant lines and seamline matching at strategic points. This verification prevents oversights, and, if your planning and pattern preparations have been thorough and accurate, laying out and cutting are not difficult.

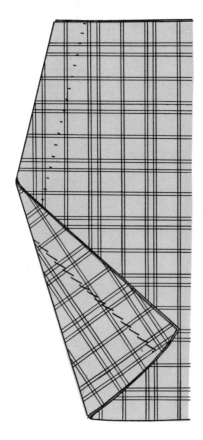

construction

When putting plaids together, you will find two techniques helpful in achieving exact matching along seam lines: slip-basting, which enables you to observe the position of each line of the design as you baste a seam; and stitching with the aid of the Even Feed machine foot, which will keep the seam layers from shifting out of line as you stitch.

Slip basting

Use slip basting to match stripes or plaids.

Work from the right side of the garment; fold under the seam allowance on one edge and pin. (Baste if necessary.) Lap the folded edge over the seam allowance of the joining section, being careful to match each stripe or plaid. Place pins at right angles to the folded edge, with heads toward the seam edge. Space the pins about $\frac{1}{2}$ inch apart, depending on the size of the stripe or plaid.

Insert the needle, from the wrong side, up through the three thicknesses of fabric near the folded edge, and pull through. Then from the top side, directly opposite the previous stitch, insert the needle through the single thickness and bring it up through the three thicknesses and near the folded edge. A long stitch appears on the underside and a short stitch appears under the folded edge. The long stitch is usually $\frac{1}{4}$ to $\frac{5}{8}$ inch long but may vary with the pattern of the stripe or plaid, or the texture of the fabric.

If you used a basting thread to retain the fold, remove it before stitching. Machine-stitch the seam from the wrong side through the center of the short basting stitches.

To remove the basting, clip the longer basting threads every two or three stitches and pull out. Use tweezers if your fingers cannot grasp the threads.

Even Feed foot

The Even Feed machine foot should be used for stitching seams in plaids because it prevents the seam layers from moving unevenly. A plaid that is accurately spaced can be stitched without basting when the seams are pinned at intervals so that the lines match at the seam lines. Some plaid fabrics are stretched unevenly in finishing so that the spacings between lines of the plaid differ slightly. These plaids must be basted, making the lines match by slightly stretching or easing as needed. Press such a basted seam before attempting to stitch. The Even Feed foot will not correct such irregularities but will accurately complete the basted and pressed seam.

diagonal fabrics

Fabrics with a diagonal weave require some special consideration. Not all pattern styles are appropriate for diagonal fabrics. Those that are not suitable are always so designated on the pattern envelope. The diagonal weave of the fabric will slant from one shoulder diagonally toward the hemline of the other side. The diagonal weave at seams, such as center, underarm, or princess, will run continuously rather than form a chevron-type pattern. Diagonal lines should be matched at strategic points, like plaids, when the lines are ¼ inch or more in width. The diagonal line of the weave will then repeat in parallel fashion continuously around the garment.

Whether the diagonal line will extend from high on the left front to low on the right front depends on the way the fabric is constructed. For example, as you look at the outside of the fabric, if the slant of the diagonal is from the right downward to the left, the diagonal line on your garment will be from your left shoulder toward your right hemline. Laying the pattern pieces in the opposite direction will not change the direction of the diagonal in a garment.

Two kinds of fabrics give you a choice of the direction in which the diagonal will run on your garment: fabrics that have no right and wrong sides, and fabrics that have the same stability in lengthwise and crosswise directions. With reversible fabrics, you may choose for the outside whichever side will place the diagonal in the direction you prefer. With directionally stable fabrics, you may cut the entire garment on the crosswise grain if you prefer the diagonal weave to run differently.

These two kinds of fabrics also allow you to create a chevron effect at center and side seams. With reversible fabrics, cut the right-hand garment sections using one side of the fabric as the outside and the left-hand garment sections using the other side of the fabric outside. With directionally stable fabrics, cut one side of the garment on the lengthwise grain and the other side on the crosswise grain. In both situations, the pattern must have a center front seam or a front closing and a center back seam.

Remember that it is safest to cut suit and coat fabrics according to a one-way lay out and with only one side being used as the outside. Whenever some sections are cut in a different direction, and when right and wrong sides are used in one garment, subtle differences in light reflection, sheen, and nap almost always become noticeable after the garment is sewn.

Chapter IV

furs– real and fake

Until recently, few home sewers even considered the possibility of sewing a fur garment. But, with the emergence of fake furs on the high-fashion scene, more and more women are discovering that they can apply many of their dressmaking skills to these pile fabrics. And, having made this discovery, they are finding it entirely possible to sew some forms of real fur.

Fake furs are abundantly available by the yard in many varieties. Some are made to look like real fur; others are original creations. The high-quality fakes are often more beautiful than some real furs, but the low-quality ones are a poor investment at any price. Just as with real fur, you should look for a thick, dense coat, one in which a fold will not reveal the base fabric. Look for suppleness; whether real or fake, the fur should compress into a small bundle. Look for sheen and lights as in beautiful hair.

A fake fur may have either a woven or a knitted base fabric, and it will reflect the characteristics of the base. Generally, knit-back furs are more flexible and easier to work with than woven-back varieties. However, some stabilizing treatments applied to knit backing impart rigidity and harshness.

Most fake furs are pile fabrics, and the pile may be any length, depending on the kind of fur it imitates. The pile may be curled or brushed and heat-set so that there is no up and down direction, or it may have an up and down direction typical of pile fabrics. In addition, it may have a right and left direction. Flocking and tufting are less common processes for creating fur fabrics.

Some other fabrics, not truly fur fabrics, are made to resemble the design of a fur by a printing process. These are handled as regular fabrics.

Most fake furs are 54 or 60 inches wide. The backing may be cotton, acrylic, or polyester. The face may be rayon, modacrylic, polyester, acrylic, or wool.

The care of your fake fur will depend on what kinds of fibers it is made from, how the fabric is constructed, and how it is finished. Read labels carefully before you buy, and plan to have your garment cleaned by a good fur-cleaning process unless the label specifically recommends washing or other dry-cleaning methods.

In a store, fake fur is either loosely rolled or suspended on a fixture similar to that used for velvet. When you bring it home, do not keep it in its wrapping; instead, suspend it from a hanger so that the pile will not be crushed and the backing will not wrinkle. Shake rather than brush it; to remove wrinkles, subject it to moist air instead of pressing.

Real fur comes from animals and, as with real leather, the pelt or skin is shaped like the animal it comes from. In addition to undergoing processing similar to that given leather in tanning, fur pelts are shaved on the flesh side to make them of even thickness. Also, the appearance of the fur side is often changed. For example, the heavy guard hairs in the beaver are often plucked; muskrat is often sheared to make it look like seal. Dying, tipping, and curling are a few of the many other processes that change the appearance of real fur.

Real fur is available in two forms: pelts and plates. **Pelts,** or skins, can be used as is or they can be let out. Letting out, or skin elongation, is possible because real fur can be seamed invisibly when the hair side is perfectly matched. We see this most frequently in mink and muskrat coats where one skin extends from neckline to hemline. The skin is slashed diagonally toward the center at intervals of an inch or less and stretched and seamed to elongate the grotzen (center back of the animal). Let-out furs are always more expensive than others because this process requires skill and time. **Plates** — that is, rectangular pieces that resemble fabric yardage — are made by seaming small skins or paws, legs, and bellies together. It is from plates that most furs are cut to make coats, jackets, or trims.

Working with fur at the pelt stage is a task for skilled professionals; but the home sewer can successfully work with fur plates, trimming bands, collar shapes, and used furs.

Pattern — Fur can be elegant or casual, sleek and slim, or large and bulky, depending on the kind of fur and the pattern styling you select. Fur, real or fake, can be used as the fashion fabric for the entire garment, for parts of the garment, for lining, or merely for trim or accent. Leather, suede, wool tweed, and many knit and woven fabrics combine well with fur. Planning fashions of fabric and fur in combination requires a well-developed fashion insight; but when done well, it results in an outstanding outfit.

Many patterns are designed for all-fur or fur and fabric in combination. Patterns that recommend fur are suitable for either real or fake furs. Many other patterns that do not specify fur are also appropriate for fur. Just keep in mind that silhouette and shape are the overriding considerations, rather than seam details, which will scarcely be seen. Avoid obvious gathers and ease because of both the bulk they create and the rigidity of many fur fabrics. A soft center back pleat that gives a slim line yet releases to give walking ease is acceptable for medium- and short-hair furs, as are soft side pleats that create a full skirt and thus the illusion of a small waistline. Otherwise, avoid pleats. Raglan sleeves are easiest to handle, but set-in sleeves can be handled well when fur techniques are used. Avoid unnecessary bulk in any form, whether it is excessive flare, full sleeves, or huge pockets. The beauty of fur lies in its texture.

Underlining is usually not required because furs have sufficient body and, owing to the thick pile, will take hand stitches without their showing. However, underlining may be used for special reasons; for example, in the upper back to support the weight of a center back pleat, or in used furs to stay and strengthen skins that have become weak.

Interfacing is required in furs for the same reasons it is required in other fabrics. Cotton flannel, thin felt, and a nonwoven interfacing fabric are good choices when loft is desirable in addition to support and shaping. Hair canvas, unbleached muslin, or permanent-press interfacing fabrics are suitable when only support and shaping are needed.

Lining is always necessary except for casual fur fabrics that are made to be used with either side out. These have fur on one side and a patterned or striped design on the other side. Classic furs or their imitations should be lined with rich, classic fabrics such as satin, brocade, or crepe. Casual types may be lined as gaily as you wish.

Interlining is optional. The combination of real fur and an elegant classic lining is often improved by adding a soft, supple interlining to protect the lining from abrasion. This interlining should be assembled as one with the lining. Otherwise, interlining is chosen because of the need for extra warmth — lamb's wool for weightless warmth and cotton or synthetic interlining flannel for conventional warmth.

Fitting the pattern — Fitting begins with selecting the correct pattern type and size for your figure. Buy the same pattern size and type as you do for dresses unless you have narrow, thin shoulders and a narrow back. In that case, buy one size smaller than you use for dresses. When altering the pattern to suit your figure, concentrate on above-the-waistline fitting. When allowing for ease, remember to consider what you will wear under the coat, as well as the lining and interlining layers that will become part of the coat. Fitting a fur coat is the same as fitting a coat of heavy, firm fabric.

Fitting a muslin — A furrier always constructs and fits a heavy muslin cut from the individually altered pattern. In this way, he can make and verify all fitting corrections before cutting into the fur. Both real and fake furs are almost impossible to rip and restitch once they are assembled, and a basted fitting of the fur sections puts needless strain on cut edges. Eliminate all unnecessary seams, such as straight-grain seams that join facings, or straight-grain center back seams.

After fitting, carefully mark all seam lines and construction symbols on the wrong side of each muslin section, including straight-grain markings and fur direction. Provide even seam allowances. (See "Choosing Seam Width," below.)

The fitted muslin sections provide a fully fitted whole pattern for layout and cutting, an opportunity to plan the direction the fur should run on each section, and an opportunity to remove ease or change ease to darts.

Choosing the fur direction — Whether the fur is fake or real, follow these guidelines:

• Smooth, short, sleek furs run downward.
• Sheared beaver, muskrat, and seal types run upward.
• Long-hair furs run downward.
• Curly furs resembling Persian lamb or caracal have no direction.
• Rabbit usually runs downward because the hairs are almost 1 inch long.
• Fur on collars runs from front to center back when the fur in the garment runs downward. However, on sheared beaver, muskrat, and seal garments, where the fur runs upward, the fur in the collar should run from the outer edge of the collar to the neckline at the center back. Special seaming is required for collars of furs that have a stripe or grotzen. (See page 98.)
• Fakes that have both an up and down and a right and left direction should be cut with the tops of all pattern sections placed in the same direction, fur running downward. The crosswise slant of the fur will then run continuously around the garment. The fur on each sleeve will run in a different crosswise direction but will match the direction of the fur in the garment section to which it joins. The collar should be seamed at the center back and cut with one section on the crosswise direction and the other on the lengthwise; this will result in the fur running downward and forward on both right and left sides of the collar. One bias under-collar section should be cut with the pattern grain line on the lengthwise fabric grain and the other with the pattern grain line on the crosswise fabric grain. [A]
• Fakes made to resemble let-out furs with a continuous grotzen or stripe may also be styled with the stripe running around the figure. [B]

Choosing seam widths—If you are working with fur fabric for the first time, delay changing pattern seam allowances from the usual $5/8$-inch width until you are ready to stitch. Cut the fabric with $5/8$-inch seam allowances. Then, from the scraps, make several test seams, some with $1/4$-inch seam allowances, others with $5/8$-inch seam allowances, and then decide which width works best. It is easy to trim a cut-out section, and you will have a more carefully cut seam edge that has not been stretched by handling. Refer to pages 78 to 84 for seams.

layout, cutting, and marking

Fabric preparations are minimal. Most fur fabrics are stabilized and do not need to be straightened or shrunk. Washable fur fabrics that you plan to launder later should be laundered before cutting to prevent further shrinkage.

In addition to deciding in which direction the fur should run, you should consider the pattern of the fur and decide what pattern-matching procedures apply. If the fur has stripes, observe stripe-matching principles. If it has a plaid-like design, observe the rules for matching plaids. When matching plaids or stripes, mark design guidelines on the muslin or on the fabric backing to help you position the muslin pattern sections accurately on the fabric.

Always cut fur fabrics one layer at a time and with the fur side down. Lay out the entire muslin pattern before starting to cut.

When using a muslin pattern, be sure all markings are placed on the inside of each pattern section. Then, when the pattern is placed, marked side up, over the face-down fur, you will be cutting correctly. This procedure is important when right and left pattern sections are different or have been altered differently. It also ensures that you will cut a pair of sleeves rather than two for the same arm.

Work on the floor if you do not have a large enough cutting surface, and cut pieces wider and longer than the pattern sections. [C] Later, do the careful edge cutting on the table. [D]

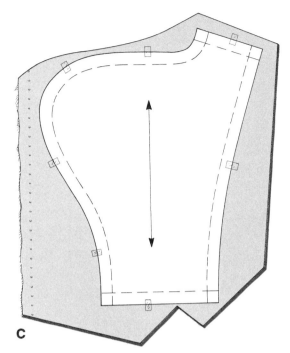

C

Attach the pattern with pins within dart and seam allowances, and place pins through the backing only, not deeply into the fur, so as to disturb the fur or pile as little as possible; or use masking or transparent tape on the edges to prevent marring. [C]

Cut most fur fabrics with sturdy shears and cut through the backing only, not the hairs. The way you cut is entirely different from the way you cut fabrics. Cut with the tips of the shears only, taking one short snip at a time. Do not rest the shears on the table or floor but hold them up enough to allow the underneath blade to separate the hairs. [D] Fur fabrics can also be cut with a single-edge razor blade, an artist's knife or a regular fur-cutting knife; but it is far easier for the inexperienced to cut with shears.

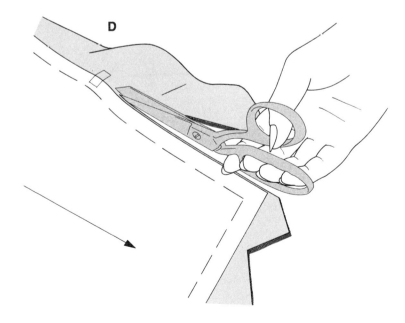

D

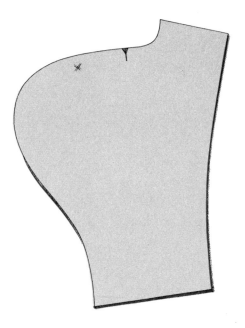

Do not cut notches; mark them with pencil, felt-tip pen, chalk, or thread tacks. If you are likely to be trimming any seam allowances before stitching, establish a marking code so that you will know which seams have been trimmed and which have not. For example, mark notches with V lines on all full $^5/_8$-inch seam allowances and with a single line on narrow seam allowances.

Keep your vacuum cleaner at hand to pick up the fall-out of fur fibers as you cut and as you stitch. Use the crevice or upholstery tool attached to the hose of your canister vacuum cleaner to remove loose hairs from cut edges and from the cutting surface. Use it also when you shear the pile from a seam allowance and, after you have completed a seam, as the final step in restoring the evenness of the pile surface.

preparing to stitch

For most heavy furs, select strong sewing thread such as spun polyester, polyester core, or 3-cord nylon in general-purpose sizes. For fine, lightweight furs, use size A silk thread.

For woven-back fake furs, select a size 14 sewing machine needle, style 15 x 1, Singer No. 2020; for knit-back fur fabrics, select a ball-point needle, Singer No. 2021 or 2045. For real fur, use wedge point, leather needles, style 15 x 2, Singer No. 2032.

The Even Feed sewing machine foot gives the best results for both zig-zag and straight stitching on all but very thick furs, on which the zipper foot is superior.

The straight-stitch or general-purpose presser foot also may be used for straight stitching and the general-purpose presser foot only for zig-zag stitching.

Stitch lengths of 10 to 12 are best for straight stitching; use the shorter length, 12, for short-pile and 10 for long-pile furs. Stitch lengths of 12 to 15 are best for zig-zag stitching; use the shorter length, 15, for short-pile and 12 for long-pile furs.

Needle-thread tension should be regulated to produce an evenly set stitch. In most fur fabrics, it must be set slightly higher than for fabrics of similar weight without pile.

Presser-foot pressure should be tested at a regular or normal setting first and then increased slightly if the stitch length appears shorter than the setting indicates or if the fur is not firmly held under the presser foot.

seams and darts

For a lined fur garment, you have a choice of two basic types of seams: 1) plain, straight-stitch seams with $^5/_8$-inch seam allowances pressed open and 2) zig-zag seams with seam allowances trimmed to narrow width before stitching. Procedures vary for making each of these basic types of seams, depending on the bulk and length of the fur pile and whether you use tape to support the seam.

For an unlined fur garment, you have a choice of straight-stitch or zig-zag seams with a decorative covering, or a flat-felled seam.

Using scraps, test-stitch different kinds of seams and procedures described in this section in order to decide which ones are best for your fur. Two or more different kinds of seams may be used in a single garment because some seams function differently from others.

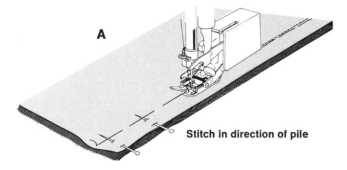

A

Stitch in direction of pile

Plain Straight-Stitch Seams
(⁵/₈-inch seam allowances)

In short-pile furs, pin, hand-baste (optional), and stitch in the same direction as the pile. Finger-press the seam allowances open. Inspect the right side and, with the eye end of a heavy, long darning needle, raise hairs caught in the stitching. Then apply steam by holding the steam iron level, an inch or two above the fabric. Roll along the seam line to press. Use long, loose diagonal stitches to hold seam allowances open.

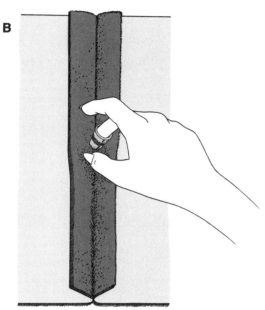

B

Finger-press seam open

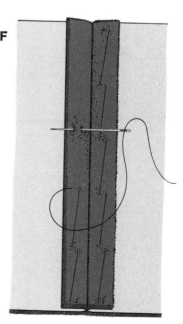

C

Raise hairs caught in stitching

D

**Steam,
holding iron above fabric**

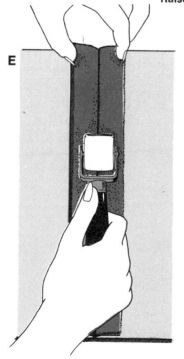

E

Roll along seam line

F

**Hold seam allowances
open with diagonal stitches**

In medium-length-pile furs, pin, hand-baste (optional), and stitch in the direction of the pile, working the pile away from the seam line with a long needle. [A] Finger-press seam allowances open. Inspect both sides of the seam and raise the hairs caught in the stitching from both inside and outside. Shear pile from seam allowances

In long-pile furs, shear pile from 1/2 inch of the seam allowances [C] and baste on the seam line. Inspect the outside and then raise hairs caught in the basting. Stitch on the seam line in the direction of the pile and, if necessary, use the zipper foot adjusted to the right of the needle to avoid the bulk of the fur. [D] Finger-press seam allowances

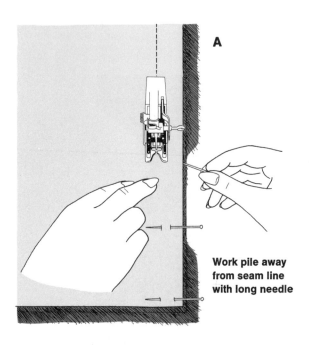

A

Work pile away from seam line with long needle

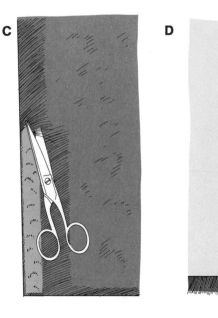

C

D

with scissors, snipping the hairs close to the backing. [B] Steam, holding the iron an inch or two above the fabric. Roll along the seam line to press.

Use long, loose diagonal stitches to hold seam allowances open.

open. From the outside, raise hairs along both sides of stitching with a long needle. Press seam allowances with steam iron, allowing the iron to rest on the two layers of seam allowance only. [E] Cover the seam allowances with a thin press cloth if testing indicates a fiber content that needs protection. Open the seam allowances with your fingers and roll to hold them open temporarily. Use long, loose diagonal stitches to hold seam allowances open permanently.

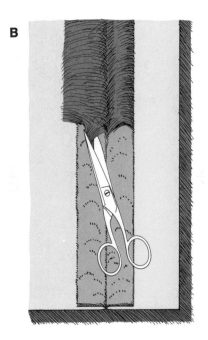

B

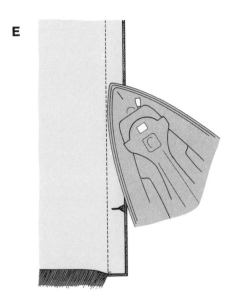

E

To tape straight-stitch seams that should not stretch, include ¼-inch shrunk twill tape in the seam as it is being stitched. [F] This procedure applies to furs of any pile length.

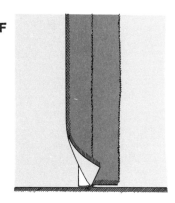

F

Zig-Zag Seams
(¹/₈- to ¹/₂-inch seam allowances)
In short-pile fabrics that are sparsely covered, do not use a zig-zag seam.

In short-but-dense-pile furs, trim seam allowances to ¹/₈-inch width, transferring notches to new seam-allowance edge. Pin edges together at seam ends and at notches. Use a plain zig-zag stitch, 3 stitch width, and 15 stitch length; stitch in the direction of the pile, letting the needle enter the seam line on one side and over the seam edge on the other side. [G] Backstitch at both the start and the finish of the seam. Finger-press seam. From the outside, raise hairs caught in the stitching. Steam, holding the iron above the inside of the fabric, and roll lightly. [H]

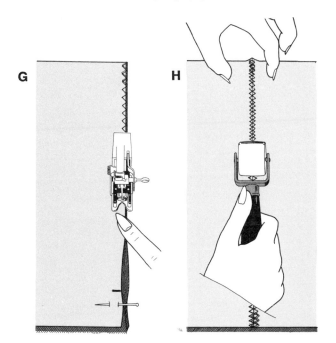

G H

In medium- and long-pile furs, trim seam allowances to ¹/₄-inch width, taking special care to snip with the points of shears through the backing only. Do not cut off the fur. Transfer notch markings as you work. Pin seam edges together at ends and notches, and at shorter intervals if necessary. Hand-baste with an overcasting stitch. [I] From the outside, raise hairs caught in the basting. Stitch with the plain zig-zag stitch, 5 stitch width, and 12 stitch length, backstitching at both ends of the seam. Finger-press seam allowances open. Raise hairs caught in stitching. Steam, holding the iron above the inside of the fabric, and roll lightly.

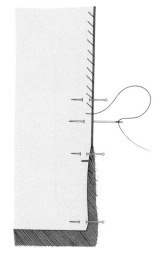

I

To tape zig-zag seams that should not stretch, add ¹/₄-inch shrunk twill tape to the basting step of the above seam preparation, catching only the outside edge of the tape in the basting and allowing the greater width of the tape to extend toward the garment. [J]

J

To cross a narrow, zig-zag seam that has been trimmed [A], reinforce the seam end. Position the seam under the needle ½ inch from the new seam end; stitch backward ½ inch, then forward ½ inch. [B]

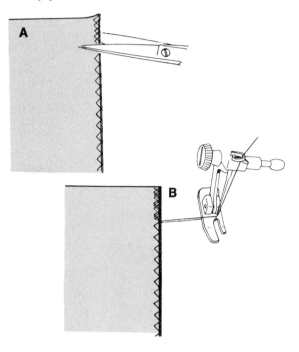

To cover seams with tape, use ½-inch shrunk twill tape and catch-stitch it over the seam. [C] and [D] This taping method prevents abrasion of the lining and gives a slightly more flexible seam than the taping method described on page 81. A covering is usually preferred for side seams and other major structural seams.

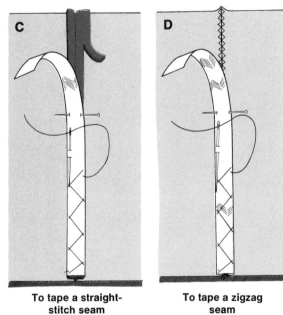

To tape a straight-stitch seam

To tape a zigzag seam

Seams in unlined furs

Covered seams and edges—Straight-stitch [E] or zig-zag [F] seams can be covered with grosgrain ribbon, leather or leatherlike fabric, braid, or folded bias-cut bands of fabric. Edges can be finished

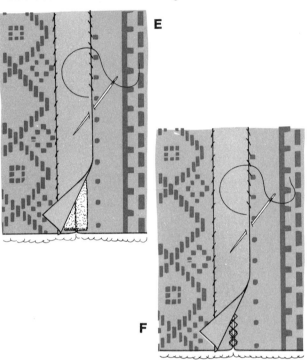

with contrasting ribbon that has been pressed to shape before being applied. [G] Experiment with this creative construction and adapt the method to suit the specific situation.

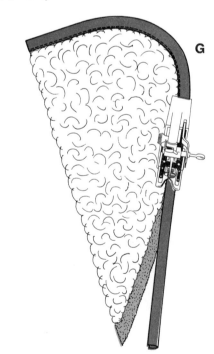

Flat-fell seams can be used for unlined garments made from fur fabrics that are boldly printed on the back and have a matted lamb's-wool face. The printed side is usually used as the outside of the garment so that the lamb's-wool side becomes the lining. Often, the lamb's wool is turned to the right side for front, sleeve, and hem trimming bands.

To make a flat-fell seam, straight-stitch the seam first. Trim the seam edge that will be covered to $1/4$ inch; shear the pile from it and from $1/2$ inch of the garment area underneath it. Also, shear the pile from the wide seam allowance for $1/8$ inch so that you can turn it under and topstitch. [H] These fabrics are often polyester and can be steam-pressed like fabric, using a moist cheesecloth to protect the fabric.

To tape edge of a turned-back facing or hem with twill tape, apply the tape with a narrow zig-zag stitch. Turn tape and stitch it to the backing with a hand overcasting stitch. [I] Fold back the facing along the taped fold line. Slip-stitch the finished taped edge to the garment. [J]

To tape folds, such as the fold of a facing [I] or a soft pleat, or the fold line of an in-seam pocket, catch-stitch $1/2$-inch twill tape on the underside of the fabric, bringing the outside edge of the tape to the fold line. The purpose of taping is to prevent the fabric from stretching. For an in-seam pocket, tape both back and front sections alike for firmness, although only the front section is folded.

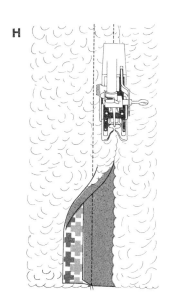

H

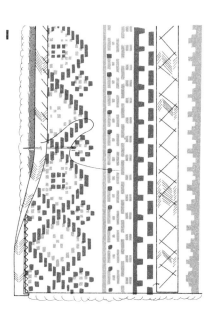

I

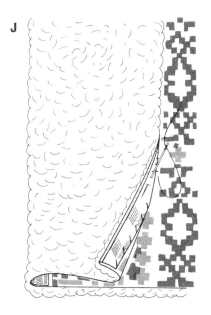

J

Darts

Darts can be straight-stitched in fur the same way as the seams. However, in all except sparsely covered short-pile furs, a narrow zig-zag seam is preferred. For a straight-stitch dart, slash the dart on the center fold line as far into the point as practical and straight-baste on the stitching line. Raise pile caught in the basting from the outside, and shear the pile from the seam allowances. Then stitch, steam-roll, and trim seam allowances to a scant ¼ inch. Catch-stitch ½-inch twill tape to cover seam allowances. [A]

When stitching darts with a narrow zig-zag stitch, trim seam allowances to ⅛ or ¼ inch, whichever width you have chosen for seaming. Slash to within ⅛ inch of point of dart. [B] Baste (optional) with an overcasting stitch, then stitch with plain zig-zag, narrowing the width of the zig-zag stitch as you approach the point of the dart and where the seam allowances become narrow. Straight-stitch the final 3 stitches. Always stitch from the wide end of the dart to the point; backstitch at the start, and tie thread ends at the point. [C] Taping is optional, depending on the firmness of the backing fabric and on the strain the dart wil be subjected to. If you use tape, use ½-inch twill and catch-stitch it to cover the seam allowances.

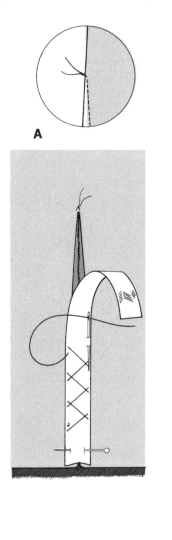

A

B

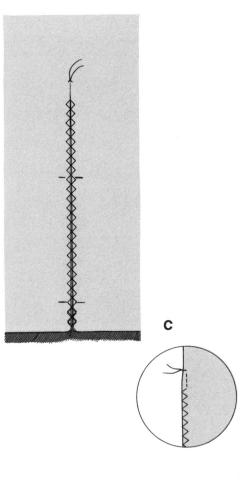

C

Ease in Seams

Slight ease can be absorbed in either plain, straight-stitched seams or narrow zig-zag seams. When you prepare the seam by pinning, match seam ends and notches first and then add a few extra pins to divide the ease equally. Baste if necessary and, when you stitch, place the eased side against the feed of the machine.

Moderate ease can be controlled with small hand running stitches placed only a thread's width outside the seam line. [D] Then pin, baste, and stitch the seam, keeping the controlled-ease side up where you can guide it as it goes under the foot and prevent little pleats from forming.

Excessive ease can be converted to one or more darts. At the elbow in a sleeve seam or in the back shoulder seam, form a single dart; in the cap of a set-in sleeve, form three darts. [E] Stitch the darts, following the method for zig-zag seams described earlier.

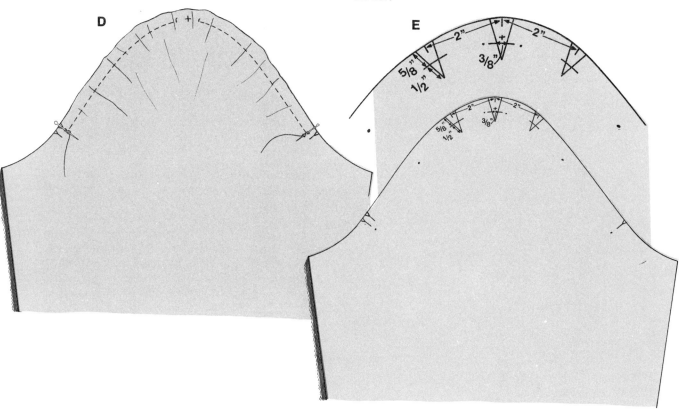

Planning for Fastenings

Decide on the fastenings for your coat before applying the interfacing so that any required provisions can be made at the proper time.

You have several choices for coat fronts, such as buttons and buttonholes, hooks and eyes designed for furs, button loops and buttons, or large covered snaps.

Bound buttonholes should be made before the interfacing is applied. Refer to page 94.

Fur-type hooks require a ¼-inch opening in the facing seam through which the hook is placed. Refer to page 95.

Button loops must be shaped and included in the right facing seam when it is stitched. Refer to page 96.

Large covered snaps require no preparations and are sewn the same way as in heavy coatings.

Belt carriers are usually drawn through openings in the side seams, and these openings should be allowed for when side seams are being stitched. Refer to page 97.

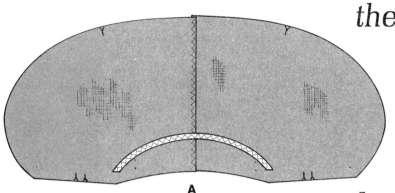

A

assembling the garment

Interfacing a Collar and Lapel (with a seamed facing)

Furs accept padding stitches well because the pile surface conceals them. Plan to attach the interfacing with long padding stitches over the entire front, inside the roll line of the lapel and within the fall of the collar. Plan to use short padding stitches within the lapel and stand of the collar. Remember to make shallow padding stitches, through the backing only, and do not catch the fur.

Preparations—On the interfacing, stay the collar and lapel roll lines with twill tape, attaching it with multi-stitch zig-zag stitching before applying the interfacing. To save hand stitching time, also attach ¼-inch shrunk twill tape with multi-stitch zig-zag stitching to the interfacing front seam line. Attach the tape below the lapel roll line only, placing it to extend ⅛ inch beyond the seam line so that it will be caught into the seam when it is stitched. Cut off the interfacing seam allowance from the taped edge only, just short of the seam line. Do not stitch tape to the outside edges of the collar or lapel interfacing yet.

Position the interfacing over the garment section, securing it with squares of transparent tape

B

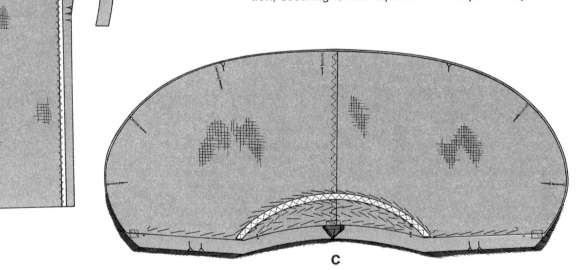

C

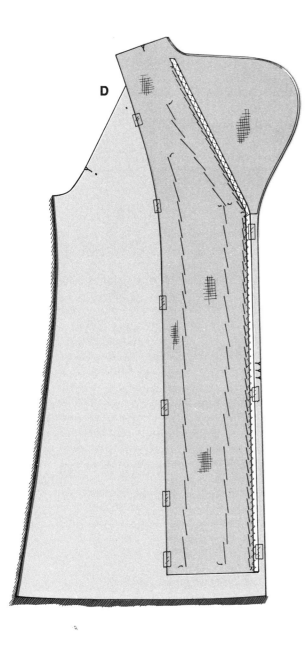

D

until you have made enough padding stitches to keep it in place. [C] and [D] Follow Method 1, pages 36 to 39, for all steps recommended for shaping the lapels and collar but do the shaping with your hands, without steam.

Pin the outer edges of the interfacing to the under collar and lapel within the seam allowances. Measure and mark the interfacing seam lines carefully. Pin the twill tape, allowing the outside edge to extend $1/8$ inch beyond the seam line, and attach it by hand with short diagonal stitches. [E] and [F] Cut off interfacing seam allowances inside seam line. When taping a curved edge, steam-press the tape to a curved shape before attaching it. Do not press it after it has been applied to the fur.

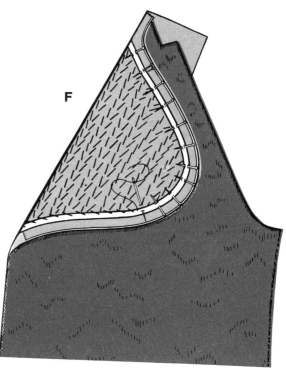

F

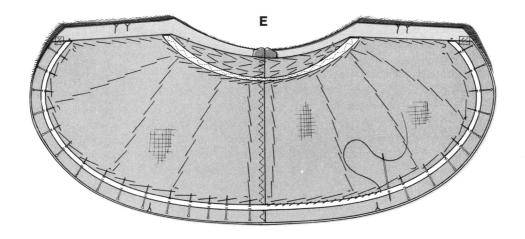

E

Preparing for and Attaching Collar and Lapel Facing

1. Instead of using fur for the back neckline facing, substitute slipper satin or lining fabric underlined with nonwoven interfacing.

2. Straight-stitch facing shoulder seams, shear, open, and hold open with short diagonal stitches.

3. Attach upper collar to facing with a straight-stitch seam, as follows:

(a) Shear fur from seam allowances for $1/2$-inch width.

(b) Stay-stitch back of neckline $1/8$ inch outside seam line, pushing fur toward garment as you stitch. Slash seam allowance to stay stitching.

(c) Pin collar to neckline, matching all symbols.

(d) Hand-baste with short running stitches.

(e) Straight-stitch from center back to lapel symbol and backstitch precisely at symbol. Overlap stitching at center back and tie threads.

(f) Trim seam allowances to $1/4$ inch and finger-press them open. Then stitch them open with short diagonal stitches to within 1 inch of lapel symbol.

4. Attach under collar to garment neckline with straight-stitch seam, as follows:

(a) Trim interfacing just short of seam line on collar and garment sections.

(b) Repeat procedure under step 3 above.

5. Decide which of the following two seaming methods (step 6 or 7) you prefer for joining the facing to the garment. Either method is suitable for long- and medium-length-pile furs and for thick, short-pile furs. Only step 7 is suitable for sparsely covered short-pile furs.

6. Zig-zag seam.

(a) Trim seam allowances on upper collar and facing unit to $1/4$ inch, and on garment unit $1/8$ inch outside the edge of the twill tape. This provides $1/4$-inch seam allowances. Remember that the tape extends $1/8$ inch into the seam allowance.

(b) Pin facing unit to garment unit, working from center back to lapel/collar joining seam. There should be slight ease in the upper collar near the point or rounded edge. Distribute it evenly.

(c) Baste collar edges together with an overcasting stitch and a matching thread. Bring the needle through the seam layers in a direction perpendicular to the fabric, catching into the outside, free edge of the twill tape. Place stitches $1/4$ inch apart. Match lapel/collar joining seams exactly.

(d) Pin lapel facing to garment, working from roll line to lapel joining seam and easing the facing to the taped garment lapel. Normally, you would stretch the garment lapel side of the seam to match the facing side, but there is little opportunity to stretch it after it has been taped.

Baste as before.

(e) Pin and baste the facing to the garment below the roll line; be careful not to stretch the facing where it is not restricted with tape.

(f) Zig-zag-stitch seams with machine settings of 5 stitch width and 12 stitch length. Stitch from center back to collar/lapel seam, from lapel roll line to collar/lapel seam, and from roll line to lower edge; overlap stitching at joinings. Keep eased side of seam next to machine feed and make certain the needle penetrates the twill tape.

(g) Turn the facing to the inside of the garment and finger-press the seam in place by reaching inside the facing.

(h) From the outside, raise any fur that has been caught in the stitching. Skip step 7 and proceed with step 8.

7. Plain, straight-stitched seam.

(a) Carefully shear the fur for a width of $1/2$ inch on all seam allowances involved except on fabrics with very short, sleek, or sparse pile.

(b) Pin and hand-baste with short, even stitches on the seam line. Starting at center back, work to collar/lapel seam joining, then from lapel roll line upward to collar/lapel seam joining, and last from roll line downward to hemline.

(c) Work from the outside to raise hairs caught in basting.

(d) Stitch, following the same sequence as for basting in (b) above. Use a straight stitch, 10 to 12 stitch length, and the zipper foot if the fur pile is bulky; otherwise, use the Even Feed foot. Backstitch for two stitches at collar/lapel seam joining points and leave threads long enough to thread through a hand needle. Hand-stitch to reinforce the cross seam joining.

(e) Turn facing, exposing the outside, and raise hairs caught in the machine stitching. These should be minimal if you have raised the hairs carefully at the basting step.

(f) Turn facing back and trim the seam allowance on the interfaced side of the seam to $1/4$ inch and on the other side to $3/8$ inch; notch on curves to remove bulk. Hand-whip both seam allowances to the interfacing to hold them in place. This takes the place of both pressing and understitching. Turn facing to right side and work the seam edge into position with your fingers.

8. To tack the facing to the interfacing, take a stitch through the interfacing and then through the turned-back facing. Repeat, making a second stitch in the same place. Draw thread tight but leave $1/8$ to $1/4$ inch of play in the tack. Make the next tack $1/2$ to 1 inch from the first, repeating the process. [A]

Closely spaced tacks are used near the outside

edges; widely spaced tacks are used along the center of the facing and near the inside edges.

Closely tack the upper collar to the interfacing, outside the roll line, working between the layers from the outside edge toward the roll line. Treat the lapel facing the same way.

Tack the collar/lapel joining seams together with closely spaced tacks.

Tack along the front from below the roll line to the bottom, making two or three rows of long tacking stitches, about 2 inches apart.

With the lapel rolled, tack the upper portion of the front facing inside the roll line to the garment interfacing with long tacking stitches.

9. Catch-stitch ½-inch twill tape over the opened back neckline seam, which joins the under collar to the garment. Then tack the back facing seam allowance to the tape.

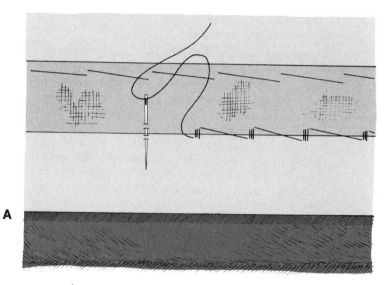

A

Interfacing
(with an unseamed facing)

When the facing is cut in one with the garment, allow hair-canvas interfacing to extend ½ inch beyond the fold line into the facing. Place two or more vertical rows of long padding stitches on the interfacing—the first 1 inch from fold line, the last near the inside edge of the interfacing, and one centered between the two if width of interfacing requires it. With catch stitches, attach ½-inch twill tape, outside edge on fold line. The outside edge of the interfacing should not be stitched.

After finishing the neckline (or after attaching the collar if there is one), fold the facing on the fold line; then, working from the inside, make a row of tacking stitches ¾ inch from the fold line to hold the facing to the interfacing. [A] This method gives a soft fold line.

Nonwoven interfacing, such as Thermolam interfacing by Stacy, may be used when loft is desired. Extend it only to the fold line and attach it with two or more vertical rows of long padding stitches. [B] On stretchy fabrics, apply ½-inch twill tape at the fold line. After the collar or neckline finish has been applied, fold facing on the fold line and tack facing to interfacing near the fold line with one or two additional vertical rows of tacking. [A]

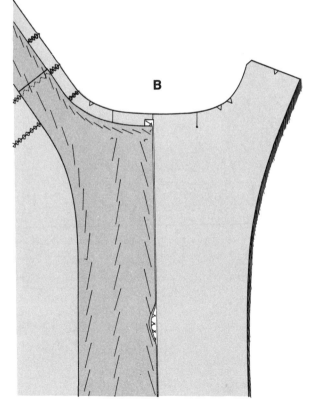

B

Interfacing a Plain Collar

Many styles call for a plain collar rather than one that rolls in conjunction with lapels. The main differences in these two collar styles are in the location of the roll line and in the placement of ease in the upper collar. In fur, both real and fake, the upper collar will be seamed at the center back to make the direction of the fur the same on the right and left collar fronts. The under collar may be of fur unless the fur is long and heavy; then the under collar should be of color-matched wool, velveteen, or slipper satin.

To interface an all-fur collar, use either hair canvas or nonwoven Thermolam interfacing. The procedures are the same except the nonwoven interfacing can be cut without a center back seam. Cut off the seam allowance at the neckline edge. Attach the interfacing to the under collar with short padding stitches, starting at the roll line and filling in the stand portion to the neckline seam line. Taping the roll line is optional. Shape the collar by rolling it over your hand at the roll line and by curving the front to form a circle representing the curve of the neckline. Place pins along the front and back edges to hold the interfacing to the under collar in this shaped position.

Measure and mark seamlines on all outer edges. Stitch interfacing to under collar with short padding stitches on all outer edges inside seamlines. Then cut off interfacing seam allowances. [A] Make vertical rows of padding stitches throughout the fall area of the collar to make the two layers act as one.

To join upper collar and under collar, shear fur from 1/2 inch of the 5/8-inch seam allowances on all edges, including the neckline edge.

Pin collar sections together and distribute the ease of the upper collar carefully at the seam lines near the collar points or rounded edges. Hand-baste the outer edges on the seam line.

Working from the fur side between the layers, raise the hairs caught in the basting. Do this job thoroughly because it is easier to do at this stage than after the seam has been machine-stitched.

Straight-stitch, under-collar side up, from center back to center front, overlapping stitching at center back and using the zipper foot adjusted to ride on the seam allowance, needle next to the interfacing. [B]

Remove hand basting, turn collar right side out, and raise the hairs caught in the seam. Inspect inside of seam allowance for caught hairs also. When you are satisfied with the appearance of the collar edge, turn collar inside out and cut under collar seam allowance to 1/4 inch and upper-collar seam allowance to 3/8 inch. Shear off any remaining hairs. Open seam allowances with your fingers and, working over a seam board, roll the opened seam allowances to shape the seam. Then turn both seam allowances over the interfacing edge of the under-collar section and hold them fast with short diagonal stitches. Notch seam allowances at rounded edges where they may overlap.

Turn collar right side out, fold it along the roll line, and hold it to form the neckline curve.

Make the first row of tacking stitches between the collar layers from the outside edge of the center back to the roll line. Make additional rows of tacking stitches throughout the collar from outside edge to roll line. The collar is now ready to attach to the neckline and facing.

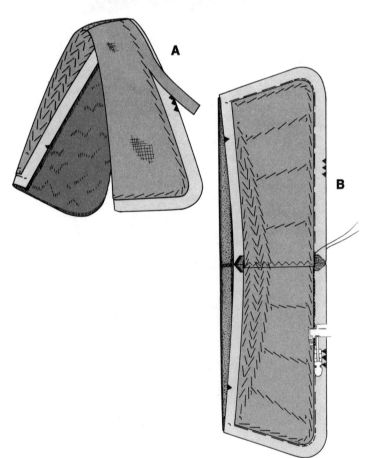

A

B

Sleeves

Raglan sleeves must be joined to the garment before the interfacing is completed; set-in sleeves may be joined after the interfacing, collar, and facing have been completed.

Raglan sleeves require no special handling steps other than those described for seams and darts. Plain or narrow zig-zag stitched seams are appropriate, and taping seams is optional, depending on the firmness of the backing and on the degree of strain the garment will be subjected to. However, do assemble the sleeves first and then make the armhole seam.

Set-in sleeves require some additional preparation beyond that given to regular woven or knitted fabrics. Ease in the sleeve cap, beyond slight ease, must be controlled by hand gathering as described on page 85, and excessive ease must be reduced by darts to slight ease as described on page 85. The armhole must also be taped whether you choose to use a plain seam or a narrow zig-zag stitched seam for the construction.

To tape the armhole, steam-press ¼-inch twill tape to curve like the armhole, then baste it to the armhole along the center, letting the outside edge extend ⅛ inch beyond the seam line. [C] Do not press.

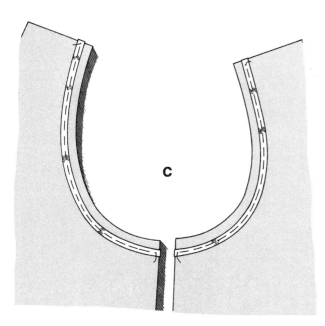

C

Join and tape (optional) the shoulder and side seams if this has not been done. Prepare the sleeves by stitching the sleeve seam.

Shear the fur from ½ inch of the armhole and sleeve seam allowances for either of the following methods for stitching the armhole seam.

For a narrow zig-zag seam, cut ⅜ inch from both the armhole and sleeve seam allowances; this leaves ¼-inch seam allowances. Remember to transfer notches and symbols. Pin sleeve to armhole matching all symbols. Baste with an over-

casting stitch. Raise hairs on right side. Stitch, sleeve side up, with zig-zag stitching, 5 stitch width and 12 to 15 stitch length, overlapping stitching at underarm.

For a plain seam, cut ¼ inch from both the armhole and sleeve seam allowances; this leaves ⅜-inch seam allowances. Remember to transfer all pattern notches and symbols. Pin sleeve to armhole, matching all symbols. Hand-baste with straight basting. Raise hairs on right side.

Then, stitch, sleeve side up, with 15 length straight stitching. Raise hairs on right side and finish seam edges together with zig-zag stitching placed over both seam edges.

To shape seam, use a roller to flatten the seam in the same way as you would press. [D]

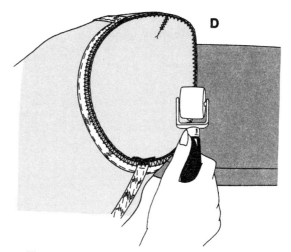

D

Then, turn the seam into the sleeve and use the roller along the stitching line and turned seam. [E] This will shape the seam and not compress the fur. Inspect the outside and raise any hairs you have previously overlooked.

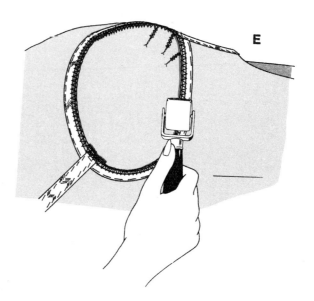

E

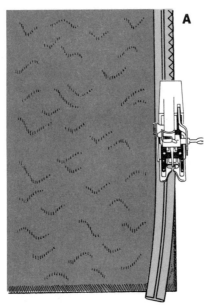

A

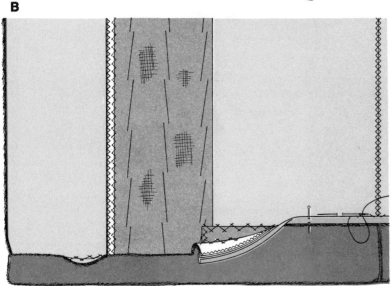

B

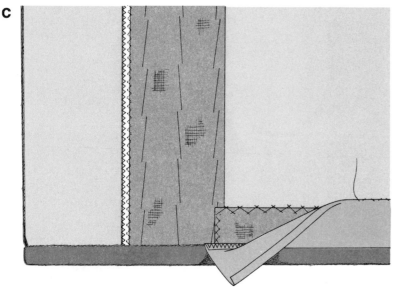

C

Hems and Edge Finishes

There are two ways to hem fur-fabric coats: with a soft-fold hem or a fabric-faced hem. The length and density of the pile dictate which method you should select.

Soft-fold hem. Short- and medium-length-pile fur fabrics may be hemmed like fabric coats. [B] A 2- or 2½-inch hem width is appropriate. Large sizes may have slightly wider hems.

Finish the hem edge as a bound edge or apply rayon seam binding [A] and finish it flat. [B]

Double-stitch the hem, placing the first row of blind catch stitching ¾ inch from hem fold line to support the hem.

Trim hem to ¾ inch width at front facing and across front interfacing.

Finish a bound hem with blind hemming or blind catch stitching and a flat finished hem with blind-stitching.

Faced hem. Long-pile and dense, medium-length-pile fur fabrics may be finished with a fabric facing to reduce bulk. Allow 1 inch below the fold line for completing the hem. [C]

Apply bias interfacing at the hem the same way as for a soft-fold hem, allowing the interfacing to extend ¾ inch below the hemline and from 2 to 2½ inches above the hemline. Cut a bias facing of firm lining fabric or slipper satin wide enough to extend above the top of the interfacing. For a 2½-inch-wide finished hem, cut facing 2¾ inches wide; and for a 3-inch hem, cut facing 3¼ inches wide.

Fold and press one edge of the facing to the underside ¼ inch and the other, ½ inch. In addition, press the facing to curve slightly, like the lower edge of the coat, curving the side with the ¼-inch fold wider.

Stitch the side of the facing with the ¼-inch fold to the fur-fabric hem edge with zig-zag stitching, as shown for attaching rayon bias seam binding. [A] Do not catch edge of interfacing.

Turn hem on hemline basting and, with a slack overcasting stitch, secure zig-zag seam allowance interfacing and fur fabric.

Turn facing over interfacing and blindstitch folded facing edge to coat. [C]

Finish sleeve ends the same as for a soft-fold hem.

Coat facing edges. Bind or cord the facing edges so that the lining can be slip-stitched to the finished edge, or attach piping to the facing edge for a machine-stitched lining application.

To bind the facing edges, attach bias rayon seam binding as illustrated [D] for finishing a hem

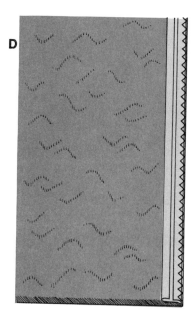

edge. Fold the binding over the seam and whip it to the backing. Slip-stitch the folded edge of the lining to cover the bound edge. [E]

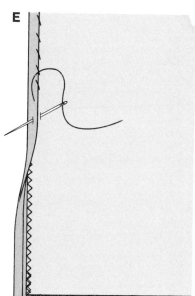

To cord the facing edges, cover soft cable cord with bias-cut lining fabric. Trim seam allowances to ¼ inch and stitch to facing edge with cording foot and straight stitching. Slip-stitch the folded edge of the lining close to the cord, covering the machine stitching. [F]

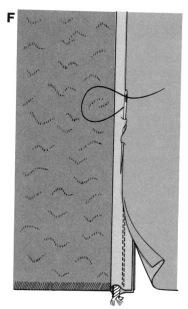

To pipe the facing edges, cut bias strips 1 inch wide and join them, making a length that will extend around the facing from hemline to hemline. Fold in center and press, making a folded strip ½ inch wide. Stitch to fur side of facing, edges matching, with zig-zag stitching, 5 stitch width, 12 stitch length. Trim lining seam allowance to ³⁄₈ inch and stitch to piped edge with straight stitching, using the Even Feed foot. [G]

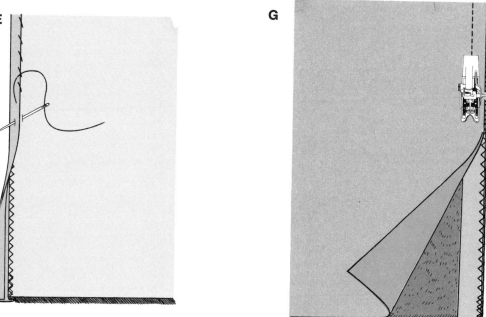

other finishing details

Buttonholes

In *short-pile* furs, bound, corded, or machine-made buttonholes are appropriate. Follow conventional methods.

In *medium- and long-pile* furs, machine-made buttonholes are not appropriate and bound buttonholes should be made by a special strip method, which prevents catching the fur in the stitching. Make the buttonholes before applying the interfacing. Strips for buttonholes may be of grosgrain or satin ribbon, leather or suede, plastic or wool.

1. Chalk-mark vertical lines for buttonhole length and horizontal lines for buttonhole location (center). [A]

2. For each buttonhole, cut one stay strip of 1/2-inch-wide twill tape (shrunk) 1 inch longer than the buttonhole. This stay prevents stretching the buttonhole. Instead of twill tape, firmly woven, color-matched crisp fabric, cut lengthwise, or woven-edge seam binding may be used.

3. Pin twill tape to garment, centered over location line, allowing ends to extend 1/2 inch beyond lines marking buttonhole length. Whip edges to backing. [A]

4. Place a pin 1/2 inch from each end of the buttonhole [A] and cut through garment and tape between these pins on the center line. Then cut diagonally to the end markings 1/8 inch from center. [B]

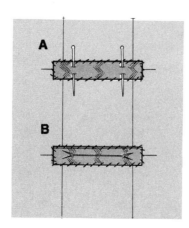

5. For each buttonhole, prepare two 5/8-inch-wide strips of ribbon or fabric 1 inch longer than the buttonhole. Fold strips in center, press folds, and tack them together 1/2 inch from each end and

in several additional places between the 1/2-inch tack and the end. [C]

6. Lift the triangular tab at one end of the buttonhole slash and shear fur pile. Place the triangle (tape and sheared fabric) against the right side of the prepared strip, locating the tack that is 1/2 inch from the end at the buttonhole length line, which is also the end of the diagonal slashes. Hand-whip the tab to the strip and hand-backstitch across the base of the triangle with very short stitches. Repeat for second end. [D]

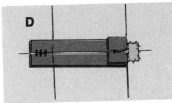

7. Lift one side of the buttonhole slash. Shear fur pile for 1/8 inch if pile is heavy and dense. Pin edge of slash to edge of strip at center, and allow the diagonal portions at each end to angle away from the edge of the strip. [E] Hand-overcast along the entire side, making the stitches 1/8 inch deep. Repeat for second side.

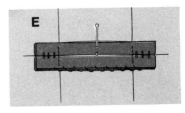

8. Set your sewing machine for a 12-to-15-length straight stitch, and stitch along each side 1/8 inch from edge. [F] On furs too heavy to place under the presser foot, substitute a short backstitch made by hand for the machine stitching.

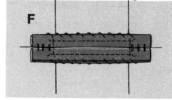

9. Cut a window in the interfacing, large enough to fit over the buttonhole opening. Draw the strip through the window and catch-stitch the edges of the strip to both the interfacing and the fabric backing along the sides and then hand-whip across the ends. [G]

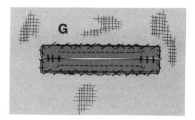

10. After the garment facing has been applied, mark the buttonhole location with pins and apply twill tape to the back of the facing as in steps 2 and 3. Slash opening as in step 4. Draw triangular tabs through opening, shear pile, and whip turned-back tabs to the twill tape stay. Using 1/2-inch tape instead of a prepared grosgrain strip, overcast one edge to one side of slash as in step 7. Using a second length of twill tape, repeat for second side of slash.

Machine-stitch or hand-backstitch 1/8 inch from edges as in step 8. Bring free side of twill tape against backing, forming a window, and whip edges to backing. Repeat for second side. [H]

11. Slip-stitch the window of the facing to the back of the buttonhole strip.

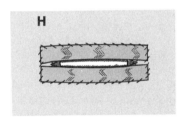

Buttons

When sewing on a button, always support it with a medium-size button on the underside of the fabric and carry each stitch through the backing button. Provide an extra-long shank to accommodate the unusually thick pile surface. Use heavy waxed thread or buttonhole twist.

Hooks and Eyes

When hooks and eyes are to be used for fastening a coat, remember to leave a 1/4-inch opening in the right facing seam. Be sure to use hooks and eyes especially designed for fur closures.

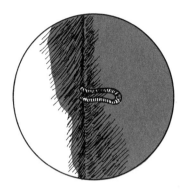

To attach hooks

1. From inside the facing, bring the hook through the opening in the seam, placing the hook over the facing edge. [A]

2. Pass a 3-inch length of 1/4-inch twill tape through the loops of the hook, cross the tape ends, and pin. Then overcast the edges of the tape to the interfacing and fabric backing. Also, overcast the hook shank and outside edges of the loops. [B]

3. Adjust the facing to turn on the seam line, and tack it securely to the tape near the base of the hook. [C]

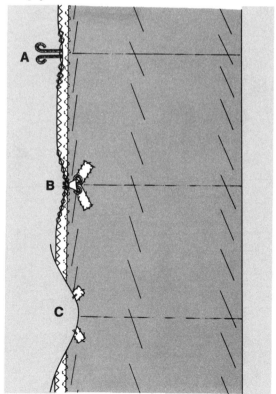

To attach eyes

1. Mark exact position for placement of eyes on left front of coat with pins.

2. With small, flat-nose pliers, straighten the loops on each end of the wire eye. [A]

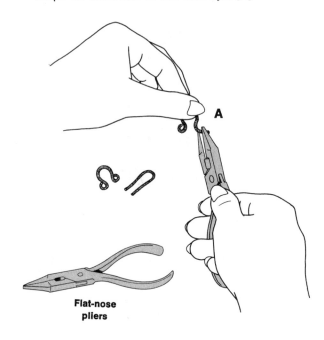

Flat-nose pliers

3. To separate the backing yarns, use an awl to pierce the coat fabric and interfacing from the right side, ⅛ inch on each side of the pin marking. [B]

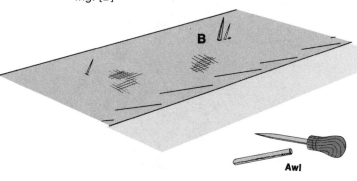

Awl

4. Pass wire ends of eye through openings. [C]
5. Using pliers, reshape wire ends to form loops.

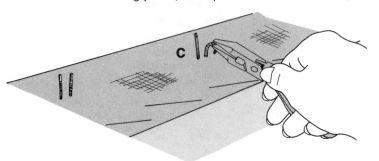

6. Pass 3-inch length of ¼-inch twill tape through the loops and cross the tape ends. Pin and stitch tape to interfacing and backing of garment fabric. [D]

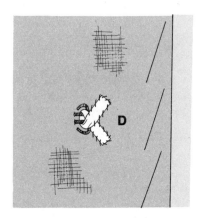

Buttonloops

Buttonloops can be applied in the same way as on coating fabrics except that the ends should be at least 1 inch longer, and they should be whipped by hand to the interfacing and backing for extra support.

The loops may be made of round or flat braid, elastic, leather, or fabric of a matching or coordinating color.

Belts

Belts on fur coats may be leather, suede, plastic, or metal, depending on fashion. Also, tie belts of fur are often fashionable. They are made from a lengthwise strip, twice the finished width plus two ¼-inch seam allowances. A fur belt should be long enough to tie gracefully. Plan to place the seam in the center of the underside of the belt, to make diagonal ends, and to turn the belt through an opening near the center of the length of the belt.

1. Prepare the opening by stitching bias seam binding to each side of the 3-inch opening with zig-zag stitching, 3 stitch width and 12 stitch length. Fold the binding on the stitching line and overcast the edge to the backing. [E]

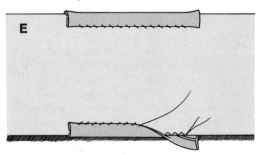

2. Prepare the seam near the ends for 2 to 3 inches by bringing seam edges together and including the end of a length of 1/2-inch twill tape in the seam. Stitch with zig-zag stitching, 5 stitch width and 12 stitch length, for 2 or 3 inches. [F]

3. Center the seam and mark a diagonal line for cutting the end. [F] Cut and stitch. Repeat for second end. [G]

4. With the attached tape on the inside, pin and stitch the edges together, leaving the prepared opening unstitched.

5. Reach into the opening, grasp the tape, [G] and turn one end at a time by drawing on the tape and helping the belt to turn at the end. Cut the tape close to the stitching.

6. Slip-stitch the opening [H] and loosely tack the seam in the center of the belt at 3/4-inch intervals; make a short stitch on the surface and a long stitch between the belt layers, catching into only the backing of the outside layer.

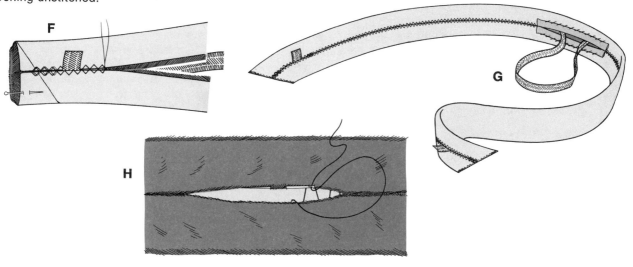

Belt Carriers

Braid, leather, or grosgrain ribbon is suitable for belt carriers, and it should match the buttonhole strip. If grosgrain or leather is used, start with a 5/8-inch-wide fold, at the edges to the center and stitch near the edges. [I] Make the carriers twice as long as the belt width. If the belt is fur, measure it loosely, without crushing the fur.

When stitching the side seams, leave 1/4-inch openings in the seam above and below the belt location to pass the carriers through. The space between the openings should be slightly less than the belt width.

Pass each end of the belt carrier through a side seam opening from the right side of the garment [J] and abut the ends in the center of the space on the back. [K] Whip the edges to the fabric backing, over the seam, and whip the seam edges together at the opening.

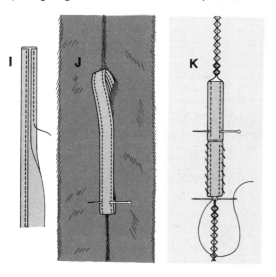

Lining

Cut and assemble lining and interlining, if there is one, and put them into the garment in the same way as you would line and interline a fabric coat.

seams in real fur

Remember that real fur is backed with the animal skin, which handles more like leather than fabric. The skin may be heavy and tough or amazingly thin and supple. Thin, delicate skins will tear easily, and it is wise to include twill tape or woven-edge seam binding in all structural seams of a garment where there will be strain. Using a fine needle and silk thread, catch-stitch either kind of tape, outer edge along the seam edge, to all structural seams. This will distribute the strain over a wider area of the skin. Then stitch the seam with a narrow zig-zag stitch, 3 stitch width and 12 stitch length, using a size 11, style 15 x 2 needle and the Even Feed foot or the general-purpose foot.

Heavy, tough skins need not be taped.

Re-using Furs

When a fur coat is being recut to use as a fur lining or for a smaller coat or a jacket, take it apart at the structural seams by cutting the stitches. Inspect the inside for weak skins or tears. If a seam has opened because of broken stitches, resew it by hand, using a whipstitch or a buttonhole stitch. Small rips can be sewn in the same way. Weak skin sections should be cut out in diamond shapes and replaced with a matching piece of fur cut from edges or sections that will become scraps. Stitch patches in by hand.

If the fur is matted from wearing, comb it gently with a furrier's metal comb to separate the hairs. If it is soiled from makeup or skin oils, moisten a piece of turkish toweling with a dry-cleaning fluid and stroke the hairs gently, being careful not to dampen the skin. General freshening should be done with a mild solution of cold-water soap or vinegar and water. Moisten toweling and stroke the fur in the direction it runs and do not saturate it. Then, with a dry towel, stroke it the same way to remove all the moisture possible. Allow it to dry, then comb it lightly.

Blocking is a process that will smooth and restore the shape of the skins. It smooths the wrinkled and stretched areas of fur just as pressing smooths fabric. You will need a piece of plywood the size of the fur section, a hammer, and tacks or small-diameter finishing nails. With a sponge, moisten the skin side of the fur with water or with a mild suds of saddle soap, which will feed the leather. Carefully stretch the section and tack the edges, skin side up, to the wood. Allow it to dry slowly before re-cutting.

To reinforce a garment section of a used fur, cut a section of permanent-press thin underlining fabric by the same pattern. Attach it to the skins with long padding stitches over the entire surface. When taping the edges, treat the underlining and fur as one.

Adapting a collar pattern. To adapt a curved collar pattern for cutting from a fur band or a skin that has a grotzen, cut the pattern from muslin and remove seam allowances. Mark the collar pattern in several places from neckline to outer edge for slashing to straighten it. Also, mark the pattern where you want the grotzen to fall. [A]

Remember, the fur should run from front to center back on the collar. If you are working with a fur band, cut the collar apart entirely at the center back and lay out each half separately so that the direction of the fur will be correct. The illustration [B] is of a fur boa that is seamed at the center back, making the direction of the fur correct.

Cut with knife or razor blade, allowing ⅛-inch seam allowances on all edges.

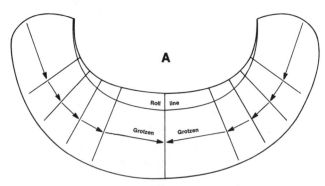

A

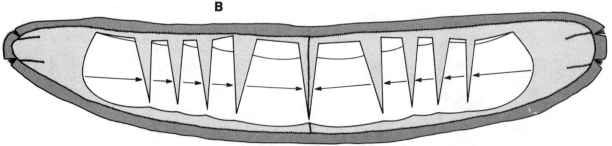

B

Constructing the collar. With a narrow zig-zag and without tape, stitch the sectional seams to form the collar. [B] Block collar by moistening and tacking to wood. Allow it to dry slowly.

Press 1/2-inch twill tape to a rounded shape to match the collar edges.

Stitch the outside edge of the shaped tape to the outside edge of the fur side of the collar with narrow zig-zag stitching. Stitch the inside curved edge of the shaped tape to the neckline edge of the collar the same way. [C]

Cut an interlining 1/8 inch larger than the collar pattern. Furriers use a quilted cotton batting covered with cheesecloth for padding. However, for home sewing Thermolam interlining is an excellent substitute. Use more than one layer if you want a lofty collar.

Pin the interlining to the inside of the taped collar. Catch-stitch the interlining to the center back and through the center from back to front. Then turn the twill tape to the inside, letting the edge of the padding roll back with it. Overcast the edge of the tape through the interfacing and skin.

Applying the collar. The constructed fur collar can be applied to a coat or suit that has a completed collar or to an incomplete garment on which the upper collar has been omitted. Turn the seam allowance on the outer edge of the under collar over the interfacing and hold it in place with overcasting or catch stitching.

Then, pin the fur collar to the garment, matching all edges. Slip-stitch the taped edge of the fur to the turned edge of the garment under collar and the neckline edge to the facing.

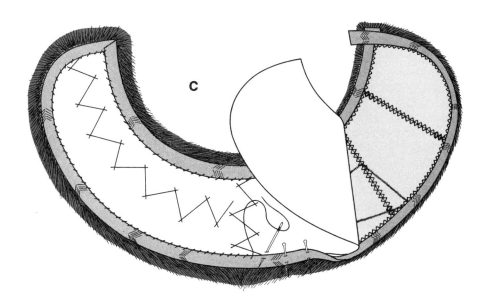

C

Fur Bands

Fur bands are available by the yard in many varieties and widths. They are padded, lined, and ready to slip-stitch to a straight edge. When you use a wide fur band at the bottom edge of a coat, it can be seamed at the center back to make the fur run in the same direction on both sides. Also, it should be shaped to fit the curve of the bottom of the coat by cutting out wedges as illustrated for a collar. [B] Cut a muslin pattern from the coat pattern the width of the finished band. Slash it from top to bottom at intervals to enable you to place it against the inside of the fur band. Cut wedges from the fur where the pattern separates when it is straightened. Handle as described for the fur collar. [C]

Chapter V

leather— real and fake

preliminaries

The leather look is easy to interpret in fashion sewing, especially when you learn a few tricks of handling leatherlike fabrics and real leather, and when you experiment a little as you sew.

Leatherlike fabrics have reached a high place in fashion. They are more practical and convenient for the home sewer than real leather because they come in the form of yardage rather than irregularly shaped skins. Also, they are less expensive, more readily available, and generally easier and less expensive to maintain. However, for sheer luxury, real leather is always preferred.

Leatherlike fabrics consist of a layer of polyurethane or vinyl over a woven or knitted base fabric. Polyurethane produces a soft, spongy fabric; vinyl tends to be more rigid. Both surfaces are nonporous, rain repellent, and can be wiped clean with a damp sponge. Those with a knit back are more supple than those with a woven back. Some have a thin layer of foam between the plastic film and the fabric back to give loft and warmth. Whether made to look like patent leather, grained leather, or suede, the new plastics are handled alike.

Suedelike fabric is usually produced by flocking, a process that adheres short fibers to a flat-surfaced fabric. It actually looks and feels like real suede but is more soil-resistant and does not crack or flake. Other leatherlike fabrics are produced by either polishing, to resemble patent leather, or embossing, to resemble grained leather. Ciré is a good example.

Flocked, polished, and embossed fabrics require the same sewing procedures as similar fabrics that do not have a leather look. Plastic-coated fabrics that do not have a leather look also require procedures similar to those used for suede and leather.

Real leather is the tanned or treated skin of an animal. It comes in pieces shaped like the animal, rather than as yardage. Most leather used for sewing comes from short-haired animals, such as cows, sheep, or goats. When finished, the surface from which the hair is shaved becomes the grain side, which may be buffed for a mat surface or polished for a shiny one. This surface may also be sueded, embossed, or glazed. The other side (flesh side) becomes suede when dyed and buffed into a soft, napped surface, and buckskin when buffed to produce a rough-textured surface. Although true buckskin is the skin of a male deer, the term is used in fashion to describe a surface finish of other skins that resembles real buckskin.

The terminology used in connection with real leather is based on the size of the animal. A *hide* is 25 square feet or over in area, a *skin* is less than 15 square feet, and a *kip* is between 15 and 25 square feet.

Sometimes sections of a hide are sold separately. A *side* is the area from the center of the hide (center back of the animal) to the outer edge; a *belly* is the softer area near the edge of the hide, and a *back* is the firmer section between the belly line and the center back. Each of these sections also varies in thickness and degree of stretch. For example, the strip along the center of the hide comes from the back of the animal and is stronger, thicker, and stretches less than the area near the edges of the hide, which comes from the belly or legs of the animal. Large thick hides are often split into two usable layers or shaved on the flesh side to make the thick areas thinner and uniform with the rest of the skin.

Grades in leather are determined by the amount

of usable surface free of scars, cuts, dye spots, knife marks, and holes. Grade A leather has the maximum usable surface. Lower grades are cheaper and often a good buy when you are cutting only small pattern sections because the usable portion is of quality equal to Grade A.

There is no exact formula for determining how much leather to buy as there is with fabric yardage. You must do a great deal of planning and some guessing. Begin by determining the number

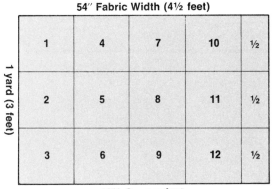

54″ Fabric Width (4½ feet)

1	4	7	10	½
2	5	8	11	½
3	6	9	12	½

1 yard (3 feet)

13½ Square feet

of square feet of fabric recommended for the pattern. Convert the 54-inch yardage requirement to square feet. One yard (3 feet) of fabric 54-inch wide (4½ feet) contains 13½ square feet (3′ x 4½′). This formula will give you only a rough estimate of your needs. The waste in hides or skins may run to 20 percent or more because of irregularities in surface and shape.

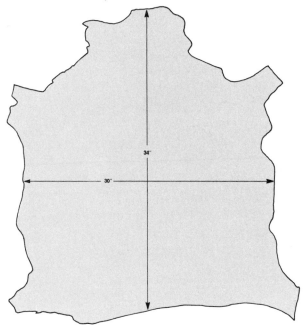

34″

30″

Skin, 34″ x 30″ = 1020 square inches, about 7 square feet

To ensure uniformity of color, buy the full quantity at one time. Although part of the beauty of leather is the subtle natural gradation of color, you do not want to combine sections where the color difference is attributable to different dye lots. For more detailed suggestions on the quantity to buy, read "Layout and Cutting," page 105.

Pattern. Leather and leatherlike fabrics may be used for small separate items and for accents on garments of woven or knit fabrics, but they have attained important status for jackets, coats, suits, capes, and other major tailored apparel. Select patterns with pure, simple lines. Avoid gathered fullness, sharp pleats, and bulk in silhouette or detail. Patterns that are shaped by seams rather than ease or darts are best, although basic darts are acceptable and sometimes can be converted to seams. Topstitching is a good fashion accent and is also functional because it substitutes for pressing, which cannot be done effectively. Buttonholes and set-in or patch pockets can be handled well.

Choose the pattern type and size that fits you best. Remember that leatherlike fabrics and real leather afford minimum give for movement so they should not be fitted too snugly. Neither are they as supple as most fabrics you are accustomed to working with, and too much ease will make them look too large.

Underlining. Since leather has a great deal of body, underlining to add body is unnecessary. However, in some situations, underlining is recommended. For example, leather does stretch and wrinkle, so it is advisable to underline the back shoulder area extending into the armholes in jackets and coats. The underlining may be of unbleached muslin (fully shrunk), woven permanent-press underlining fabric, nonwoven all-polyester interfacing fabric, or lightweight hair canvas. In a coat or jacket front, a partial underlining, extending from the center front to the first long dart or seam, will provide a fabric layer to receive the hand padding stitches that anchor the interfacing.

Because seam allowances in leather garments cannot be pressed, they are usually held open with glue. Underlining heavy grades of leather interferes with this process.

Interfacing. Choose nonwoven interfacing for shaping and softness; tailor's canvas or hair canvas for thin, sharp support; and polyester nonwoven fleece, such as Stacy's Thermolam interfacing, for loft. Do not use fusibles because of the amount of heat needed for fusing.

Lining. For leather and leatherlike garments, lining is essential. You would expect to line jackets and coats, but for comfort you should also line other apparel such as pants, jumpers, skirts, vests, and dresses. A color that does not show soil readily, in a dry-cleanable permanent-press fabric, makes a good choice for leather and suede. For leatherlike fabrics, choose a fabric that is also washable. Zip-in linings of fake fur and satin-faced thermal fabric, such as Skinner's Sunback lining make excellent linings for winter wear.

The amount of leather required can often be reduced by bringing the lining to the garment edges, eliminating facings.

Interlining. Interlining may be used in leather or leatherlike garments for two purposes: to prevent abrasion of the lining that might result from the harsh seam edges, and to add warmth. Preshrunk cotton flannel, challis, cotton interlining, and other soft, stable fabrics are good choices for preventing abrasion. Lamb's wool, wool flannel, and wool underlining are good choices for adding warmth. Assemble the lining and interlining as one unit.

---

preparing the pattern, testing the fit, and cutting

Almost all fitting must be done before the garment is cut. Remember that leather and leatherlike fabrics do not provide the amount of give that woven and knit fabrics do, so all of the ease for comfort and fashion must be contained in the pattern itself. Alter your pattern carefully and thoroughly, as you would for a garment of firm fabric, and then make a few special changes.

Special changes to make your pattern more suitable for leather:

1. Provide additional length to compensate for folds that result from wear.
• 1 inch more in total length in a free-hanging garment.
• $3/8$ inch more in length above the waistline and $5/8$ inch below the waistline in a garment that has a defined waistline.
• $1/2$ inch more in total sleeve length.
• $3/8$ inch more in pants for crotch depth, and $5/8$ inch in leg length.

2. Provide additional ease across the back shoulders for freedom of arm movement.
• Broaden back $1/2$ inch beyond a good fit in fabric,
• Or, add a release pleat at the center back,
• Or, increase curve of center back seam at armhole level,
• Or, increase curve of princess seams.

3. Remove from the sleeve cap the extra ease that cannot be handled because of the rigidity of leather and plastic.

One-piece sleeve
• Fold a small dart in cap of sleeve pattern at shoulder-line symbol.
• Slash pattern above notches at front and back, allowing slashes to spread.
• Redraw the sleeve-cap curve to lower or shorten it. [A]

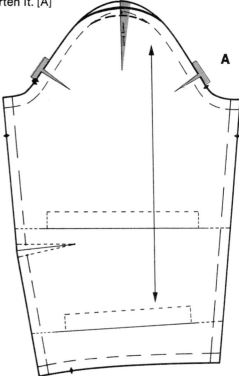

102

Two-piece sleeve
• Redraw the sleeve-cap curve to lower it.
• Take in seams slightly near armhole. [B]

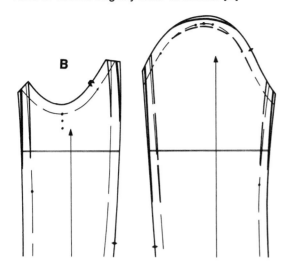

4. Convert eased fullness to a dart at the elbow of a one-piece sleeve or use a two-piece sleeve pattern.

5. If shoulders are muscular, convert eased fullness in back shoulder seam to a dart; if shoulders are thin, reduce the amount of eased fullness by pinning a dart in the pattern. [C]

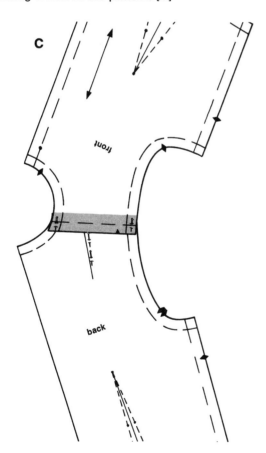

6. Eliminate intersecting seams in facings for coats and jackets. For example, if there is no center back seam in the garment, create one in the facing and eliminate the facing seam at the shoulder by overlapping the shoulder seam allowance of the facing pattern. [D] If there is a center back seam in the garment, create a facing seam in a new position. [E]

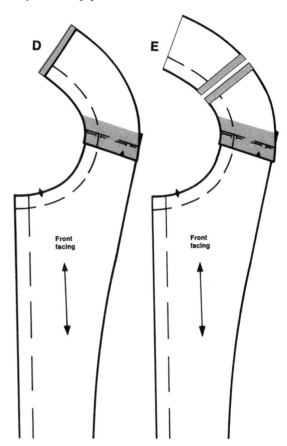

7. Eliminate seamed-on facings in styles where facing and garment can be cut in one. This suggestion applies primarily to straight-front styling and to coats of vinyl or polyurethane, but it is also suitable for leather.

Make a test fitting. Cut the altered pattern sections from medium-weight or heavy nonwoven interfacing. Trace all seam lines, grain lines, and pattern symbols from the pattern onto the fabric. Machine-baste darts and sectional seams, and assemble the test garment. Attach under collar at neckline seam and baste sleeve seams, but do not baste sleeve to armhole. Try on the test garment, wearing the same kind of clothing as will be worn with the finished garment. Evaluate the fit, keeping in mind the thickness of the other fabric layers that will be part of the garment, and the firmness of the leather or leatherlike fabric. Make whatever fitting changes are needed, and transfer them to the pattern pieces, remembering to change facing, interfacing, and lining pattern sections if the fitting changes affect them. Then fit sleeves, pinning them at shoulder-line symbol, notches, and underarm seams. Baste the sleeves to the armholes if you feel the need of further evaluating the ease in the sleeve cap.

When you are satisfied with the fit, have made all corrections, and have redrawn the seam lines that were changed, remove the basting, press, and true seam-line markings. Also, mark right and wrong sides so that you can make a trial layout on the skins. For leatherlike fabrics, the trial layout is unnecessary.

Trial layout on real leather. Inspect the skins for marks, holes, or dye irregularities and mark them on the wrong side. With skins right side down on the cutting surface, lay pattern right side down, avoiding the irregularities.

As you handle the leather, you will feel the difference in thickness and firmness between the center area of the skin and the stretchier area near the outer edge. Lay out like pattern sections on like parts of the skin. The best practice is to use the backbone line as the straight grain and place all major pattern sections parallel to the backbone line with the tops toward the neck. Small pattern sections may be placed wherever they fit and without regard for grain if necessary. With suede, nap is a major consideration, and pocket sections and outer collar sections should match the nap direction of the major garment sections just as in fabrics. For the trial layout, use weights to keep the sections in place, and plan the entire layout before securing pattern. [A]

If not all pattern sections can be accommodated, experiment with alternative layouts that will save leather or break up the size of large pattern sections that cannot be cut in one piece. The alternatives are: 1) Reduce seam allowances to $1/2$ or $3/8$ inch where they would later be cut off anyway, such as the outside collar, lapel, or facing seam allowances, armhole and sleeve-cap seam allowances. Then reduce shoulder, side, and sleeve seam allowances, if necessary. Deal cautiously with sectional seams because, where topstitching is used, one seam allowance may need to be a full $5/8$-inch width while the other can be reduced to $1/4$ inch. 2) Breaking up large pattern sections is the most creative step in working with real leather and requires consideration of proportion and fashion lines. Study the fashion illustration and sketch trial seams, such as yokes and panels. Some darts can be continued to form new seam lines. Remember, if you create horizontal seams in the area below the waistline, they should not be straight across, but should follow the curve of the hemline. Keep in mind that space divisions must enhance the proportions of the garment as well as suit the skin size. [B] and [C]

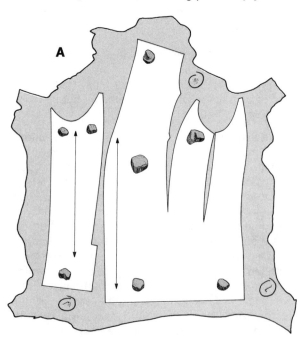

Once you have tentatively decided where the new seams should be placed, mark them on your test-fitting garment sections. Try on the garment and evaluate the proportions. When you are satisfied with the new lines, cut the garment apart on the new seam lines, add extra fabric to provide for seam allowances, and mark the new seam edges with corresponding notches.

Layout and Cutting

For leatherlike fabrics, follow the same rules for pattern layout and cutting as for other fabrics, except: 1) place pins only within dart or seam allowances, and 2) let the face design of the fabric determine whether the top of each pattern section must be placed in the same direction.

For real leather and suede, remember to place all large pattern sections with the tops toward the neck of the skin, and to use the backbone line as the lengthwise grain line. If you have made a test-fitting garment of nonwoven interfacing fabric, use it for layout and cutting rather than the tissue pattern. It is far easier to handle and lessens the possibility of not having a large enough section of leather on which to lay out the second half. Use the strongest parts of the skin for the most prominent parts of the garment. Do not use pins except on very thin leather or suede, and then place them within the seam or dart allowances. Instead, use small squares of magic transparent tape or masking tape along the edges to keep the pattern secure. [D] Sharp, heavy-blade shears will cut single layers of most sewing-weight leathers; but for heavy leather, it is best to use a razor blade or artist's knife over a hardwood board.

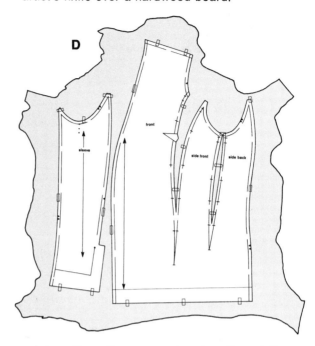

Leave the pattern on each cut section until you are ready to use it. Then mark with soft pencil, felt-tip pen, or chalk just prior to sewing the section. Guard against smears on the right side. Magic transparent tape may also be used for wrong-side markings, but test it on a scrap first to be sure it does not mar the backing. Leave it on only a very short time.

putting leather
garments together

Preparing to Stitch

Thread.
• For soft leather, real suede, and ciré, use size A silk thread.
• For firm leather, use spun polyester thread in the general-purpose size.
• For suedelike and plastic-coated fabrics, use spun polyester or polyester-core thread.

Needle.
• For real leather, suede, and leatherlike plastic-coated fabrics, use a wedge-point sewing machine needle, style 15 x 2, catalog #2032.
• For soft leather, use a size 11 needle, style 15 x 2.
• For medium-weight leather, use a size 14 needle, style 15 x 2.
• For thick leather and leatherlike fabrics, use a size 16 needle, style 15 x 2.
• For ciré, use a size 11 ball-point needle (catalog 2021).
• For suede-like fabrics, use a regular 15 x 1 needle, size 14.

Sewing machine fittings.
Equip your sewing machine with the straight-stitch throat plate. Use the straight-stitch presser foot for soft leather, suede, and ciré, and the general-purpose presser foot for medium and thick weights. The Even Feed sewing machine foot may be used for all weights. The top feeding action of the Even Feed foot overcomes the natural tendency of leather, suede, and plastic-coated fabrics to adhere to the underside of the presser foot and thus retard the movement of the top seam layer.

To improve stitching on leather when you are not using the Even Feed foot:
1. Add a layer of pulpy paper or crisp, thin fabric underneath and on top of the seam layers as you stitch. Then tear the paper or trim the fabric along the stitching.
2. To topstitch on polyurethane or vinyl fabrics, use clear oil† or powder‡ as you stitch to keep the top layer from adhering to the underside of the presser foot. Test before applying to the garment for complete removal of oil or powder.

† SINGER* oil or clear baby oil.
‡ Talcum powder, cornstarch, chalk spot remover.

Test-stitch several seams in real leather or suede, using scraps from both thin and thick parts of the skin. Test seams on leatherlike fabrics, also. Usually you will need to increase the needle-thread tension slightly to compensate for the lack of porosity of these materials. Medium or normal presser-foot pressure is usually adequate. However, if the stitch length appears shorter than set for, increase the pressure slightly; or if feed marks show on the underside and the machine runs hard, decrease the pressure. Use your test-stitched seams to test the new ways of treating seams that follow in the next section.

Darts and Seams

Preparations. Remember to leave the pattern on the cut-out sections and to defer marking until you are ready to use each section. Mark seam widths that vary from the standard ⁵/₈ inch, and mark notches with short, perpendicular lines.

Darts. Fold right sides together, matching markings. If you use pins, place them within the dart allowance because of the permanent holes they will leave, or use paper clips over the fold.

Darts, which are placed over rounded parts of the figure, should be stitched on a slight outward curve, and the last few stitches near the point should be on the edge of the fold. Tie threads at both ends. Slash through the fold as far as possible, and finger-press the allowances open. Trim to ¼ inch. [A]

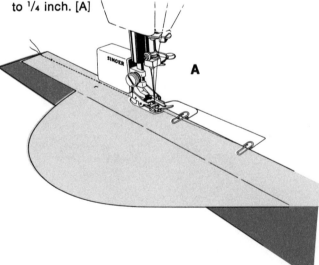

Pounding, Rolling, and Gluing. Pounding seams open on leather and leatherlike fabrics is equivalent to pressing to embed the stitches and to pressing a seam open with the point of the iron. With the garment held over a padded and rounded hardwood surface (or a firm tailor's ham), pound along the stitching line with short, staccato strokes, using a wood mallet. Pound near the dart point to flatten the fold, distributing it equally on each side of the stitching. [B] When working with real suede, always place a scrap of suede, right sides together, under the section to be pounded as additional protection against marring the surface of the garment.

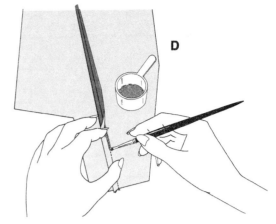

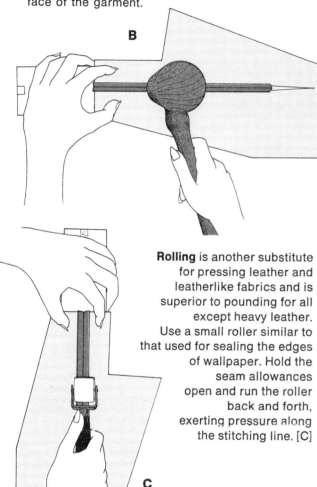

Rolling is another substitute for pressing leather and leatherlike fabrics and is superior to pounding for all except heavy leather. Use a small roller similar to that used for sealing the edges of wallpaper. Hold the seam allowances open and run the roller back and forth, exerting pressure along the stitching line. [C]

Gluing is the process by which seam allowances are held in an open position. Use a glue recommended for leather, such as Sobo brand, or rubber cement. Place a thin line of glue under the seam allowance, slightly inside the seam edge. [D] Finger-press the seam allowance against the garment. Pound lightly or roll to compress the two layers, and allow to dry.

Plan to do as much gluing at one time as possible. Be meticulous and avoid smears. A fine stiff-point brush for applying the glue and a small glue cup will help you to do a neat job. To protect the face of real leather, work with the garment section over a Turkish towel. Plastic-coated fabrics are less subject to blemishes and do not require such protection.

Plain Seam. Place garment sections right sides together. Match edges, if seam allowances are equal, or match seam lines, if seam allowances are unequal. Match seam ends and notches first, and hold together with paper clips or small squares of magic transparent tape. Add clips or tape as needed. [E]

If there is slight ease in one layer of the seam, stitch with that side against the feed. Stitch slowly and keep a firm hold on the seam. [F] Remember, you cannot remove stitches and restitch without leaving holes. Tie threads at both ends, remove tape, and finger-press seam open. Pound or roll along stitching line and glue seam allowances open.

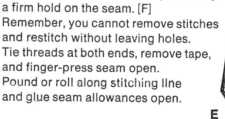

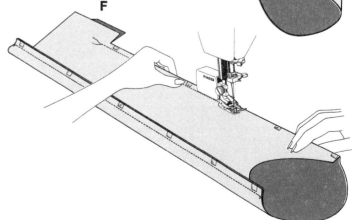

Taped Seam. When extra strength is required, include shrunk twill tape or woven-edge seam binding in the seam as you stitch. [A] Pound or roll along the stitching line and glue seam allowances open, following the method given for a plain seam.

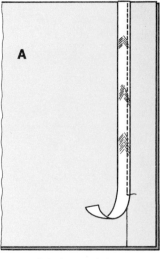

Double-Topstitched Seam. Stitch a plain seam, pound or roll it open, but do not glue. Topstitch an equal distance from center on each side through garment and seam allowance.

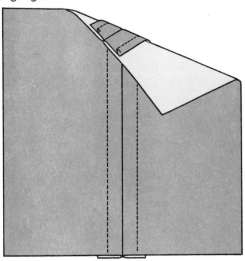

Welt Seam. Seam allowances may be equal or unequal for the welt seam. Stitch a plain seam on the stitching line. Pound or roll seam open

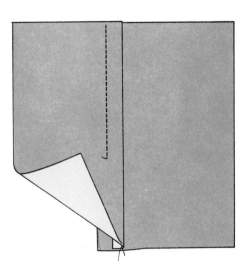

first. Then turn seam allowances to one side and pound or roll again. Trim the seam allowance next to the garment to ¼ inch. Topstitch through garment and one seam layer. Use no glue.

Slot Seam. Turn both seam allowances under along seam line. Pound or roll and glue. Cut a strip of leather, suede, or plastic twice the seam width plus ½ inch. Center the strip, right side against one seam allowance, and topstitch one side. Hold the strip and abutted edges in place with strips of magic transparent tape or masking tape, and stitch second side. Do not stitch through the tape.

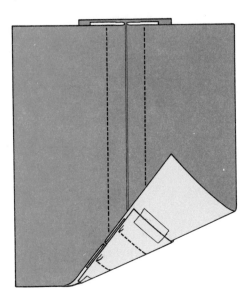

Seams in Heavy Leather. Variations of slot and flat-fell seams can be made in heavy leather by using unturned edges.

For a mock slot seam, cut leather strip twice the

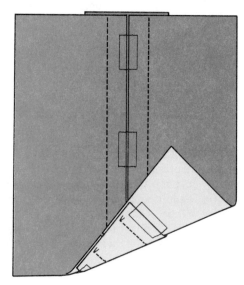

width of the topstitching from center edge plus $\frac{1}{2}$ inch. Center strip, right side against underside of seam. Topstitch one side, holding abutted edges in place with strips of tape, Topstitch second side.

For a mock flat-fell seam, overlap seam edges $\frac{1}{2}$ inch. Secure one seam edge with tape on underside. Stitch close to the other seam edge from the top. Remove the tape and stitch that seam edge. This seam requires only $\frac{1}{4}$-inch seam allowances when cutting. Other seam widths may be used if desired.

Clipping, Notching, and Trimming Seam Allowances. Straight seam allowances [A] present few problems in handling, but curved seam allowances must be carefully clipped or notched so that they form a smooth and continuous line. Clip small wedges to flatten seam allowances that ripple [B], and slash into seam allowances that draw too tightly [C] and restrict the shape of the garment. Diagonally cut seam allowances at cross seams. Cut seam allowances that are inside faced edges to unequal widths, such as $\frac{1}{4}$ and $\frac{1}{8}$ inch. [D]

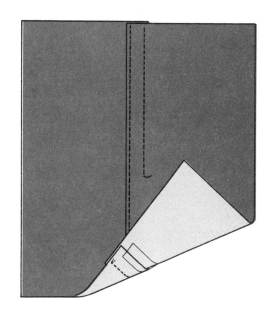

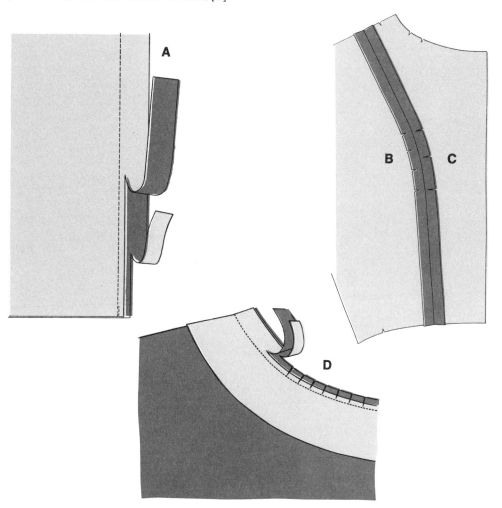

making pockets and buttonholes

Pockets and bound or corded buttonholes should be completed before garment sections are interfaced and assembled. Hand-worked and mock-bound buttonholes should be stitched after the garment is completed.

Real leather and leatherlike fabrics have three characteristics that affect their handling in making buttonholes: 1) they do not ravel so that an unsupported slash or a cut edge is acceptable; 2) they are more rigid than fabrics so that a conventional patch or strip is difficult to turn to the inside; and 3) they do not compress as readily as fabrics so that bulk under the presser foot is undesirable.

The mock bound buttonhole is very easy to do well and quickly. The strip buttonhole is a true buttonhole but the procedure for making it in leather varies slightly from that for making it in fabrics.

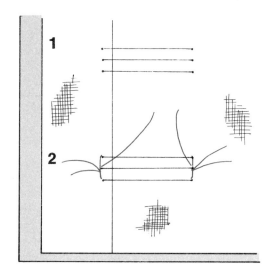

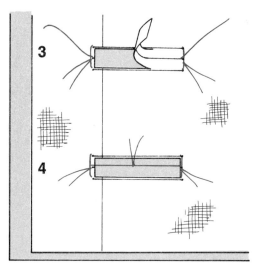

Mock Bound Buttonhole in Real or Fake Leather

1. Mark buttonhole position, length, and width on the interfacing with pen, chalk or pencil. Mark a center line and mark additional lines $\frac{1}{4}$ or $\frac{3}{8}$ inch above and below the center line.

2. Mark corners of rectangle and the center line with silk thread on the outside of the garment as shown in illustration 5. Working from the inside, take one stitch across each end by bringing the needle down through one corner and up through the other. Tie thread ends together. Take one long stitch to mark the center line. Do not tie these thread ends until after you have completed step 3.

3. Cut out rectangle from interfacing, but do not cut silk marking threads.

4. Then tie the ends of the center-line-marking thread together.

5. Delay further steps for buttonholes until after the facing has been applied and anchored on the inside edge.

6. Stitch buttonhole from the outside of the garment with a 10 to 15 stitch length and a straight stitch, using a matching thread color.

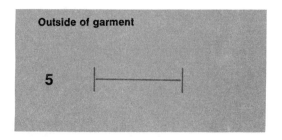

Outside of garment

To stitch, refer to diagram. Start at the center of one end, stitch to the corner mark, pivot on the needle, and continue stitching and pivoting until the rectangle is completed.

Then reposition needle and stitch along one side of the center marking to within one stitch of the end. Pivot on the needle and take one stitch. Using the reverse stitch control, stitch backward one stitch and forward one stitch, and then repeat to reinforce the end. Stitch second side, and reinforce starting end.

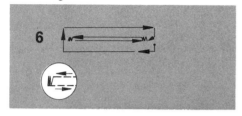

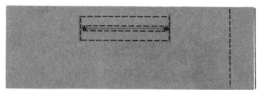

7. Draw thread ends to underside and tie. Remove marking threads.

8. Cut on center line through both garment and facing layers.

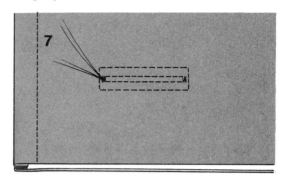

Strip Buttonhole in Real or Fake Leather

• Make buttonholes before applying interfacing.

Cut two strips for each buttonhole. Cut the strips 1 inch longer than the buttonhole. Determine the most appropriate strip width by making test buttonholes, using the following chart.

Buttonhole Width	Lip Width	Strip Width
$1/4$ inch	$1/8$ inch	$1/2$ inch
$3/8$ inch	$3/16$ inch	$3/4$ inch
$1/2$ inch	$1/4$ inch	1 inch

• Fold strips in half, glue lightly, roll to compress, and allow glue to dry.

1. Abut folded edges of two strips and wrap ends with magic transparent tape for exactly $1/2$ inch.

2. Mark rectangle for buttonhole on garment and mark cutting lines for center and angular cuts to corners.

3. Cut on center and angular lines. Cutting must be accurate.

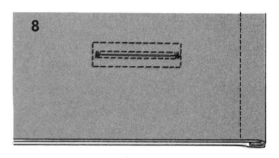

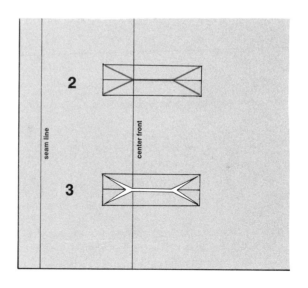

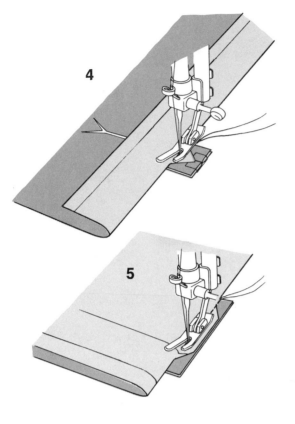

4. To stitch strips to ends of buttonhole slash: With garment right side up, fold it along the right-hand end of the buttonhole, triangular tab extended.

Place strips under buttonhole, folds of strips centered and seam allowance extending under tab. Stitch across tab and strips at garment fold line and $\frac{1}{2}$ inch from end of strip.

• Repeat for second end.

5. Turn garment and stitch one side of buttonhole at a time, keeping the three seam edges of the buttonhole slash and strip even, centering the stitching on the strip, and stitching slightly inside the slashes at the corners.

• Flatten the buttonhole from the right side with your fingers and the roller.

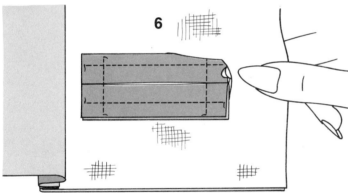

6. After interfacing has been applied to garment, cut out a rectangular box from the interfacing to coincide with buttonhole stitching lines. Lift seam allowances of buttonhole strip through opening and lightly glue them to the interfacing.

7. To finish buttonhole through facing, stitch from the outside in the buttonhole seam crevice along edges and ends. Tie thread ends.

8. Trim facing inside stitching lines.

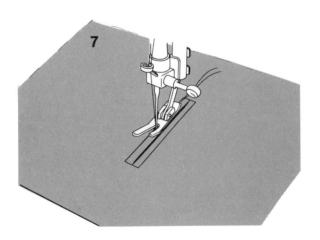

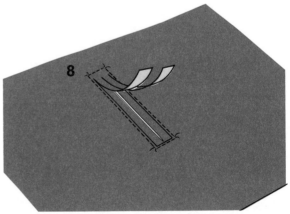

assembling the garment

To Attach Underlining and Interfacing

The method you choose to apply the underlining or interfacing depends on the styling of the garment, the kind of underlining or interfacing you have chosen, and whether your garment is of real leather, real suede, or plastic.

Back. For most leather or suede garments, apply hair canvas as illustrated. [A] Cut off hair-canvas seam allowances at the back neckline and shoulders, and cut all internal seams and darts on stitching lines. Do not cut off armhole seam allowances. Join internal seams and darts in hair canvas with abutted seams, supported with a woven fabric underlay and topstitched with multi-stitch zig-zag stitching. Attach to leather or suede with a thin line of glue at shoulders, back of neck, and side or side back seams. Do not glue at armholes or bottom edge. Allow glue to dry before continuing work on the back section.

For leatherlike, thin leather, and suede garments, apply a firm, woven or nonwoven fabric reinforcement at the back as illustrated. [B] Join internal sectional seams and darts in the back reinforcement with edges overlapped, seam lines matching, and using one line of multi-stitch zig-zag stitching. Machine-baste reinforcement to garment at shoulder and side seams, placing machine basting 1/4 inch from seam edges, and staystitching back neckline 1/8 inch outside the seam line. As you assemble the garment, include the reinforcement fabric in the seams. Then remove the machine basting and trim the reinforcement seam allowances close to the stitching.

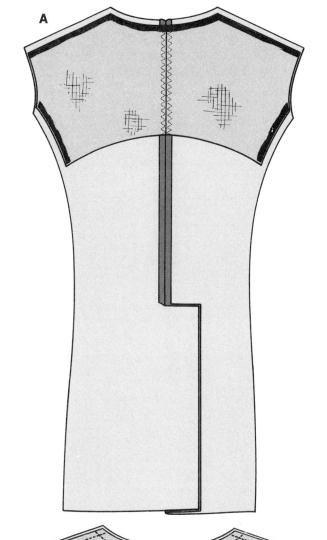

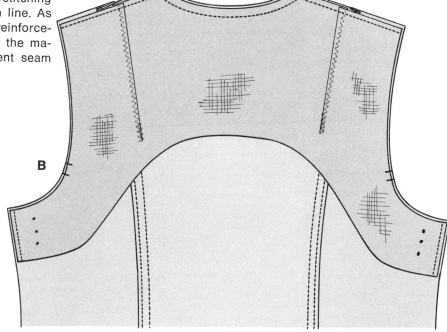

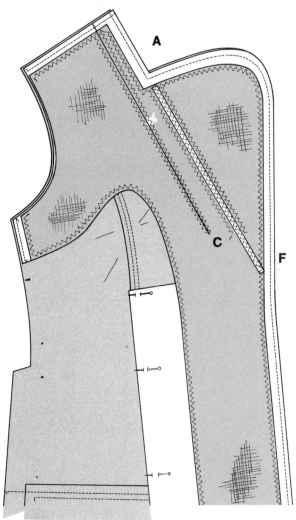

Tailored lapels and collar. For garments of real or fake leather with tailored lapels and collar, follow Method 2, pages 40 and 41 for partially underlined jackets. Use a thin, crisp, permanent-press underlining fabric rather than organza for the partial underlining. As interfacing, use hair canvas for a crisp effect or nonwoven polyester fleece, such as Thermolam interfacing for loft. Attach the interfacing to the partial underlining with multi-stitch zig-zag stitching. Then stitch ¼-inch twill tape to the underlined interfacing along the collar and lapel roll lines, using straight or multi-stitch zig-zag stitching. Use paper clips sparingly instead of hand basting to hold the underlined interfacing to the garment temporarily. Machine-baste ¼ inch from seam edges at shoulder, side, and front below roll line. [A] Substitute multi-stitch zig-zag stitching for hand padding stitches in the stand of the under collar. [B] Make one line of stitching on each side of the lapel roll line but stop at least 2 inches from the junction of the front seam line and roll line. [C]

Shape collar and lapels as described for tailoring, Method 1, but do not use steam. Additional multi-stitch zig-zag stitching that would function as padding stitches is optional. Use paper clips along edges to hold underlining to the under collar [D] and lapels. Then machine-baste ¼ inch outside seam line through garment and underlining of under collar [E] and lapels. [F]

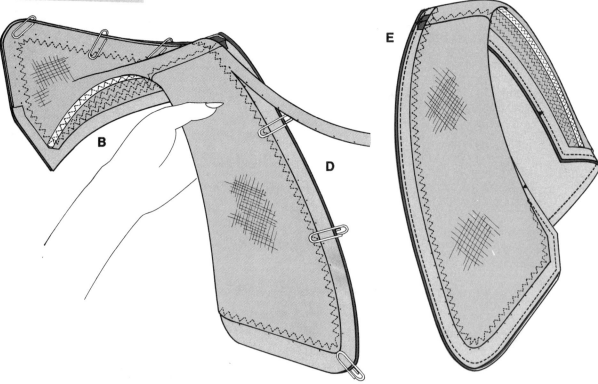

Collarless neckline. For a collarless garment without lapels, plan to use topstitching as a final finish because it will hold the interfacing securely in place. Prepare darts and seams in the interfacing [G] and trim off front, shoulder, and side or side-back seam allowances. Attach hair canvas or nonwoven interfacing to front with a very thin line of glue, bringing the interfacing, which has been trimmed at the seam line, to the garment seam line. Hold the inside edge of the interfacing in place with squares of magic transparent tape until after the facing has been applied. [H] Then, when the facing has been completely attached and topstitched, machine-baste the free interfacing and facing edges together.

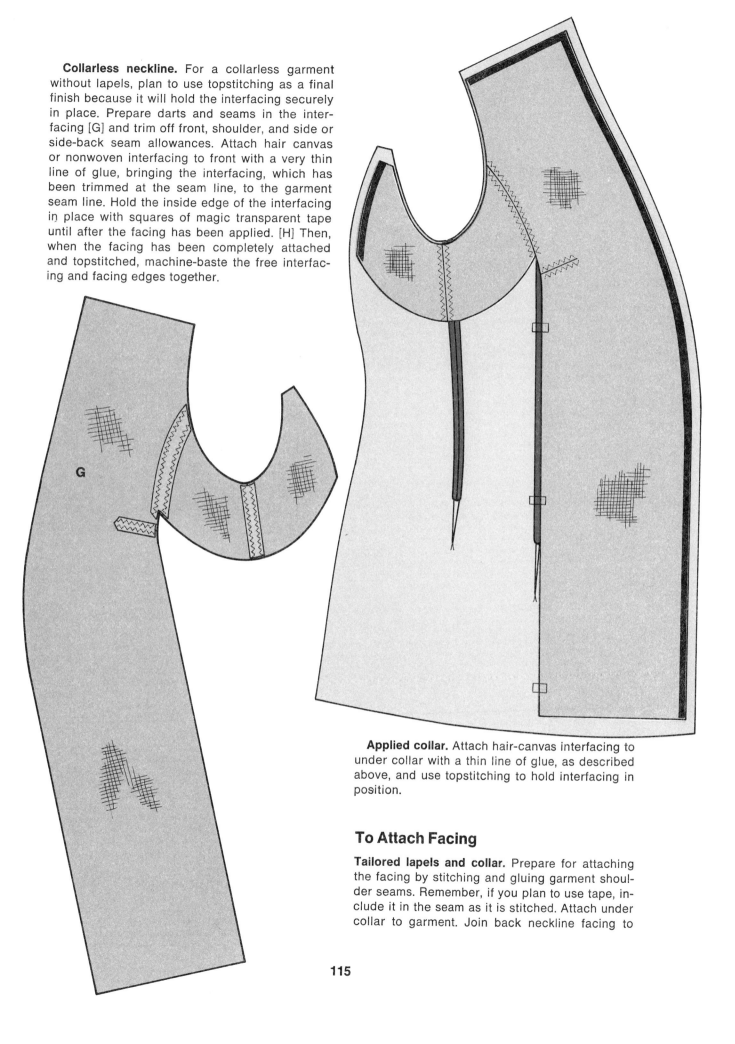

Applied collar. Attach hair-canvas interfacing to under collar with a thin line of glue, as described above, and use topstitching to hold interfacing in position.

To Attach Facing

Tailored lapels and collar. Prepare for attaching the facing by stitching and gluing garment shoulder seams. Remember, if you plan to use tape, include it in the seam as it is stitched. Attach under collar to garment. Join back neckline facing to front facing and join facing unit to upper collar. Pound all of these seam allowances open and glue them. To reduce bulk, the back neckline facing may be made of one layer of lining fabric and one of polyester nonwoven interfacing handled as one.

Use paper clips or squares of magic transparent tape to hold garment and facing seam edges together. Stitch in the directions described on page 47. Complete the collar and lapels as described on pages 36 to 39. Remember to pound or roll rather than to press, and to glue seam allowances. Topstitch rather than baste. When topstitching is not used, machine understitching is acceptable where it will not show when the garment is worn.

Collarless neckline. Prepare for attaching the facing by stitching the shoulder seams of the garment and facing sections. Pound or roll along seam lines and glue seam allowances open. If you plan to tape the facing seam, hold the pressed-to-shape twill tape over the seam line of the garment with squares of magic transparent tape. Hold the facing to the garment, right sides together, with paper clips. Stitch from center back to hem edge with garment side against the feed, overlapping stitching and tying threads at center back. Pound or roll the seam allowances open. Trim seam allowances to unequal widths, keeping the garment seam allowance wider. Notch and slash into seam allowances so that they will be smooth and even. Use glue sparingly to hold the seam allowances open. Turn the facing to the inside and pound or roll the turned edges from the facing side to compress the layers. Delay topstitching until hem is prepared.

To Set Sleeves

Follow the method described on pages 51 and 52 except trim the seam allowances from both the armhole and sleeve to 3/8 inch. Mark notches and shoulder-line locations on the trimmed seams. Control ease in the sleeve cap with a long machine stitch placed between the notches only a thread's width outside the seam line. Hold sleeve to armhole with paper clips placed at underarm seam, shoulder-line symbol, at each set of notches, and above each notch if required. Stitch on the seam line from the sleeve side of the seam. Pound or roll seam allowances open over sleeve cap to flatten ease and sharpen seam, but turn both seam allowances toward the sleeve after pounding. Apply shaped 1/4-inch twill tape at underarm next to the garment between notches by stitching one edge of the tape 1/8 inch outside seam line and allowing the other edge to extend toward the

garment. Continue stitching through seam allowances over the sleeve cap, but do not tape. Trim seam allowances at the underarm between notches to 1/4 inch. Pad sleeve cap (optional) as described on page 52, using either method unless leather is too heavy for hand stitching.

To Hem

To mark the hem length in a leather garment, measure and mark the garment an inch below the hem fold line so that the marks will not show on the finished garment. Remove garment and turn hem an inch above the marks, placing paper clips over the fold line. Pound or roll along the fold line (not over clips) to form a crease and to shape the hem. Trim seam allowances within the hem to half width and measure and cut hem to an even width.

Plain hems in leather garments should be held with glue. Spread glue thinly over the inside of the hem and the part of the garment the hem will cover, to within 1/2 inch of the top of the hem. Let the glue dry for a few moments, then fold and finger-press the hem in place. Using the roller, roll from edge to top of hem. Let the glue dry before handling further.

Topstitched hems are suitable for some styles of leather garments on which topstitching has been used elsewhere. Do not use glue before topstitching because it may foul the needle and cause skipped stitches. Instead, use squares of magic transparent tape to hold hem temporarily while stitching. Avoid placing the tape over the stitching line.

To Attach Lining

To line an unfaced garment, cut lining and garment alike. Trim 1/8 inch from lining at armholes, neckline and front edges to make lining slightly smaller and to allow for turning edges so that lining is concealed.

When lining a jumper, sleeveless vest, or a similar garment, leave side seams open until after the lining is attached at armholes, neckline, front, and hems. Machine-stitch lining to garment. Cut seam allowances to uneven widths, turn to right side, and understitch almost to side seams. Machine-stitch garment side seams through side-seam openings in lining. Slipstitch lining side seams.

To line a faced garment you have two choices. The lining may be machine-stitched to the leather facing edge or you may machine-stitch fabric cording or piping, or braid, to the leather facing edge and then hand-slipstitch the lining to the facing finish. Refer to page 93.

Chapter VI

buttonholes

Buttonholes are either bound with fabric or worked with thread. Those bound with fabric enhance the appearance of a garment and thus are preferred for fashion apparel. A bound buttonhole is made by stitching strips or squares of fabric to a garment to form lips through which the button passes. There are many methods of making bound buttonholes. Four of these methods — patch, simplified bound, two-piece piped, and corded — are explained in this chapter. Special methods for fur and leather are explained in the chapters on these special fabrics.

Worked buttonholes, in which the opening is finished with thread, may be made by machine or by hand. A machine buttonhole is the simplest and easiest to make of all buttonholes.

Hand-stitched buttonholes can be handsome, but they take practice and skill, and few women today make them often enough to do them well. Both machine and hand-made buttonholes are generally used in a utilitarian way rather than as a fashion accent.

preparatory steps

Position of Buttonhole

The rules for positioning apply to all types of buttonholes:

Buttonholes in women's and girls' clothes are placed on the right side of the garment; in men's and boys' wear, on the left side.

Horizontal buttonholes are placed to extend 1/8 inch beyond the center line basting; vertical buttonholes are placed so that the center line basting falls in the center of the buttonhole.

Buttons are sewn on the opposite side of the garment, with the center of the button positioned exactly on the center line basting. When the garment is buttoned, the center lines on the right and left sides coincide. If a closing overlaps more or less than the pattern indicates, the fit of the garment is altered.

The pattern usually designates the button size the garment is designed to carry. The space from the center line basting to the finished facing edge must be from three-quarters to once the diameter of the button. With this spacing, the button will not extend beyond the facing edge when the garment is buttoned. If you plan to use a button different in size from that indicated on the pattern, allow the proper distance between the center line and finished edge. Adjust facing width the same amount.

Spaces between buttonholes should generally be equal although fashion may show a different arrangement, especially in loosely fitted garments. Your pattern will designate the spacing required. However, if you have lengthened or shortened the pattern, or if you use a larger or smaller button

117

than the size indicated on the pattern, you will have to modify the spaces between the buttonholes accordingly.

Normally, buttonholes should be spaced in harmony with the figure. When they are incorrectly spaced, the closing will gap, giving the appearance of a poorly fitted garment.

The three key points for positioning buttonholes are at the fullest part of the bust, at the neckline, and at the waistline. Mark the position of the buttonhole at the fullest part of the bust, then at the neckline, and then at the waistline. After locating these key points, space additional buttonholes evenly between them. If the pattern has buttons all the way down the front, place the last buttonhole at least 4 inches from the hem edge.

Determine the positions of the buttonholes and mark the fabric while the pattern is still pinned to it. During the first fitting, check the positions to prove that they are accurate.

Length of Buttonhole

Since the length of the buttonhole depends on the size of the button, select your buttons before making buttonholes. To determine the length, measure the diameter plus the thickness of the button. To test the length, cut a slash in a double thickness of fabric. If the button slips through the slash easily, the size is correct.

Always make a test buttonhole of the length you have just determined in a scrap of the fashion fabric. Make the buttonhole through a layer of fashion fabric and a layer of underlining or stay fabric (or both), keeping the fabric grains the same as the garment. The buttonhole should be long enough so that the button will slip through easily, yet snug enough so that it will stay buttoned.

Stay for Buttonholes

A stay for buttonholes is a strip of firm, thin fabric that acts as a reinforcement for the lines of stitching for the buttonhole.

Bound buttonholes are never made through haircanvas interfacing, but they are sometimes made through pliable interfacing such as tailor's canvas that does not contain hair. Such interfacing acts as a stay when the fashion fabric is loosely woven like a tweed fabric. Otherwise, bound buttonholes are always made through the fashion fabric and at least one layer of stay fabric or crisp underlining fabric that acts as a stay. When the underlining fabric is soft or loosely woven, a stay may be used in addition to the underlining.

The stay may be of a closely woven fabric such as crisp lawn, organdy, organza, or lightweight interfacing fabric. Or, the stay may be of a non-

woven, press-on interfacing fabric, which is adhered to either the underside of the fashion fabric or to the underlining. All press-on interfacing fabrics should be tested on the fashion fabric before being used in a garment to make certain the edges will not show as ridges on the outside.

Guidelines for Bound Buttonholes

Study the lines [A], [B], [C], and [D] on the diagram. These lines of basting are made on the lengthwise and crosswise grains of the fabric and are your guidelines for stitching the buttonholes. For basting, use thread contrasting in color to that of the fabric so that it can be easily seen and removed.

On the right side of the garment, place a vertical line of machine basting 1/8 inch outside the center line basting [B]. The center line [A] is not necessarily the center front line. In reference to button-

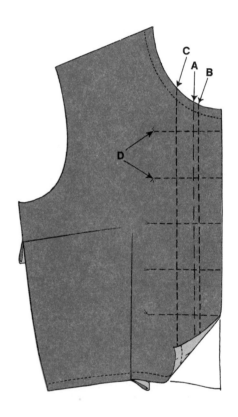

holes, the center line is the line on which the centers of all buttons rest when the garment is closed. Measure the length of the buttonholes and place the second vertical line of machine basting the measured distance from [B], as at [C]. Machine-baste the position of each buttonhole on a horizontal line, extending each end of the stitching about 3/4 inch beyond the vertical markings [D]. Use hand basting if machine basting will mar the fabric.

Patch Method

The patch method is best for light-to-medium-weight fabrics that do not ravel but do crease easily. The patch method requires additional markings for accurately stitched buttonholes.

1. Machine-baste the vertical and horizontal guidelines, [B], [C], and [D], as described on opposite page. Then, on the stay, draw a pencil line on each side of, and ⅛ inch from, the horizontal basting [E]. These are the stitching lines. If the fabric is bulky, draw the lines ¼ inch or ⅜ inch from the basting.

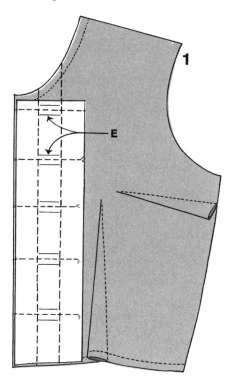

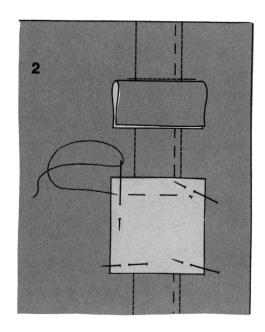

to the end; leave the needle in the fabric, raise the presser foot, and turn the fabric on the needle. Lower the presser foot and stitch across the end, taking four or five stitches. Continue stitching around the buttonhole, turning each corner in the same way; make the same number of stitches at each end and overlap about four stitches at the starting pointing. Press.

2. For each buttonhole, cut a patch of fabric on the crosswise grain or on the true bias, 2 inches wide and 1 inch longer than the finished buttonhole. Unless the patch is bias, the fabric grain in the patch should run the same way in the finished buttonhole as the grain of the garment. Crease lightly through the center, following the crosswise grain (or true bias) of the fabric.

On the right side of the garment, center a patch over each buttonhole marking, right sides together. Pin in position; baste if necessary. [F]

3. On the wrong side, stitch around the buttonhole, following the markings. Use a 20 stitch length. Begin at the center of one side and stitch

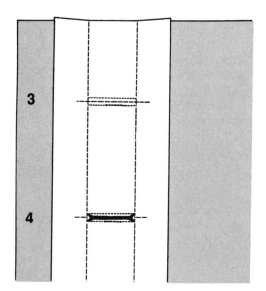

4. Remove basting threads across each end of the buttonhole. Carefully cut through the center of the buttonhole to within ¼ inch of each end; then cut diagonally to each corner. Do not clip through the stitching.

119

5. On the right side of the garment, draw the patch through the opening to the underside.

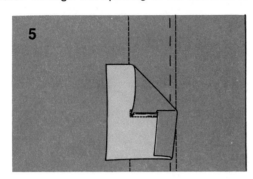

6. Carefully pull out the triangular ends to square the corners. If the slashes are made deeply enough into the corners, the opening will be smooth. Press the triangular ends and side seam allowances away from the opening.

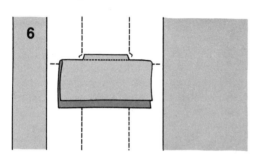

7. From the right side, pin and fold each side of the patch to form pleats that meet at the center of the buttonhole and cover the opening. Carry the folds to the edge of the patch. Baste along the center of each fold, then overcast the fold together. Remove machine-basted guidelines. Press.

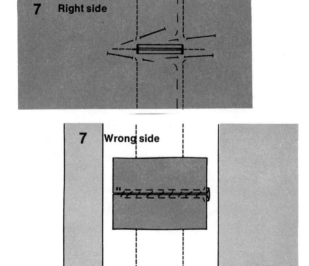

8. Place the garment right side up on the machine, fold it back to expose the triangular ends and stitch across the triangular ends and the pleats, starting and ending at the edges of the patch.

Then stitch along the seams on each side, just a hair's width from the original stitching line, beginning and ending at the raw edge of the patch.

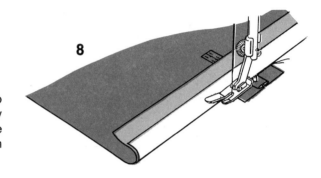

The side stitching crosses the end stitching and squares the corners. The stitching is not visible on the right side.

9. Remove all hand bastings except the overcasting holding the pleats together. Press. Trim the patch to within ¼ inch of the stitching.

Treat the interfacing as described on page 124, and finish the back of the buttonhole after the facing is attached as described on page 125.

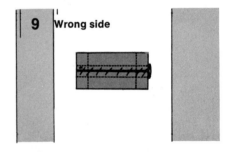

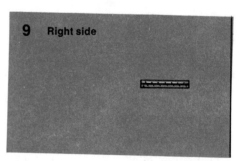

Corded Method

The corded method is best for light-to-medium-weight woven fabrics and for all knit fabrics. It is also recommended for spongy fabrics and for fabrics that are crease resistant.

1. Prepare corded bias strips from true bias 1 inch wide and long enough for all buttonholes to be made. Determine the length needed by allowing twice the length plus 2 inches for each buttonhole.

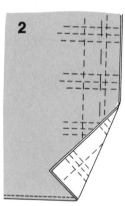

Use No. 9 cable cord, available at notion counters. Replace the presser foot with the adjustable zipper foot. Fold the bias strip, right side out, around the cord. Stitch close to the cord, but do not crowd. Press.

2. Make additional markings required for corded buttonholes. On the stay, draw a pencil line on

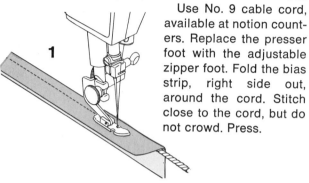

each side ¼ or 5/16 inch from each buttonhole position line. Machine-baste on these lines to transfer the markings to the right side. The spacing of these lines from the buttonhole marking will vary, depending on the weight of the fabric used.

3. For each buttonhole, cut two strips of cording 1 inch longer than the buttonhole. Center the strips

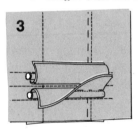

over each buttonhole marking, aligning the corded edges with the outside markings and keeping the raw edges toward the center. Hand-baste in position.

4. Using a short stitch and the zipper foot, stitch the cording to the garment. Stitch just inside the stitching line that encases the cord, and begin and end the stitching at the guidelines that designate

the buttonhole length. Stitch the other side in the same way. Inspect the stitching on the underside to be sure that the lines are parallel and end evenly at the markings. Bring the threads through to the underside and tie them. Remove the bastings that hold the cording to the garment.

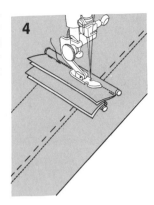

5. From the underside, cut at the center between the two lines of stitching, through the garment and stay, to within ¼ inch of one end of the buttonhole and then the other; then cut diagonally to each corner. The basted guidelines across the ends will prevent fraying at the corners until the ends are stitched in place.

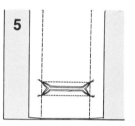

6. Draw the strip through the opening to the underside. Carefully pull the triangular ends away from the opening to square the corners. Press. With the corded edges meeting at the center of the opening, diagonally baste the corded edges together.

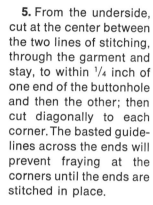

7. With the straight-stitch presser foot on the machine, place the garment right side up, fold it back and stitch the triangular ends to the cording strips at each end of the buttonhole. Remove the vertical guidelines. Trim the ends and sides of the cording strips to wthin ¼ inch of the stitching. Press. Treat the interfacing as described on page 124, and finish the back of the buttonhole after the facing is attached as described on page 125.

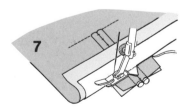

Simplified Method

The simplified bound-buttonhole method can be used on all types of fabrics that are not marred by machine stitching.

1. Remember to baste the buttonhole position line to extend $^3/_4$ inch beyond the vertical lines that indicate the buttonhole length.

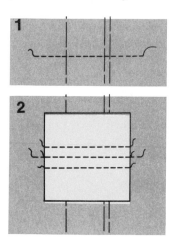

2. Cut a patch for each buttonhole on the same grain as the garment, 2 inches wide and 1 inch longer than the buttonhole.

With right sides together, center the patch along the position line and machine-baste it exactly on the position line.

Machine-baste $^1/_4$ inch above and below the position line.

3. Fold down and press the top edge on the basting. With the straight-stitch presser foot, stitch exactly $^1/_8$ from the folded edge for the exact length of the buttonhole. Do the same on the bottom free edge.

Bring the thread ends to the underside and tie.

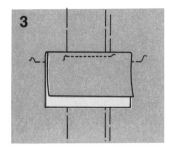

4. Working from the inside of the garment, cut from the center to within $^1/_4$ inch of one end

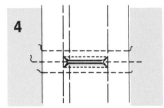

of the buttonhole and then the other. Then cut diagonally into each of the four corners. Do not cut through the machine stitching. Remove all three bastings that hold thte patch to the garment.

5. Working from the right side, cut through the center of the patch only from outer edge toward the center. The patch now has become two strips.

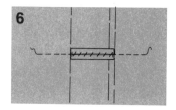

6. Draw the seam allowances of the strips through the buttonhole opening and pull the diagonal ends away from the opening. Working from the right side, diagonally baste the lips together.

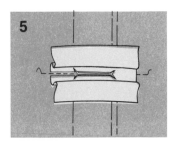

7. Working from the wrong side, slip-stitch together the folded outer edges of the lips [A] to [B].

8. Place the garment right side up on the machine, fold it back and, using a short stitch, stitch the triangular ends to the patch. Remove all basting and press. Trim ends and sides of patch to within $^1/_4$ inch of stitching. Treat the interfacing as described on page 124, and finish the back of the button-hole after the facing is attached as described on page 125.

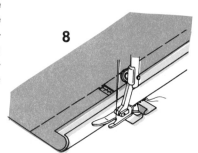

Two-Piece Piped Method

For heavy, bulky, or loosely woven fabric, this is the method to use. Because these fabrics require heavy interfacing, apply the interfacing after making the buttonholes to eliminate bulk.

1. With a stay of lightweight fabric positioned on the underside, baste guidelines to mark the buttonhole positions as described on page 118. Draw pencil lines about 3/16 inch from both sides of the horizontal basting line on the stay as markings for the stitching. See page 119.

2. Cut a patch of organza 2 inches wide and 1 inch longer than the finished buttonhole. (The color of the organza must match the fabric exactly.) Center the patch over the buttonhole marking on the right side of the fabric. Pin in place and baste if necessary.

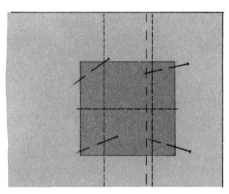

3. Place the garment on the machine, wrong side up. Using a 20 stitch length, stitch around the buttonhole, following the markings exactly. Begin at the center of one side and stitch to the end; pivot and take four or five stitches across the end. Pivot again at the corner and continue stitching around the buttonhole, pivoting again at the other end in the same way. Be sure to make the same number of stitches across each end and overlap about four stitches at the starting point. Press. Carefully remove the basted guidelines that pass through the center and across the ends of the buttonhole.

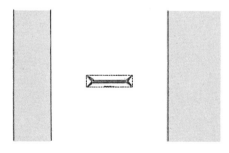

4. Starting at the center of the buttonhole, cut to within 3/16 inch of each end; then cut diagonally to each corner. Do not clip through the stitching.

5. Turn the organza patch through the opening to the underside. Carefully pull out the triangular

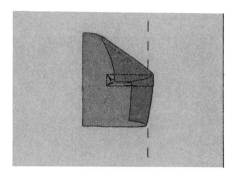

ends to square the corners and press them away from the opening. Turn the seam allowances and the organza patch away from the opening along the sides, fold on the stitching line, and press flat against the fabric.

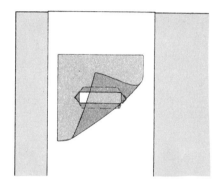

6. *For the piping,* cut two strips of garment fabric on the crosswise grain, 1½ inches wider and 1 inch longer than the finished buttonhole. With their right sides together, machine-baste through the center, following the grain line of the fabric. Leave sufficient thread at each end for easy removal of the basting.

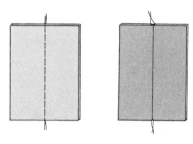

7. Press, then press the basted seam open, using a press cloth to protect the right side of the fabric. (Each strip should now be folded, wrong sides together, and both strips should be temporarily basted together along the folds.)

8. With the garment right side up, place the strip over the wrong side of the opening with the basted seam centered and the ends extending $1/2$ inch beyond the opening. Pin the strip in place with fine needles close to the ends of the opening.

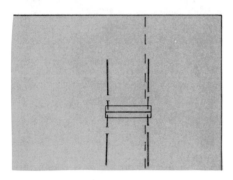

9. Place the garment right side up on the machine; turn back the edge and stitch the seam allowances and organza patch to the strip. Use a 20 stitch length, and place the stitching barely beyond the previous stitching so that the organza patch will not be visible on the top side of the garment. First pin the triangular ends to the strip

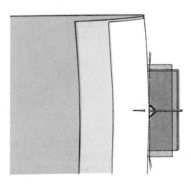

with fine needles and stitch across the ends; then, just before stitching along each side, remove the needles on the top side and pin the seam allowances and organza to the strip on the underside to

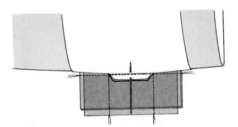

prevent them from slipping during the stitching. Trim the ends of the strip to within $1/4$ inch of the stitching; along the sides, trim the seam allowance on the top layer of the strip to $1/4$ inch and on the bottom layer to $3/8$ inch. Before pressing, slip

brown paper between the garment and seam allowance to prevent the outline of the seam allowance from being pressed onto the fabric.

Treat the interfacing as described below. Finish the back of the buttonhole after the facing is attached, following the directions on page 125. Remove the basting joining the buttonhole strips.

Treating heavy interfacing

Hair canvas or heavy canvas interfacing is attached to the underside of the garment after bound buttonholes have been made through a stay. Be sure that the interfacing lies smoothly against the garment section.

Pin around each buttonhole through all layers. From the right side, insert a pin straight through each of the four corners to mark the positions of the stitching lines of the buttonhole on the interfacing.

From the underside, using the pins as a guide, cut out a rectangle from the interfacing barely outside the pins. The cut-out will be slightly longer and wider than the buttonhole. Lift the seam allowances of the buttonhole through the opening in the interfacing.

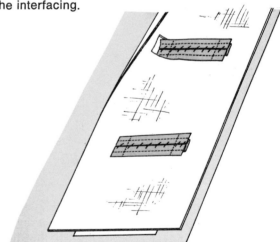

Finishing the Back of Buttonholes

After the interfacing and facing have been applied to the garment, finish the buttonhole through the facing by one of the following three methods:

The rectangle method is suitable when the fabric will not ravel easily and when the facing side will not be visible when the garment is open.

Hand-baste around the buttonhole through all fabric layers. From the right side, insert pins straight through each of the four corners to mark the position of the buttonhole stitching on the facing.

On the underside, cut the facing between the end pins, through the center, to within 1/4 inch of the ends; then cut diagonally to each corner.

Use the point of a fine needle to turn the edges under. Then slip-stitch the facing, covering the buttonhole stitching lines, to the patch or strip. The facing side has the same shape as the front of the buttonhole.

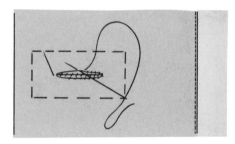

The oval method is suitable for tweeds and fabrics that ravel easily and for jackets and coats that will not be worn opened.

Hand-baste around the buttonhole through all fabric layers. From the right side, insert one pin through each end of the buttonhole to mark the position and length of each buttonhole on the facing.

On the underside, cut the facing between the pins.

Use the point of a needle to turn the edges under to form an oval shape, and slip-stitch the facing to the lips of the buttonhole.

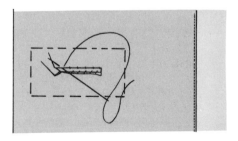

The windowpane method should be used whenever the facing side of the buttonhole will be visible when the garment is worn, in which case it must be as neatly finished as the garment side.

Instead of hand-basting the facing to the buttonhole, pin it in place. Mark the buttonhole stitching lines by inserting pins straight through at the four corners from the right side of the garment. Then insert another set of pins straight through, in the same places, from the facing side. Remove the first set of pins.

Carefully lift and separate the facing from the garment, leaving the pins to mark the buttonhole location on the facing. Baste the outline of the buttonhole, using the pins as a guide.

1. Using organza that matches the garment fabric, cut a piece 2 inches wide and 1 inch longer than the buttonhole. Center the patch over the basted marking on the right side of the facing, and baste as in "Patch Method," Step 2, page 119. Continue to follow "Patch Method," Steps 2 through 5 for stitching, cutting, and turning the organza patch to the underside.

Turn the seam allowances and organza patch away from the opening on the stitching lines, at the ends and along the sides and press.

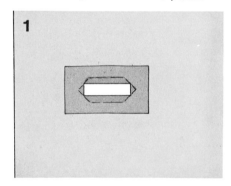

2. Center this rectangular opening over the back of the buttonhole and baste in place. Slip-stitch the opening to the buttonhole.

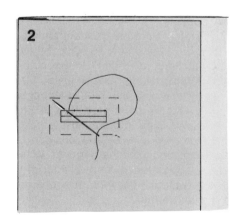

125

pockets

Pockets are usually included in a tailored coat or jacket for both fashion interest and utility. Since they call attention to the part of the figure where they are placed, they should be considered in the initial planning and fitting of your garment, so that your particular figure requirements may be taken into account. For example, you can avoid using pockets where they are called for if they increase your apparent size where you prefer to diminish it. Also, when you must lengthen or shorten your pattern, consider whether the position of the pockets must be changed to preserve the balance of the design. Read and heed all special preparation steps for the kind of pocket application you plan to make before cutting the pocket sections.

Pockets designed to set into a seam are the easiest kind to make, but you must follow the pattern markings exactly for seam lines and other symbols that must be matched so that the parts go together smoothly.

Set-in pockets are made through the garment fabric by stitching, slashing, and turning the pocket section to the inside of the garment. Some of the names given to these pockets are: buttonhole, stand, corded, and welt. The welt pocket, which is the most popular of the set-in variety, is described in this chapter.

Patch pockets, as the name implies, are prepared separately from the garment and applied to it later in one of the following ways: by hand with invisible stitching; by hand or machine with a welt type of topstitching, spaced inside the pocket edge; or by machine stitching, placed near the edge. They may be plain or cuffed, or they may have a separate flap. In planning a patch pocket, consider not only its size and position but also how it will be applied to the garment. With a welt-type application, for example, the underneath layer of the welt will show, so it should be made of the fashion fabric.

Pocket Set into a Seam

Follow pattern seam-line markings and symbols exactly. If you are making a heavy coat, make the front pocket section of lining fabric or of color-matched slipper satin, and the back pocket section of the garment fabric.

1. Stay the fold line of both back and front garment sections with ½-inch twill tape that has been shrunk and pressed to curve with the fold line. Cut the tape to extend ½ inch beyond the top and bottom symbols. Baste tape, inside edge along fold-line mark. Whipstitch both edges of the tape to the underlining only. [A] Press both sections flat. Do not form the front fold line yet.

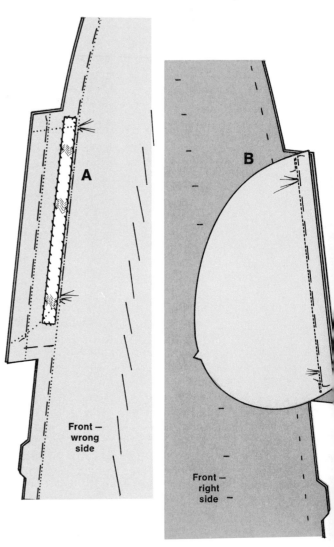

Front — wrong side

Front — right side

2. Baste and stitch the front pocket section to the garment front, right sides together, matching notches and symbols. [B] Press seam allowances toward the pocket, and cut off notches at edges. Also, baste front fold line, press lightly, and then remove basting.

3. Baste and stitch the back pocket section to the garment back, right sides together, matching notches and symbols. Press seam as stitched; then open. Cut underlining seam allowance to ¼ inch. [C]

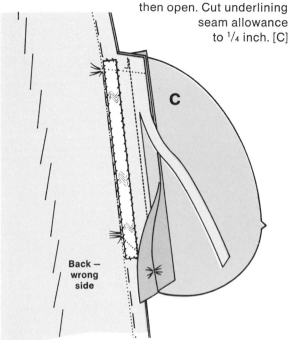

Back — wrong side

4. Pin and baste garment seams, matching all construction markings. Also baste back and front together along pocket fold line. The tailor's tacks above and below the pocket on the seam line indicate the pivot points. [D] Remember that the back seam allowances at the pocket joining are

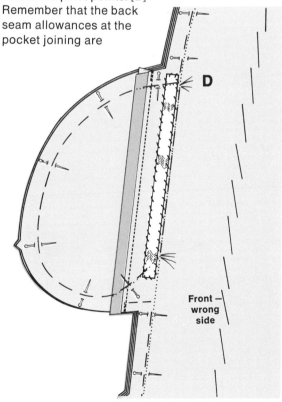

D

Front — wrong side

pressed open and both front seam allowances turn into the pocket as previously pressed.

5. Stitch the garment and the pocket seams in one continuous stitching, pivoting and backstitching for one stitch at the pivot points for reinforcement. [E]

Stitch the garment seam from the lower edge to the pivot point at lower end of pocket and stop with the needle in the fabric. Raise presser foot and turn the fabric a quarter turn, pivoting on the needle. Lower the presser foot and take one stitch forward, one stitch backward, and one stitch forward, again leaving the needle in the fabric. Raise the presser foot and pivot again, bringing the pocket seam line in front of the needle. Lower the presser foot, and continue stitching around the pocket to the pivot point at the top, stopping with the needle down. Without raising the presser foot, take one stitch backward and one stitch forward, stopping again with the needle down. Raise the presser foot; turn the fabric, pivoting on the needle, until the seam line is in front of the needle. Lower the presser foot and continue stitching the upper portion of the garment seam.

Remove bastings. Press seams as stitched. Press garment seam allowances open, slashing through the back seam allowance above and below the pivot points as shown. Cut other seam allowances diagonally to reduce bulk. Trim seam allowances around the curve of the pocket to half width.

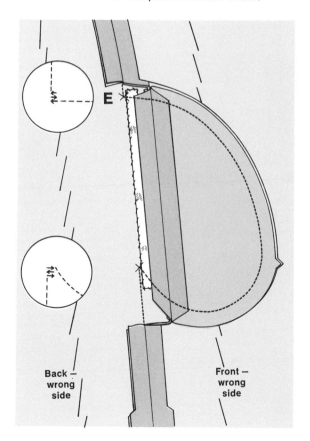

E

Back — wrong side

Front — wrong side

Welt Pocket

Preparation. Mark the position of the pocket with tailor's tacks before removing the pattern from the garment section. Mark the underlining with tracing wheel and tracing paper, making a vertical line at each end and a horizontal line at the center, extending the center line ¾ inch beyond the end marking lines. When a firm underlining is not used, place an underlay of firm, crisp underlining fabric under the pocket stitching lines to reinforce the opening and retain the shape of the pocket. Cut the underlay 1½ inches wider than the pocket opening and about 3 inches long. Center it over the markings on the wrong side of the garment. Pin in place.

1. From the right side, machine- or hand-baste across the ends of the pocket through the garment and the underlining fabrics to mark the width. Then machine- or hand-baste through the center, extending the stitching about ¾ inch beyond the ends, to form guidelines. Follow the grain of the fabric unless the pocket is positioned diagonally on the garment.

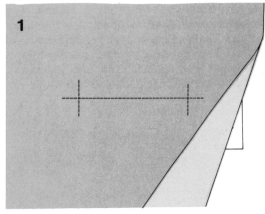

2. On the wrong side, draw pencil lines on each side of and ¼ inch away from the center basting to designate stitching lines. This distance may vary, depending on the pattern specifications, the

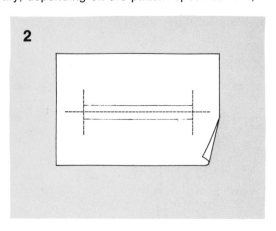

style of the garment, or the bulkiness of the fabric. However, if the distance is increased, in later steps also increase the seam allowances for the length of the welt and, instead of cutting the longer pocket section only 2 inches longer than the pocket length, cut it 1½ inches longer plus twice the distance from center line to stitching line.

Welt. If a pattern for the welt is not included, cut one the width of the pocket opening plus two ¼-inch seam allowances and twice the length of the finished welt plus two ¼-inch seam allowances. The fabric grain of the welt should match that of the garment when the pocket is placed on either the lengthwise or crosswise grain of the garment; but when the pocket is placed diagonally on the garment, the welt may be cut with either the bias or lengthwise grain of the fabric parallel to the welt fold line.

3. In coats, suits, and other garments of heavy fabric, interface the welt with hair canvas. Cut the interfacing the width of the welt and one half the length. Trim off the ¼-inch seam allowances on each end and along the lower edge. On the wrong side of the welt, place the edge of the interfacing along the center fold line of the welt. Pin and baste in place; then catch-stitch along edges.

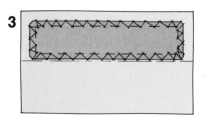

4. Fold the welt in half, right sides together. Stitch the ends, backstitching for reinforcement. Cut seam allowances diagonally at corners near fold. Trim facing seam allowances to ⅛ inch. Press seams as stitched, then open.

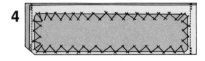

5. Turn the welt right side out and press. Machine-stitch a scant ¼ inch from the lower edge to hold the layers of fabric together.

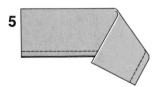

Pocket. If a pocket pattern is not included, cut one pocket section from the garment fabric the length of the pocket plus 2 inches, and 1 inch wider than the opening to allow for two ½ inch seam allowances. Cut another pocket section from the lining fabric the length of the pocket, and 1 inch wider than the opening.

Construction steps

6. Turn garment right side up. Place the welt below the pocket center basting line, right side down, with the raw edge on the basting line. The ends must be even with the vertical guidelines. Pin and hand-baste. On the inside of the garment, pin at each corner (as shown in step 8), using fine needles to prevent the welt from slipping.

7. On the right side of the garment, place one pocket section (the one cut from the garment fabric) over the markings, right sides together, extending the edge 1½ inches below the pocket center marking. Pin. Baste if necessary.

8. From the wrong side of the garment, stitch around the pocket opening, following the pencil lines. Use a short stitch, and begin stitching at the center of the upper side. Pivot the fabric on the needle at the corners and take the same number of stitches across each end. Overlap about six stitches at the starting point. Check the right side to be sure the end stitching does not extend beyond the welt. Remove all bastings and press.

9. From the underside, cut between the two lines of stitching, through all thicknesses, to within ½ inch of the ends. Cut diagonally to each of the four corners. Do not clip through the stitching.

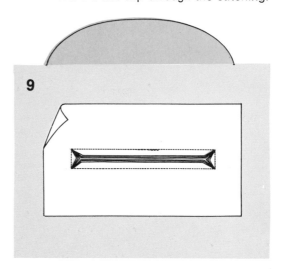

10. Draw the pocket through the opening to the inside. Pull the triangular ends away from the opening to square the corners; turn the welt up to cover the opening; and turn the lower edge of the pocket down from the opening. Press the two ends and the lower side of the opening. Turn the larger part of the pocket up and pin it to the garment to avoid catching it in the stitching of the next step, but do not press.

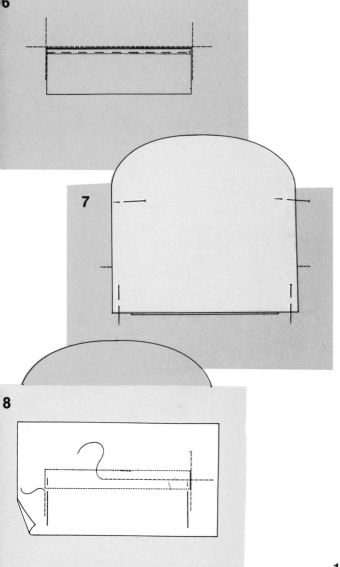

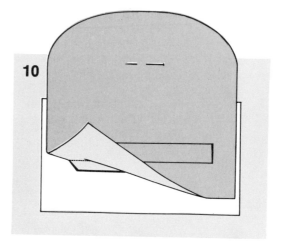

11. Place the lower pocket section (the one cut from the lining fabric) and the extended lower edge of the attached pocket section, right sides together, keeping the edges even. Stitch the two pocket sections together ⅝ inch from edges. Begin and end the stitching with backstitching at the outer edges. Press; then turn down the lining section and press again, keeping seam allowances together.

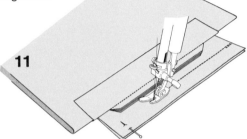

12. Turn down the upper pocket section; press the seam allowances open along the top of the opening; and pin the pocket and lining sections together along the side and bottom edges. Trim both sections to the same length. Place the garment right side up on the machine and fold back the garment to expose one end of the pocket. Stitch across one triangular end on the original line of stitching, around the pocket, and across

the triangle at the opposite end. Tie the threads. Remove all basting, and press.

Trim the underlay to within ½ inch of the stitching.

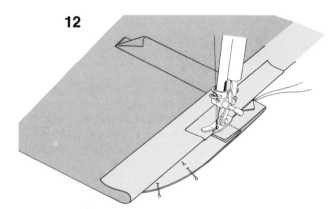

13. On the right side, slip-stitch the ends of the welt to the garment.

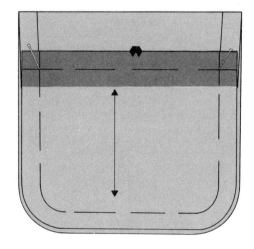

Plain Patch Pocket

A plain patch pocket for a tailored jacket or coat is assembled quite differently from a patch pocket for a dress. The pocket consists of three layers: fashion fabric, bias-cut hair-canvas interfacing, and lining. It may also have a fourth layer, the underlining, depending on the method you choose for attaching the interfacing, and whether your fashion fabric requires an underlining for a color shield or for support. The pocket facing is usually an extension of the pocket itself, and the lining extends only to the facing seam line rather than to the top edge of the pocket.

1. The pocket lining pattern should be about ¼ inch narrower than the pocket pattern, and the facing and lining should be ¼ inch shorter than the pocket to allow the lining to be finished inside the folded pocket edge. Thick fashion fabrics should have an even narrower and shorter lining. Since the pocket construction is done primarily

by hand, you can fit the lining to the prepared pocket section during the assembly step as you turn and baste the lining edge.

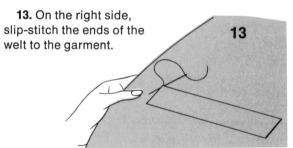

Cut and mark

2. Cut the fashion fabric and underlining on the lengthwise grain of the fabric, unless the pattern indicates a different grain or unless you are making a bias pocket for contrast in a plaid fabric.

3. On the fashion fabric, mark the fold line with simplified tailor's tacks and the symbols with tailor's tacks in threads of different colors. [A] On the underlining, mark the seam and fold lines with tracing wheel and tracing paper. [B]

4. Cut the hair-canvas interfacing on the bias from the pocket pattern, including the facing. This will result in a soft fold at the top edge. With tracing wheel and tracing paper, mark the seam and fold lines. Cut off all seam allowances slightly inside the seam-line markings. [C]

Cut the lining fabric from the lining pattern but do not mark the seam lines.

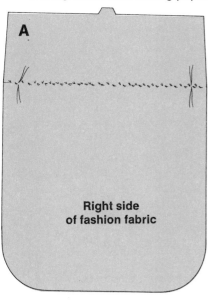

A

Right side of fashion fabric

B

Underlining

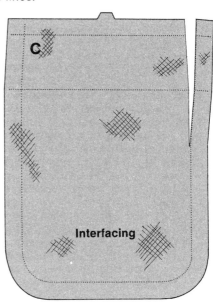

C

Interfacing

Attach underlining and interfacing

This step will vary, depending on the method you have selected for attaching the interfacing.

Method I. With diagonal basting, attach the underlining to the wrong side of the pocket section in the center. Then hand-baste just outside the seam-line markings. [D] Pin the interfacing to the underlined pocket, matching the fold lines, and catch-stitch the edges to the underlining only. [E] From the right side, backstitch through the three layers along the fold line so that the stitches are invisible. [F]

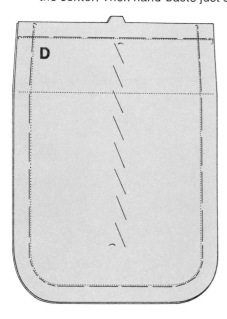

D

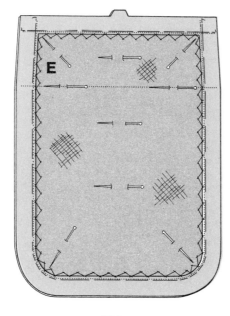

E

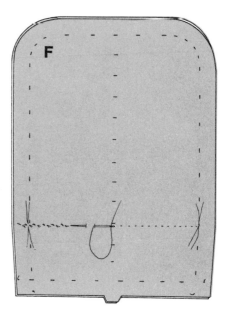

F

131

Method II. Pin and baste interfacing to underlining, matching fold lines. With multi-stitch zig-zag stitching, attach the interfacing to the underlining inside the seam lines. [A] Pin interfaced underlining unit to the wrong side of the pocket, matching the fold lines. With diagonal basting, stitch the layers together in the center; and with straight basting, stitch the underlining to the fashion fabric outside the seam lines. [B]

From the right side, backstitch through the three layers along the fold line so that the stitches are invisible.

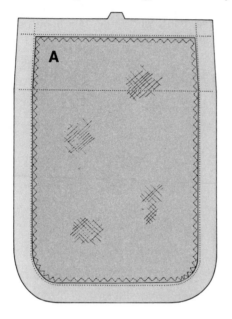

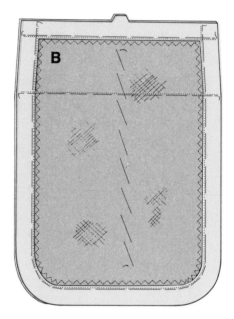

Method III. Pin and, with diagonal basting, attach interfacing to wrong side of pocket in the center. Catch-stitch interfacing to fashion fabric on all seam lines. [C] From the right side, backstitch through fashion fabric and interfacing along fold line so that the stitches are invisible.

Join lining and prepare rounded edges

Pin, baste, and stitch top of lining to facing, backstitching at each end. Remove basting. Trim underlining seam allowance to half width. Fold facing on fold line and press seam allowances together toward the lining. Square-cut seam allowances on each end. [D]

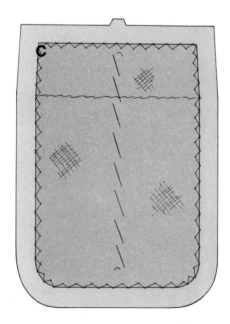

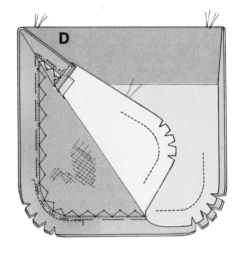

Using a 10 or 12 stitch length, stitch 1/8 inch outside the seam line at each rounded edge on both pocket and lining sections. This stitching will be used to control the ease in the seam allowances where the seams are turned and basted. In addition, trim small wedges from the seam allowances at evenly spaced intervals at each curve. [D]

Turn and baste seam allowances

On all straight edges of the pocket, turn seam allowances to the wrong side and pin. Draw the threads of the ease stitching at the rounded pocket edges and turn and pin. Hand-baste, using short stitches along the curves and long stitches along straight edges. [E] Do not turn edges of lining yet. Press the turned edges. Remove ease stitching and all basting except the basting just completed.

Draw the threads of the ease stitching on the lining; turn under the lining seam allowance, adjusting the amount to bring the lining edge at least 1/8 inch from the pocket edge. Pin all around, and then adjust the pins to penetrate only the lining. Baste the folded lining edge, remove pins, and press. Cut lining seam allowance to half width, and remove ease stitching. [F] Also remove the remaining basting from the pocket section. Then pin lining edges to the pocket, keeping the lining 1/8 inch from the pocket edges. [G]

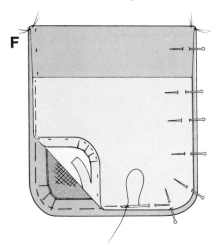

Slip-stitch lining. Starting at the fold line, slip-stitch facing to pocket. Continue to stitch lining to pocket, and then complete the pocket by slip-stitching the remaining side of the facing to the pocket. [H] Remove the basting from the lining fold. Steam-press the pocket, protecting it with a press cloth. Press from each side.

The pocket is now ready to apply to the garment. Refer to "Ways to Apply Patch Pockets," pages 138 to 141.

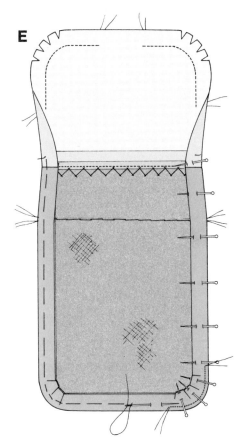

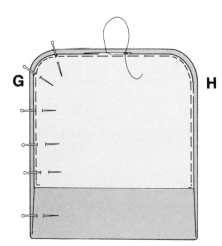

Cuffed Patch Pocket

A patch pocket in which the cuff or flap is cut in one with the pocket must have an ease allowance in the outer layer of the cuff so. that the cuff will roll smoothly. Additional ease allowances must be provided on the edges of all outside layers to allow for turning the seam line slightly to the underside out of view.

If you are making your own pocket pattern, the diagrams clearly indicate where ease is added to the basic pattern rectangle. If you are comparing pattern sections, the diagrams will indicate where the ease should have been provided. If it has not been provided in the pocket cuff, add $\frac{1}{8}$ inch above and below the roll line by slashing and spreading [B], and add $\frac{1}{8}$ inch along the edges of the lower edge of the pocket [A] and the edge of the pocket cuff [B] by redrawing the seam and cutting lines as shown.

The pocket should be interfaced with bias hair canvas. It may also be underlined. When the pocket is to be topstitched to the garment, the lining should be of the fashion fabric. [C] When the pocket is to be slip-stitched along the edge to the garment, the lining may be applied to the pocket section below the roll line by hand, following the procedure described for a plain patch pocket.

Cut and mark

Cut all sections, except the interfacing, on the lengthwise grain of the fabric. Cut the interfacing bias. Cut the underlining from the pocket pattern section.

Mark the pocket section if an underlining is not used. Make simplified tailor's tacks along the fold line and tailor's tacks at the symbols above and below the roll line. These symbols indicate where the ease is to be placed.

Mark the underlining with a tracing wheel and tracing paper along the roll and seam lines. Also mark the symbols above and below the roll line.

Mark the cuff section with tailor's tacks at the seam-line symbols that indicate the roll line and the distribution of ease above and below the roll line.

Mark the interfacing with a tracing wheel and tracing paper at the roll line and at all seam lines except at the edge of the cuff. Cut off the seam allowances inside the seam-line markings on all edges except the edge of the cuff, which you will cut off later. The lining section requires no markings.

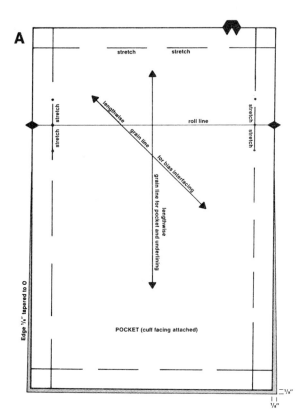

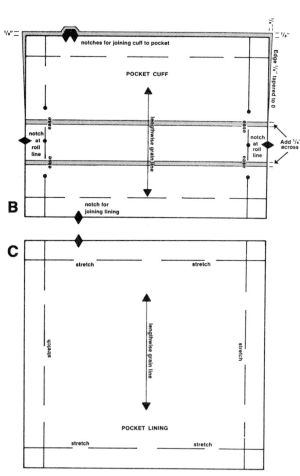

134

Attach underlining and interfacing

This step will vary, depending on the method you have chosen for attaching the interfacing.

Method I. With diagonal basting, attach the underlining to the wrong side of the pocket section in the center. Then, hand-baste just outside the seam-line markings. Pin the interfacing to the underlined pocket, matching the roll lines, and catch-stitch the edges to the underlining only, from the roll line to the lower edge on both sides and across the bottom.

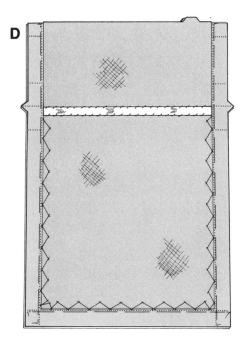

Pin and whipstitch ¼-inch twill tape (shrunk) with the top edge along the roll line and the bottom edge below the roll line. [D]

Place pocket right side up, and roll the cuff over your left hand while you make parallel rows of short padding stitches over the entire cuff through

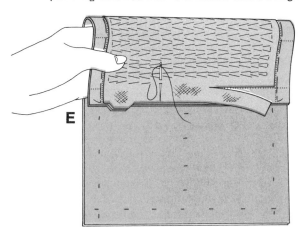

the interfacing, underlining, and fashion fabric. Trim the interfacing seam allowance from the edge of the cuff when all rows of padding stitches, except the last, have been made. [E] Steam-press pocket and cuff sections, keeping cuff rolled, but do not press a crease at the roll line. Remove diagonal basting on center of pocket.

Method II. Pin and baste interfacing to underlining, matching fold lines. With multi-stitch zig-zag stitching, attach the interfacing to the underlining inside the seam lines from the roll line to the lower edge and across the lower edge. Leave the interfacing unstitched from roll line to edge of cuff.

Pin the interfaced underlining unit to the wrong side of the pocket, matching the roll lines. With diagonal basting, stitch all layers together in the center; and with straight basting, stitch the underlining to the fashion fabric outside the seam lines. Pin the twill tape at the roll line, top edge along the roll line and bottom edge extending into the pocket. Whipstitch both edges of the tape, catching all three layers of the fabric.

Place pocket right side up, and roll the cuff over your left hand while you make parallel rows of short padding stitches over the entire cuff through the interfacing, underlining, and fashion fabric. Trim the interfacing seam allowance from the edge of the cuff when all rows of padding stitches, except the last, have been made. [E] Steam-press pocket and cuff sections, keeping the cuff rolled, but do not press a crease at the roll line.

Method III. Pin and, with diagonal basting, attach interfacing to wrong side of pocket in the center. Catch-stitch interfacing to fashion fabric on all seam lines below the roll line. Whipstitch tape, top edge at roll line, bottom edge below roll line.

Place pocket right side up, and roll the cuff over your left hand while you make parallel rows of short padding stitches over the entire cuff through the interfacing and fashion fabric. [E] Trim the inter-facing seam allowance from the edge of the cuff when all rows of padding stitches, except the last, have been made. Steam-press pocket and cuff sections, keeping the cuff rolled, but do not press a crease at the roll line.

Join lining

When a self-lining is used, pin and baste the cuff and lining sections together. Then machine-stitch for only one inch at each end of the seam, and begin and end each stitching with backstitching. Steam-press the seam as stitched, and then open before removing the basting. [A] This open seam will allow you to turn the pocket to the right side after stitching all edges. Trim the seam allowances to half width.

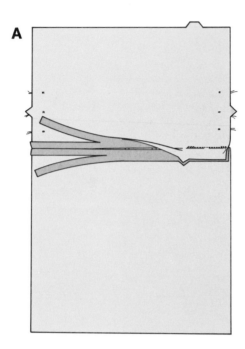

When a lining fabric has been used, pin and baste the cuff and lining section together, and stitch the entire seam. Press all seam layers in one direction toward the lining. Square-cut the seam allowances at the ends.

Join cuff and lining unit to pocket unit

For a pocket lined with *self-fabric*, place cuff and lining unit over pocket unit, right sides together, matching roll-line tailor's tacks at the side seam lines. Pin first at the roll line; then, match and pin at each tailor's tack above and below the roll line. The cuff section will have ⅛ inch of ease between each two pins. Continue to match the edges and pin all around the pocket. Hand-baste with short stitches slightly inside the stitching line all around the pocket. Curve the seam over the fingers of your left hand as you baste, stretching

the shorter side of the seam and easing the longer side. Distribute the ease evenly. [B]

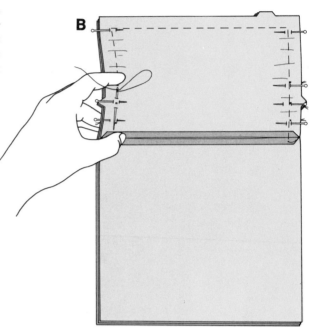

Steam-press pocket flat from facing side. Then turn pocket interfaced side up, roll cuff over press mitt, and steam-press to shrink fullness along seam lines.

Stitch on the seam line, interfacing against presser foot, outside the edge of the interfacing. Make two stitches diagonally across each corner to blunt the corners slightly. Overlap the stitching at the beginning and end.

For a pocket lined with *lining fabric*, follow the steps above, but pin, baste, and stitch the cuff along the seam line from one tailor's tack below the roll line around the cuff to the other tailor's tack below the roll line. Complete the remaining part of the edge by hand, as outlined for the plain patch pocket.

Trim seam allowances and turn pocket

Press the pocket seams as they were stitched to embed the stitching. Then, cut off the seam allowances diagonally close to the stitching at each corner. Cut the remaining seam allowances to unequal widths of ¼ inch and ⅛ inch, keeping the wider seam allowance on the edge that will be nearest to the outside layer of the pocket and cuff. Press these trimmed seam allowances open over a seam pressing board.

Turn the pocket and cuff right side out, drawing the sections through the opening in the lining seam on the self-lined pocket, and though the open edge of the pocket lined with lining-fabric.

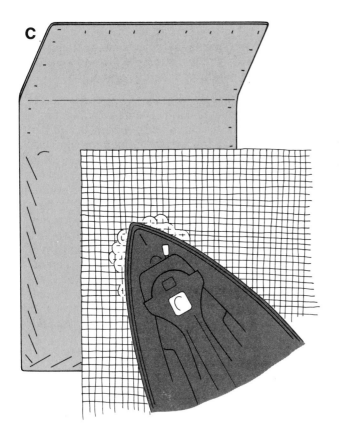

With diagonal basting made with silk thread, hold the edges for pressing. Remember when you baste to place the seam to favor the side that will show when the pocket is worn. Steam-press from the right side of the pocket and the cuff, protecting the fabric with a press cloth. Do not press over the roll line; do not press a crease in the roll line. [C]

Slip-stitch the open portion of the seam that joins the lining to the cuff. [D]

Apply the pocket to the garment, using one of the methods described in "Ways to Apply Patch Pockets," pages 138 to 141.

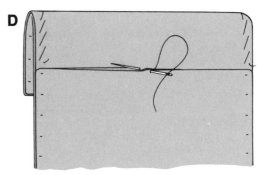

Ways to Apply Patch Pockets

Placement. On patterns, the upper back and front corners of the pocket are usually indentified with different symbols, such as a large square and a large circle. These symbols appear on both the garment and the pocket. It is a good idea to mark them with tailor's tacks of different-color threads. These marks are important because they will affect either how the pocket fabric grain matches the garment, or the shape of the pocket in relation to the garment design. If the pattern calls for more than one pocket, it is a good idea to compare the pockets for size and shape before you place them on the garment. If they differ in size because of errors in seam allowances, correct the size or make a new pocket, because a significant difference will show on the finished garment.

Pin the pocket to the garment at the top corners and at 2-inch intervals near the pocket edges. Try the garment on to verify the location. Then, with diagonal basting and silk thread, baste the pocket to the garment at the center from top to bottom. Diagonally baste, also, from side to side at center or slightly above the center. These bastings will keep the pocket from shifting as you work. Straight-baste 1/8 inch inside the edges. [A]

Hand stitching

You have a choice of three kinds of hand stitching for attaching a patch pocket to your garment: the slip stitch, the pick stitch, and the saddle stitch.

The slip stitch results in an invisible application, while the pick stitch and saddle stitch add a decorative accent and form a welt-type application.

Slip stitch. Using strong, matching thread and a fine, short needle, fasten the thread end securely on the inside of the garment at one corner of the pocket, and bring the needle through the garment at the pocket edge. Make several short stitches, catching the underside of the pocket edge and the garment layers. Knot the thread on the underside, and bring the needle up through the garment. Pass the needle through the underside of the pocket edge for 1/4 inch, then into the garment layers for 1/4 inch, and upward through the garment. Continue this sequence of stitching down one side, across the bottom, and up the other side of the pocket. Do not draw the thread so tight that it dents the pocket. Knot the thread on the underside of the garment at 1-inch intervals. Fasten the second corner as you did the first. [A]

To increase the firmness and durability, place a second line of stitching 1/4 inch inside the first, working from the inside of the garment. Use a diagonal stitch the same as diagonal basting (except, for this purpose, it becomes a permanent stitch), and do not penetrate the outer layer of the pocket. This stitch is entirely invisible when the garment is worn and is one of the hidden steps in tailoring that improve a garment. [B]

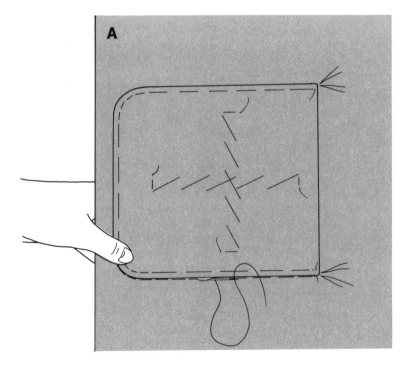

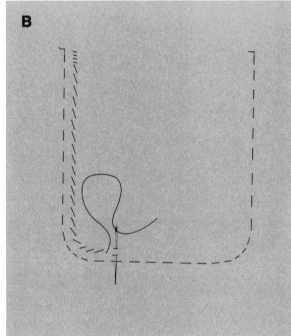

Pick stitch. The pick stitch is a form of back-stitching made with heavy thread, such as button-hole twist, or three or more strands of fine thread, such as size A silk, mercerized, or synthetic sewing thread or embroidery floss. A fine embroidery needle is recommended. The pick stitch is suitable for a welt-type, hand-stitched pocket application, but it should be used only when it is also used elsewhere on the garment, e.g., on the lapel, collar, or front edge or on all three edges. It requires the additional preparatory step of a hand or machine basting line, equally spaced from the pocket edges, slightly inside the welt stitching line. Do this basting step before the pocket is pinned and basted to the garment.

For a cuffed patch pocket where both the top and underside of the cuff or flap may be visible, the pick stitch is made differently from the way it is made when the underside is not visible, and it is made on the cuff before the pocket is positioned on the garment. [C] The pick stitch may be made to be reversible or to show only on the outside.

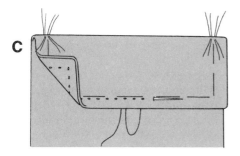

To make a reversible pick stitch, fasten the thread end invisibly and, working from the top, bring the needle up through the fabric, pulling the stitch tight. Direct the needle down through the fabric, in a perpendicular direction, one or two yarns in back of the supply thread. Pull the stitch fairly taut. Working from the underside, direct the point of the needle into the underlayer of fabric in a diagonal direction and, watching the top, bring the point of the needle up ¼ inch ahead of the previous backstitch. Draw the needle through the fabric, and pull the stitch fairly taut. [D] Repeat the four-step sequence until the cuff or flap is completed.

To make a pick stitch that is visible only on the outside, fasten the thread end invisibly and then bring the needle up through the interfacing and outside fabric layers. Direct the needle diagonally into the fabric and interfacing layers only, one or two fabric yarns in back of the supply thread, and bring the point up ¼ inch ahead of the last stitch. Draw the stitch taut, but leave enough slack to allow the short stitch to be bead-like on the surface of the fabric. Repeat the stitch until the cuff is completed. [E]

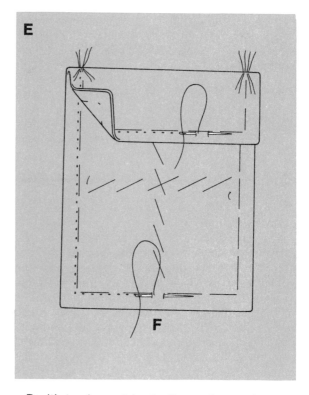

Position, pin, and baste the pocket to the garment, as described on page 138. Fasten the thread end securely on the underside of the garment at one top corner of the pocket, and bring the needle up through the pocket, pulling the stitch fairly taut. Direct the needle point down, in a perpendicular direction, one or two yarns in back of the supply thread. Then slant the needle to bring the point up through all layers ¼ inch ahead of the previous stitch. Draw the needle through the fabric layers, and pull the stitch fairly taut. Repeat the stitch until the pocket is attached. [F]

Saddle stitch. The saddle stitch is an even, running stitch used decoratively and made of heavy thread or several strands of fine thread through a fine embroidery needle. Stitches and spaces are equal and of $1/4$ inch or more in length. [A]

The saddle stitch is suitable for a welt-type, hand-stitched pocket application, but it should be used only when it is used elsewhere on the garment. By itself, the saddle stitch is not firm or durable enough to secure a pocket that will be used. To increase the firmness and durability, make a second line of hidden stitching at the same location as the saddle stitching, working from inside the garment, and catching all but the top pocket layer. Use a permanent diagonal stitch, as described on page 138.

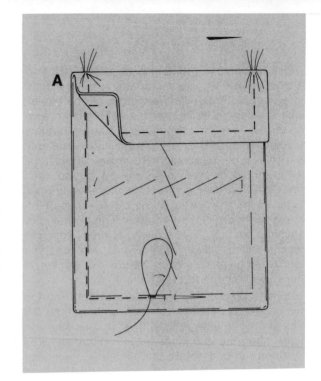

Machine stitching

You have a choice of several effects when you plan for machine-stitching the pocket to your garment. The stitching may be placed near the pocket edge or $3/8$, $1/2$, or $5/8$ inch from the edge as a welt-type application. The stitching may be of regular-weight sewing thread or of heavy thread such as buttonhole twist. When a welt-type application is planned, the pocket should be lined with self fabric, the edges faced with self fabric, or the edges turned and lining attached inside the topstitching line.

Mark the topstitching line on the pocket with hand or machine basting before placing the pocket on the garment. The Even Feed machine foot and the seam guide are valuable aids in placing a machine-basting line. For machine basting, use a 6 stitch length and set the needle-thread tension at a lower number than for regular stitching so that the basting will be easy to remove. [B]

Pin and baste the pocket to the garment, as described on page 138.

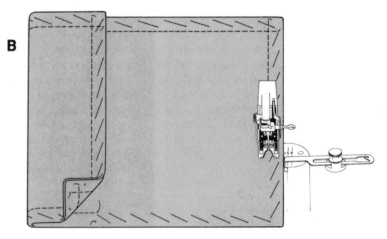

Plain topstitching. When topstitching a pocket near the edge, use the Even Feed machine foot, regular sewing thread of matching color, a size 14 needle, and a 12 or longer stitch length, depending on the weight of the fabric. Heavy fabrics should be stitched with an 8 or 10 stitch length. Place the stitching about 1/16 inch from the pocket edge, and stitch slowly and evenly. [C] Draw the thread ends to the underside, thread them into an embroidery needle, and make several backstitches by hand before securing the thread ends.

When using plain topstitching for a welt-type application, add another basting step to those described on page 138. Baste the pocket to the garment inside the topstitching line with short diagonal basting to hold it firmly. Then, using the Even Feed machine foot, stitch next to the topstitching basting line. Fasten thread ends as described above. [D]

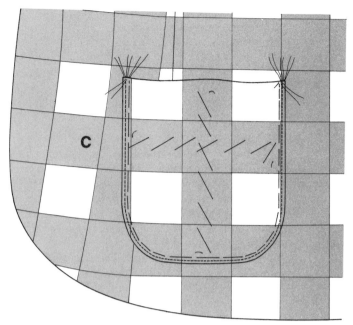

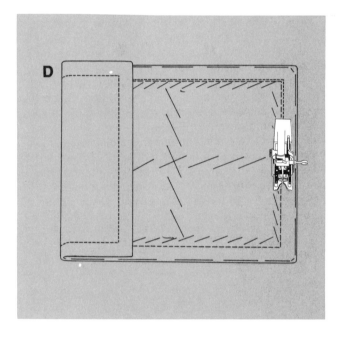

Remove all bastings, and make a horizontal bar tack 1/2 inch long under the cuff at the ends of the stitching. For the bar tack, use a zig-zag stitch, 3 stitch width, and "fine" stitch length. [E]

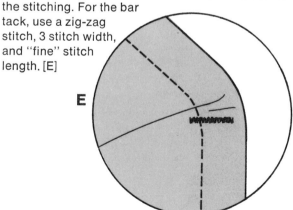

Buttonhole-twist topstitching. Prepare the pocket in the way described for plain topstitching, but thread the machine with buttonhole twist through a size 16 or 18 needle. Use regular sewing thread on the bobbin and a stitch length of 10 or longer. Always test the stiching on the same number and kinds of fabric layers before working on your garment. The Even Feed machine foot will make this step more efficient, but the regular presser foot may also be used. Increase the presser-foot pressure to above normal if you use the regular presser foot.

When test-stitching, start with your regular sewing tension setting. Make a few stitches, and look at the underside of the stitch. If the buttonhole twist loops, increase the needle-thread tension and test. Repeat these steps until the stitch sets into the fabric securely and the loops disappear.

Stitch alongside the topstitching basting line, and draw the thread ends through to the underside. Thread them through an embroidery needle, make several backstitches, and fasten the ends.

Combined hand- and machine-stitching methods
Topstitching for a welt-type application may be done before the pocket is placed on the garment. Some prefer this procedure because it does not place the bulk of the garment on the machine while the careful stitching is being done.

Stitch the pocket first along the topstitching line. Then pin and baste the pocket in position on the garment. Hand-stitch the pocket invisibly, as described on page 138, using the slip stitch near the edge (optional) and the permanent diagonal stitch at the topstitching line.

Pocket Flap

Pocket flaps are used for three purposes: to suggest a pocket where one has not actually been made; to conceal a buttonhole-type set-in pocket or one designed in a horizontal or diagonal seam; or to cover the top edge of a patch pocket. The flap is either stitched to the surface of the garment or included in a styled seam.

Cut and mark

Cut the flap, underlining (optional), lining, and interfacing on the same fabric grain as the garment section to which it will be attached, unless for accent reasons another grain is preferred, such as for a bias-plaid flap. The lining may be of either the fashion fabric or a firm lining fabric, if the fashion fabric is bulky.

On the flap, make a tailor's tack at each upper corner to identify the placement on the garment. On the underlining, mark the seam lines with tracing wheel and tracing paper to achieve accuracy when stitching.

On the interfacing, also mark all seam lines, and then cut off the seam allowances just inside the seam-line markings.

On the lining section, whether it is of the fashion fabric or a lining fabric, cut off 1/16 inch from all seam edges except the top edge. This will make the lining slightly smaller than the outside layer and will let the seam roll to the underside in a later step.

Attach underlining and interfacing

Pin and baste the underlining to the wrong side of the fashion-fabric flap outside the seam line. Pin and baste the interfacing to the underlined unit inside the seam lines. Catch-stitch over all edges of the interfacing, stitching into the underlining only, not the fashion fabric.

Pin and hand-baste the lining and interfaced flap unit together, keeping all edges even. Machine-stitch on the seam line, from one upper corner around the flap to the other upper corner, starting and ending one stitch outside the top seam line, and backstitching at both ends. [A]

Cut the seam allowances to uneven widths, leaving the one on the interfaced side wider. Cut wedges from rounded edges, and cut square corners diagonally. Press trimmed seam allowances open over a seam pressing board.

Turn and complete flap. Turn flap to right side through top opening. Roll seam to underside and hold with diagonal basting of silk thread. Steampress. Complete topstitched detail. Baste seam layers together at top of flap slightly inside seam line. [B]

Apply flap. Position and pin flap to garment, matching tailor's tacks. Baste slightly outside seam line. Machine-stitch on seam line between basting lines, backstitching at each end. Do not let stitching extend beyond either end of the flap. Draw thread ends to inside of garment and tie. Cut off all seam allowances except on the lining close to the stitching line. Turn the lining seam allowance under and pin to the garment. If seam allowance is too wide, cut it to a convenient width. Slip-stitch seam edge to garment. [C] Press as stitched with flap turned up, then turn flap down, diagonal-baste to garment with loose stitches, and steam lightly. Do not remove basting until garment is finished.

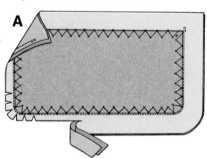

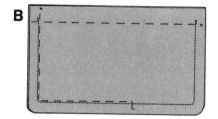

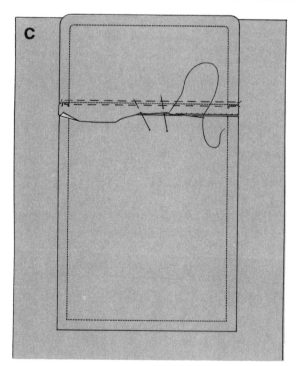

how to alter patterns

This chapter explains how to make pattern alterations to accommodate many different figure variations. It also explains how to make these alterations on different types of patterns, such as patterns with or without waistline seams; patterns shaped with darts, princess seams, or modified princess seams; patterns with one- or two-piece set-in sleeves; and patterns with one- or two-piece raglan sleeves.

Whether you are altering the pattern for a dress, a jacket or a coat, the principles are the same. But the ways you determine which alterations are needed and how large they should be are different. Refer to pages 1 to 4. Remember, also, when altering a coat or jacket pattern, that you must repeat the alteration in the pattern sections for all corresponding layers, such as the upper collar, facing, interfacing, and lining.

Pattern Alterations
Are Made by Increasing or Decreasing

Generally, to increase, slash and spread the pattern, adding tissue and redrawing the affected cutting lines. To decrease, fold a dart or tuck. Use pins to hold the alteration in place temporarily, then, after you have verified the alteration, remove the pins and apply magic transparent tape for permanence.

Sometimes, on the other hand, you can increase or decrease at the cutting line. This method can be used when the curve of a seam is contrary to a body curve, when only a slight increase or decrease is required, and when you want to provide a temporary wider-than-normal seam allowance for fitting a muslin shell. Add tissue along the edge of the pattern, if necessary; then redraw the cutting line, only, for a temporary increase of the seam allowance; or redraw both the cutting and stitching lines for a permanent increase or decrease of the pattern section.

The pattern alterations are presented in the following eight groups:

Alterations for Taller- or Shorter-than-Average Proportions

A • To lengthen (one-piece dress):

1. Cut pattern apart on lengthening/shortening lines.
2. Place tissue under the slashes.
3. Spread pattern the amount to be lengthened. Tape in place.
4. Redraw seam lines and construction markings.

B • To shorten (one-piece dress):

1. Draw a line parallel to the lengthening/shortening line the amount to be shortened in each section.
2. Fold the pattern so that the two lines meet. The tuck will be half the amount to be shortened. Tape across fold.
3. Redraw seam lines and construction markings.

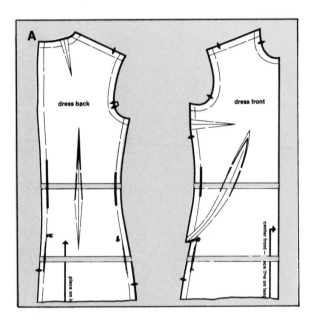

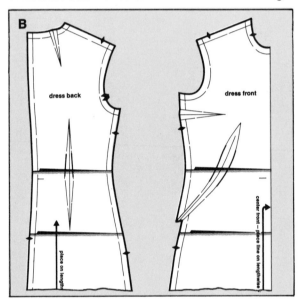

C • To lengthen the bodice, skirt, or sleeve:

1. Slash pattern pieces on lengthening/shortening lines.
2. Spread pattern the amount to be lengthened.
3. Insert tissue paper under the slash and tape in place.
4. Redraw seam lines and construction markings.

D • To shorten the bodice, skirt, or sleeve:

1. Draw a line parallel to the lengthening/shortening line, with the distance between the lines equal to the amount to be shortened.
2. Fold the pattern so that these two lines meet. The tuck will be half the amount to be decreased. Tape the fold in place.
3. Redraw seam lines and construction markings.

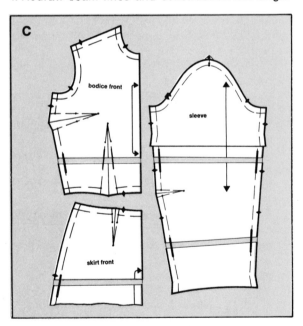

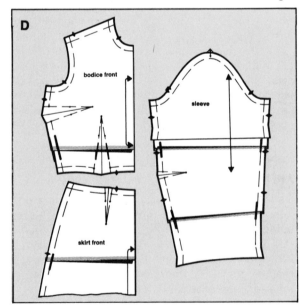

E • To lengthen armhole:

1. Draw a line straight across the bodice front, bodice back, and sleeve cap just above the notches.
2. Slash along these lines and spread the same amount on all pattern pieces. Place tissue paper under the pattern and tape in place.
3. Redraw the armhole and sleeve-cap seam lines and cutting lines.
4. To return the bodice to its original length, take a tuck just above the waistline on the lengthening/shortening lines.

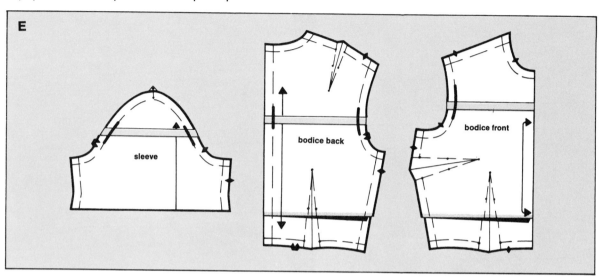

E

F • To shorten armhole:

1. Draw a line straight across the bodice front, bodice back, and sleeve cap just above the notches.
2. Draw a parallel line, with the distance between the lines equal to the amount to be shortened.
3. Fold the pattern so that these two lines meet. Tape in place.
4. Redraw the armhole and sleeve-cap seam lines and cutting lines.
5. To return the bodice to its original length, slash and spread above the waistline on the lengthening/shortening lines.

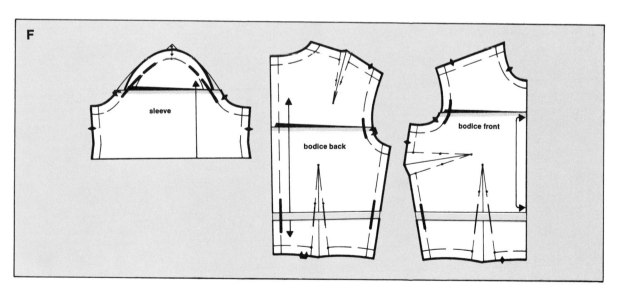

F

A • To raise or lower the underarm bust dart:
1. Draw a line above and below the dart perpendicular to the grain line.
2. Connect the two horizontal lines with a vertical line parallel to the grain line. Cut pattern on the three lines.
3. Place tissue under the pattern pieces.
4. Raise or lower the dart section the amount needed, lapping edges of pattern evenly. Tape on three sides.
5. If the pattern has a waistline or French dart, the point of that dart must also be extended or lowered the same amount as the underarm dart. Connect the seam lines.

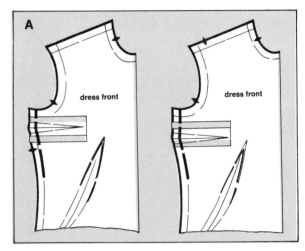

B • To raise the bustline (modified princess style):
1. Halfway down the armhole seam on the front, fold a tuck the needed amount to raise the bustline. Tape in place.
2. Cut apart both pattern pieces below the bust curve.
3. Place tissue under each slash.
4. Spread pattern the amount needed to restore original waist length. Tape in place.
5. Redraw the cutting line on the side front by measuring down the needed amount (twice the tuck width) on the underarm seam line.

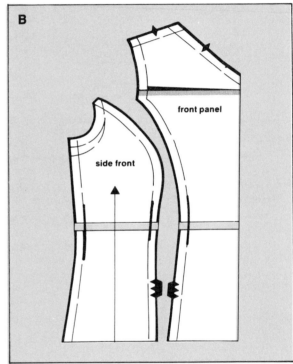

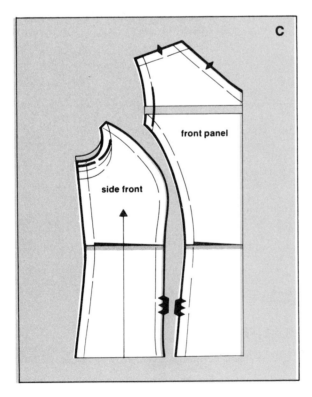

C • To lower the bustline (modified princess style):
1. Halfway down the armhole seam, draw a line parallel to the crosswise grain on the front. Cut across the pattern piece on the drawn line.
2. Place tissue under slash.
3. Spread pattern the amount needed. Tape in place.
4. Raise the armhole on the side front piece the amount spread. Taper from mark to top of the curve.
5. Fold a tuck at the waistline on both pattern pieces the necessary amount to restore the original waist length.

Alterations for Smaller- or Larger-than-Average Bust

A • For small bust (one-piece dress):

1. Draw a line, extending the waistline marking straight across pattern piece.
2. Draw a line through center of underarm dart to high point of bust.
3. Draw a vertical line from high point to waistline, keeping line parallel to the lengthwise grain line.
4. Draw another line from high point of bust to center of shoulder.
5. Slash across waistline to within ⅛ inch of center front. Slash the vertical line from waistline to within ⅛ inch of shoulder. Slash through center of bust dart to within ⅛ inch of bust point.
6. Lap edges of vertical slash at bust point ½ the total decrease, tapering lap to nothing at shoulder and at waistline. Tape in place. The horizontal slash through the underarm dart will automatically overlap as the front is narrowed. Tape dart line.
7. Place tissue under the spread slash at waistline. Keeping center front on straight grain, tape edges of slash to tissue.
8. Decrease the side seam length at lower edge of pattern the amount of the spread waistline slash. Redraw hem edge, starting at side seam, tapering gradually to nothing.

C • For small bust (two-piece dress):

1. Draw a line through the underarm dart to the high point of the bust and vertically down to the waistline. Draw the vertical line parallel to the grain line or through the center of the waistline dart.
2. Draw another line from high point of bust to center of shoulder seam.
3. Slash on the vertical line from waistline seam to within ⅛ inch of shoulder seam line. Slash through center of underarm dart to within ⅛ inch of high point of bust.
4. Lap edges of vertical slash the needed amount at the high point of the bust and taper the lap to nothing at both the shoulder and the waist. This causes the slash to overlap at the underarm dart. Tape in place.
5. Redraw the darts and the seam and cutting lines.

D • For large bust (two-piece dress):

1. Follow closely steps 1-3 for small bust.
2. Spread the vertical slash the needed amount at the bust point. The spread will taper to nothing at shoulder and waistline. This causes the slash at the underarm dart to spread. Tape in place over tissue paper.
3. Redraw darts, and cutting and stitching lines.

B • For large bust (one-piece dress):

1. Follow steps 1 to 5 for small bust.
2. Place tissue under the slashes. Spread slash at bust point ½ total increase, tapering from bust point to nothing at shoulder and waistline. Tape in place. The slash at the underarm dart will automatically spread apart; tape edges to tissue.
3. Keeping center front on straight grain, tape overlapping edges of waistline slash.
4. Redraw point of dart and shoulder seam.
5. Increase the side seam length at the lower edge of the pattern the amount of the overlap of the waistline slash. Redraw hem edge, adding tissue if necessary, tapering gradually to nothing.

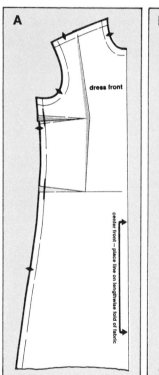

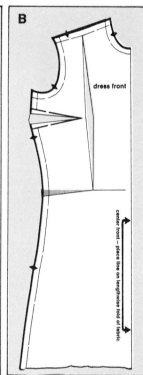

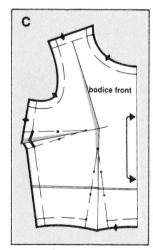

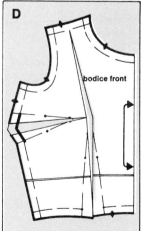

**E • For small bust
(princess or modified princess style):**

1. Raise or lower the bustline curve or dart if necessary; then proceed. Refer to page 104.
2. Divide total decrease by four to determine the amount of decrease for each seam line. Total decrease should not exceed 2 inches.
3. Measure and mark the new seam-line locations inside the old ones at the high point of the bust, on the pattern front, and on side-front sections.
4. Redraw seam and cutting lines, starting from the high-point mark and tapering to nothing at the waistline and shoulder or armhole seam line.

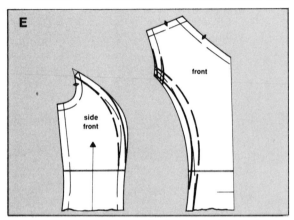

Note: *Curved seam-line length changes when redrawn:*

The seam line becomes *longer* when it is redrawn on an outside curve, outside the original line; and on an inside curve, inside the original seam line.

The seam line becomes *shorter* when it is redrawn on an outside curve, inside the original seam line; and on an inside curve, outside the original seam line.

Measure the seam lines, divide the difference by two, add one half to the shorter side, and take out the other half from the longer side at the armhole.

**F • For large bust
(princess or modified princess style):**

1. Raise or lower the bustline curve or dart, if necessary; then proceed. Refer to page 104.
2. Divide total increase by four to determine the amount of increase for each seam line. Total increase should not exceed 2 inches.
3. Tape tissue under the pattern front and side-front sections, extending the edges along the princess seam from waistline to armhole or shoulder.
4. Measure and mark the new seam-line locations outside the old ones at the high point of the bust, on the pattern front, and on side-front sections.
5. Redraw seam and cutting lines, starting from the high-point mark and tapering to nothing at the waistline and shoulder or armhole seam line.

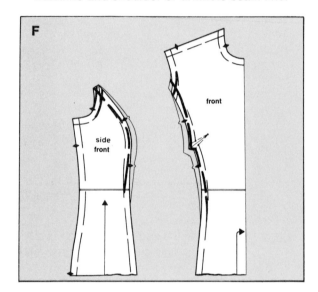

G • For small bust (one- and two-piece raglan sleeve)

1. Mark shoulder point on sleeve front.
2. Lap and pin sleeve front to garment front at raglan seam line.
3. On garment front, draw a horizontal line extending the waistline marking straight across the pattern. Draw a line through center of underarm dart to high point of bust. From bust high point to waistline, draw a vertical line, keeping it parallel to the lengthwise grain line. On garment front and extending into the sleeve, draw another line from bust high point to center of shoulder.
4. Slash on waistline mark to within $1/8$ inch of center front. Slash on vertical line from waistline to within $1/8$ inch of shoulder slash, through center of bust dart, to $1/8$ inch of bust point. (On one-piece raglan sleeve, slash along front stitching line of shoulder dart from neckline to within $1/8$ inch of vertical slash.)

5. Overlap edges of vertical slash at bust high point one-half the total decrease, tapering the decrease to nothing at both the shoulder and waistline. (The slash at the one-piece raglan-sleeve dart will spread automatically, so place tissue under it and tape edges.) Tape the overlapped edges at the bustline in place. The slashed edges of the underarm dart will automatically overlap; tape them. Keeping center front on straight grain, place tissue under the edges of the spread waistline slash and tape it in place.
6. Redraw darts and shoulder seam.

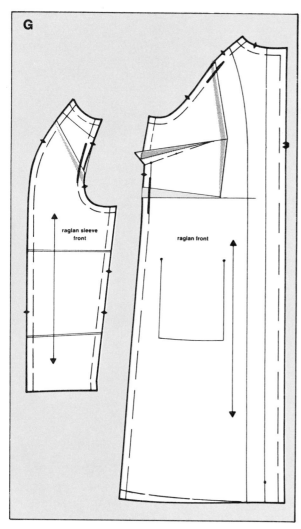

G

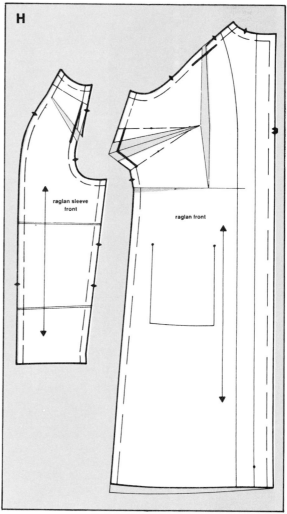

H

sleeve, slash along front stitching line of shoulder dart from neckline to within 1/8 inch of vertical slash.)

5. Place large piece of tissue under slashes and tape front edge of vertical slash to tissue. Spread the side edge of the vertical slash at bust high point one-half the total increase, tapering the spread to nothing at both the shoulder and waistline; tape the edge. (The slash at the one-piece raglan-sleeve dart will automatically overlap; tape the edge.) The slashed edges of the underarm dart will automatically spread; tape them to tissue. Keeping center front on straight grain, tape the edge of the overlapped waistline slash.

6. Redraw darts and shoulder seam.

7. Increase the side seam length at lower edge of pattern the amount of the lapped waistline slash. Extend side seam and redraw hem edge, starting at side seam and tapering gradually to nothing.

8. Separate front and sleeve pattern sections and redraw raglan-sleeve seam and cutting lines.

7. Decrease the side seam length at lower edge of pattern the amount of the spread waistline slash. Redraw hem edge, starting at side seam, tapering gradually to nothing.

8. Separate front and sleeve pattern sections and redraw raglan-sleeve seam.

H • For large bust (one- and two-piece raglan sleeve):
1. Mark shoulder point on sleeve front.
2. Lap and pin sleeve front to garment front at raglan seam line.
3. On garment front, draw a horizontal line extending the waistline marking straight across the pattern. Draw a line through center of underarm dart to high point of bust. From bust high point to waistline, draw a vertical line, keeping it parallel to the lengthwise grain line. On garment front, and extending into the sleeve, draw another line from bust high point to center of shoulder.
4. Slash on waistline mark to within 1/8 inch of center front. Slash on vertical line from waistline to within 1/8 inch of bust point. (On one-piece raglan

Alterations for Smaller- or Larger-than-Average Waist

A • To decrease the waistline 2 inches or less:
1. If your waistline measures less than that of your pattern, 2 inches or less can be taken in by dividing the total amount to be decreased by four and removing this amount from each side seam allowance.
2. Taper from waistline to underarm dart in the bodice and from waistline to hipline in the skirt.
3. If you need to remove slightly more, take in each dart (not more than ¼ inch) at waistline and taper to point of dart.

B • To increase the waistline 2 inches or less:
1. Two inches or less can be added to the waistline by dividing the total amount by four and increasing each side seam by this amount.
2. Taper from the waistline to underarm dart in bodice and from waistline to the hipline in skirt.
3. If you need to increase the waist slightly more, let out each dart (not more than ¼ inch) at the waistline and taper to the dart point.

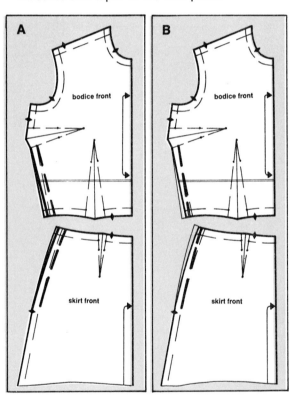

C • To decrease the waistline more than 2 inches:
1. To adjust the bodice, draw lines from the waistline toward the shoulder on the pattern front and back.
2. Slash these lines and lap to take out the necessary width at the waistline. (Divide the width to be subtracted by four to determine how much to take out of each bodice section.) Tape the lapped tissue in place.

3. To adjust the skirt, draw lines from the waistline down toward the hipline on the pattern front and back.
4. Slash and lap until the waistline corresponds to the waistline of the bodice section. Tape the lapped tissue in place.
5. When less width is required only in front or back, subtract one-half the total amount from that pattern section only.

D • To increase the waistline more than 2 inches:
1. On the bodice, draw a line from the waistline toward the armhole parallel to the lengthwise grain line on the pattern front and back.
2. Slash on these lines; place tissue underneath, and spread the slash to add the necessary width at the waistline. (Divide the total increase by four to determine how much to add to each bodice section.) Tape the tissue in place.
3. On the skirt, draw a line from the waistline down toward the hipline parallel to the lengthwise grain line on the pattern front and back.
4. Slash, place tissue underneath, and spread the slash the same amount as the bodice section. Tape the tissue in place.
5. When extra width is required only in front or back, divide the total increase by two and alter only the front or back pattern section.

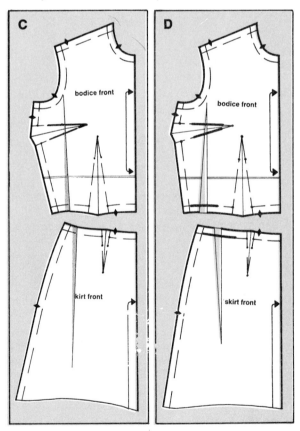

Alterations for Smaller- or Larger-than-Average Hips

A • To decrease the hipline 2 inches or less (all styles):

Divide the total decrease by four and take this amount off side seam on the skirt front and back. Taper from hipline to nothing at the waistline and from the waistline to hem. Redraw cutting and stitching lines.

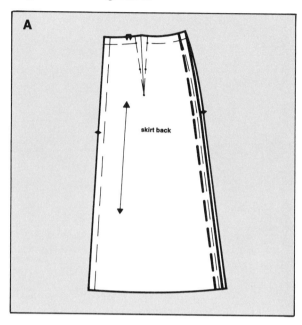

B • To increase the hipline 2 inches or less (all styles):

Divide the total increase by four and add this amount to each side seam on the skirt front and back. Taper from hipline to nothing at the waistline and from waistline to hem. Redraw cutting and stitching lines.

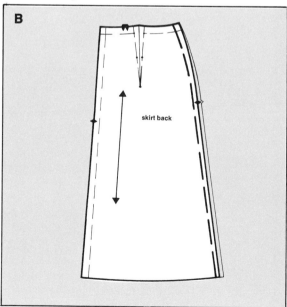

To decrease hipline more than 2 inches (princess style):

Decrease first at side seams a total of 2 inches. Subtract 2 inches from the total decrease and divide the remainder by eight. Decrease each princess seam line $\frac{1}{8}$ of remainder. Measure and mark the full width of decrease at the hipline. Redraw seam and cutting lines, tapering to nothing at waistline and holding the full width to the hemline.

To increase hipline more than 2 inches (princess style):

Increase first at side seams a total of 2 inches. Subtract 2 inches from the total increase and divide the remainder by eight. Increase each princess seam line $\frac{1}{8}$ of remainder. Measure and mark the full width of the increase at the hipline. Redraw seam and cutting lines, tapering to nothing at waistline and holding the full width to the hemline.

C • To decrease the hipline more than 2 inches (two-piece dress):

1. Near the side seam, draw a vertical line on the skirt front and back from the lower edge to the waistline.
2. At the hipline, form a lengthwise tuck on the line to decrease the hipline one-fourth the total amount. Taper the tuck to nothing at the waistline, but keep it the same width from hipline to lower edge.
3. In the side pattern section, a dart will form below the hipline. Crease and tape the dart fold.
4. Redraw the seam and cutting lines.

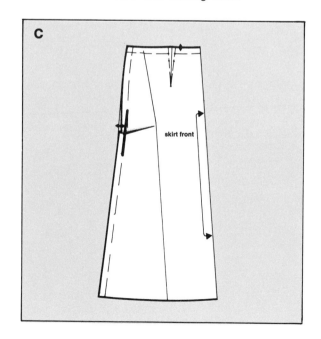

D • To increase the hipline more than 2 inches (two-piece dress):

1. Near the side seam, draw a vertical line on the skirt front and back from the lower edge to the waistline.
2. Slash on line, and place tissue underneath.
3. Keeping the grain line straight, spread the outer edge of the pattern to add the necessary width at the widest part of the hip area. (Add one-fourth the amount needed to both the skirt front and back.) Tape the entire inside edge of slash to tissue and the outside edge from waistline to hipline.
4. Hold the outside edge parallel to the inside edge of the slash from hipline to hemline. This will form a dart below the hip tapering to nothing at the side seam. Tape the outer edge to the tissue from the dart to the lower edge.
5. Add the necessary length to the hem edge to compensate for the dart.

E • To decrease hipline more than 2 inches (one-piece dress)

1. Draw a line parallel to the lengthwise grain, near the side seam on the front and back skirt, from hem edge almost to the waistline. (Do not go across darts.)
2. Use the line to form a tuck on the front and back to take up one-fourth the decrease at hipline. Taper the tuck to a point near the waistline, but keep width even from hipline to lower edge.   3. Tape tuck flat.

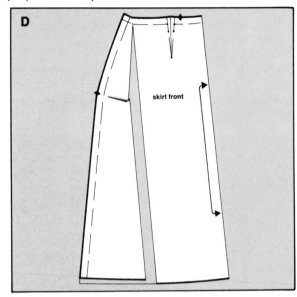

F • To increase hipline more than 2 inches (one-piece dress)

1. Draw a line parallel to the lengthwise grain on the front and back skirt, near the side seams, from hem edge almost to the waistline. (Do not go across darts.) Cut on lines.
2. Place tissue under slash. Tape the inside edge of the slash to tissue.
3. Spread the outer edge of the pattern to add the necessary width at the hipline. Add one-fourth the amount needed to both front and back sections of the skirt. Tape the outer edge to tissue.

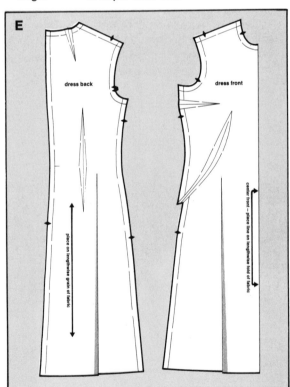

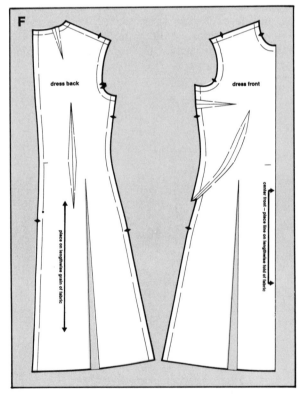

G • For large buttocks:

1. Draw a line through the center of the waist-line dart to the hemline.
2. Draw another line from the center back to the side seam line at the fullest part of the hips.
3. Slash the pattern on these lines and place the tissue underneath.
4. Spread the upper section of the pattern to add one-half the required width across the hips. Tape in place.
5. Spread the lower center section to add the desired length to the center back. Tape in place.
6. Spread the lower outside section to add length and width, then join the upper and lower sections at the seam-line edge and tape in place.
7. Form a dart below the hipline to avoid excess fullness at the hem edge. Tape in place.
8. Redraw the outside edge of the hemline. Taper from side seam to lengthwise slash.
9. Restore waistline darts to original placement.

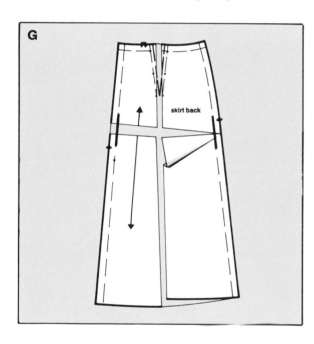

H • For flat buttocks:

1. Draw a line through the center of the waistline dart to the hemline.
2. Draw another line from the center back through the side seam at the fullest part of the hips.
3. Slash the pattern on the drawn lines and place the tissue underneath.
4. Lap the vertical slashed edges of the upper and lower sections to take up one-half of the excess width across the hips. Tape in place.
5. Then lap the upper and lower section to take out the extra length, and tape in place.

6. Redraw the hem by extending the side seam down the amount it was lapped in the hip area and taper to the center back.
7. Redraw the dart from waistline marking to original point.
8. Redraw side seam.

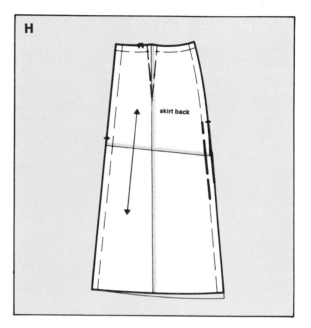

I • To adjust for a sway back

1. Slash across the skirt from the center back to the side seam line about 2 inches below the waistline.
2. Lap the slashed edges at the center back (usually about $1/2$ inch) and taper to nothing at the side seam line. Tape in place.
3. Restore the center back line and the dart.

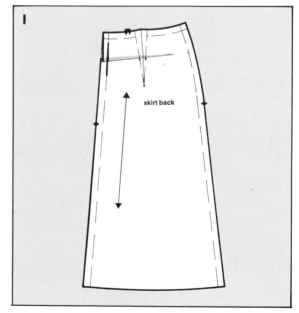

J • For one high hip:

If one hip is noticeably higher, alter the pattern as follows:

1. Cut paper duplicates of the back and front skirt patterns.
2. Transfer all construction markings.
3. Working on the front piece for the side with the high hip, make the following adjustments:
   a. Draw a line from the side of the pattern at the hipline to the point of the waistline dart nearest to the center front line.
   b. Slash on this line; place tissue paper underneath, and tape the lower edge of the slash in place.
   c. Spread the required amount, and tape the top cut edge in place.
   d. Dart out excess fullness into waistline. Extend the waistline seam at the side the same amount that was taken into this dart.
   e. Mark the new seam and cutting lines.
4. Make the same adjustment in the back piece for the side with the high hip.
5. Where the pattern pieces are cut on the fold, place the edges side by side and tape in place to make a complete skirt front or back. Do not tape the skirt sections together where a seam allowance is provided.
6. Now cut skirt back and front sections on a single thickness of fabric.

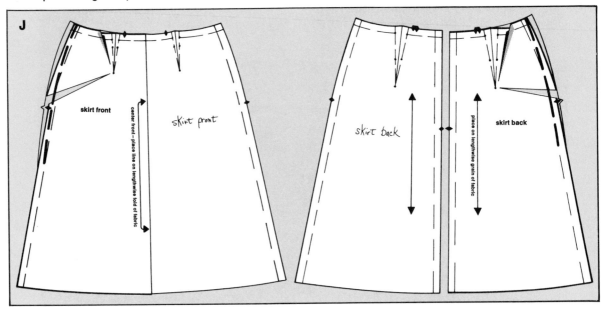

Alterations for Upper-Back and Chest Variations

A • For a broad back (plain style):

1. On the back bodice pattern, draw a vertical line, parallel to the grain line, from the shoulder, near armhole, about 10 inches long; slash on this line.
2. Place tissue under slash. Tape inside edge of slash to tissue.
3. Spread slash one-half the amount needed across back.
4. Bring shoulder edges together, forming a small dart on the outside of slash.
5. Clip armhole seam allowance opposite dart so the pattern will lie flat.
6. Tape in place.
7. Redraw the shoulder seam.

B • For a broad back (princess style):

1. From waistline to shoulder, add tissue to princess seam edges on the back and side back pattern sections; tape in place.
2. At fullest part of back, measure out from each princess seam line one-fourth the amount needed across back; mark pattern.
3. Redraw seam and cutting lines, tapering from each mark to nothing at waistline and shoulder.

C • For a broad back (modified princess style):

1. Lap and pin pattern fronts together along princess seam, seam lines coinciding.
2. Draw a line about 10 inches long, parallel to the back grain line, starting at the shoulder and extending through the princess seam into the side back.
3. Cut on this line. Place tissue under the slash and tape side nearest center back.
4. Spread slash at the fullest part of the back one-half the amount needed across back.
5. Bring edges of slash together at shoulder, forming a small dart on the armhole side of the slash at the fullest part of the back. Clip armhole seam allowance opposite dart so that the pattern will be flat.
6. Tape remainder of slash and dart in place.
7. Separate pattern sections and insert tissue where necessary.
8. Redraw shoulder, armhole, and princess seams and cutting lines.

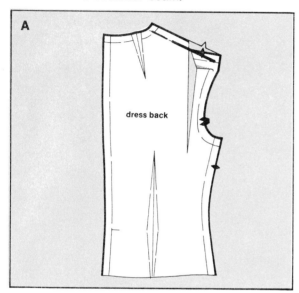

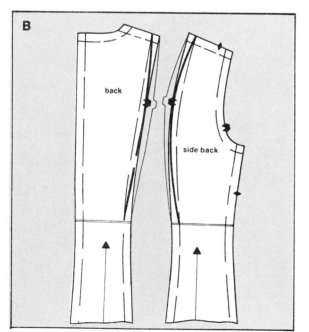

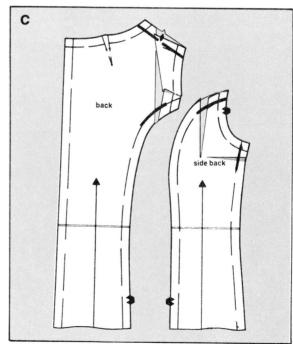

D • For round shoulders (plain style):

1. On the back pattern section, draw a line perpendicular to the grain line at the fullest part of the back; slash on the line from center back to armhole seam line.
2. Place tissue under the slash, to extend from center of back to neckline. Tape the lower edge of slash to tissue. Draw center back line straight up from taped edge of slash.
3. Raise upper section for length required and tape edge in place.
4. Add a narrow dart on shoulder to take up amount added at center back.
5. Make shoulder dart shorter. Redraw neckline.

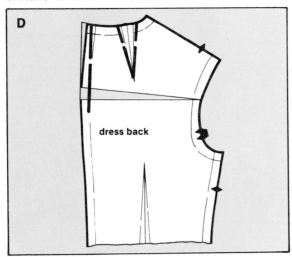

E • For round shoulders (princess style):

1. Lap and pin princess seam below the fullest part of the back, seam lines coinciding. Do not pin the seam above the fullest part of the back.
2. At the fullest point, draw a line perpendicular to the back grain line.

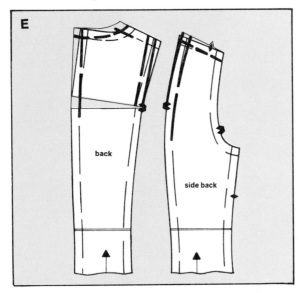

3. Slash on the line from center back to the cutting line of the princess seam. Place tissue under the entire upper part of the pattern. Tape lower edge of slash to tissue and anchor pattern to tissue at armhole.
4. As you spread the slash the amount needed, you will notice that the princess seam allowances overlap slightly more.
5. Redraw the center back seam and cutting lines at and above the slash. Add to the shoulder length at the neckline, the same amount as the pattern slash was spread. Redraw neck seam and cutting lines. Redraw the princess seam and cutting lines, decreasing each at the shoulder one-half the amount added to the shoulder length at the neckline and tapering gradually to nothing. Redraw shoulder seam and cutting lines.
6. Unpin pattern sections.

F • For round shoulders (modified princess style):

1. Draw a line perpendicular to the grain line at the fullest part of the back.
2. Slash on the line from center back to cutting line of princess seam.
3. Place tissue under the slash, tape lower edge of slash to tissue, and anchor armhole edge to tissue.
4. Spread the slash the required amount and tape upper edge of slash. A dart will form in the pattern from the end of the slash to the shoulder. Crease the dart and tape it.
5. Redraw center back seam and cutting lines. Add to the shoulder length at the neckline the same amount as the slash. Redraw neck and shoulder seam and cutting lines.

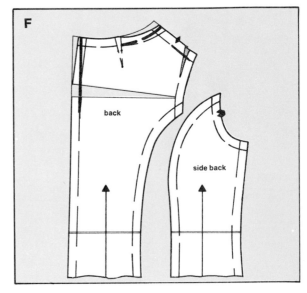

G • For a wide chest:

1. Draw a lengthwise line from center of front shoulder line to a point just above armhole notch and a horizontal line from armhole straight across to meet first line.
2. Cut on line from armhole to point and up to, but not through, shoulder line.
3. Place tissue under slash.
4. Spread vertical slash at point one-half amount to be added across chest. Tape edges to tissue.
5. Redraw shoulder and armhole seams.

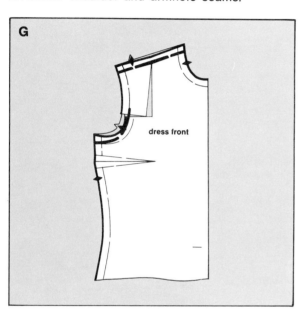

H • For a hollow chest:

1. Draw line about 4 inches below neckline from center front to armhole seam line. Cut on line.
2. Lap edges of slash amount needed to be removed at center front and taper to nothing at armhole.
3. Tape overlapped edges. Tape top of pattern to tissue.
4. Redraw center front line.
5. Trace on tissue the outline of neck, shoulder, and armhole of pattern above slash.
6. Using that as a guide, restore neckline to its original size and redraw shoulder and armhole edges.

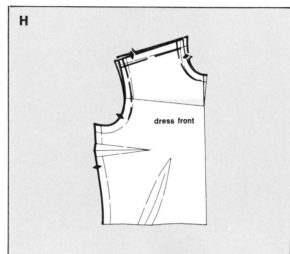

Alterations for Shoulder Variations

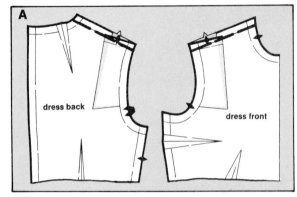

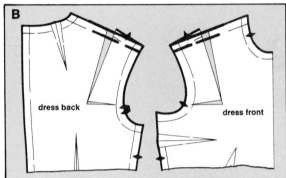

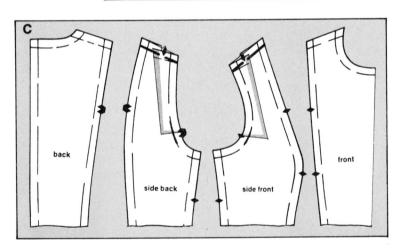

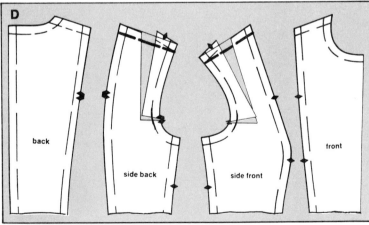

A • For narrow shoulders (plain style):

1. Draw diagonal line from shoulder line to point even with armhole notch and a horizontal line from armhole notch straight across to meet first line. Mark back and front pattern pieces.
2. Cut on line from shoulder to point and across almost to armhole notch.
3. Lap edges at shoulder seam needed amount.
4. Tape in place.
5. Redraw shoulder seam from neckline to armhole.

B • For broad shoulders (plain style):

1. Draw a diagonal line from shoulder line to a point even with armhole notch and a horizontal line from armhole notch straight across to meet first line. Mark back and front pattern pieces.
2. Cut on line from shoulder to point and across almost to armhole notch.
3. Place tissue under slash and tape inside edge of pattern to tissue.
4. Spread armhole piece needed amount and tape to tissue.
5. Redraw shoulder seam.

C • For narrow shoulders (princess style):

1. On the side front pattern at the armhole notch, draw a horizontal line, perpendicular to the grain line. From the center of the pattern section at the shoulder, draw a line parallel to the princess seam and intersect the first line.
2. Cut on the line from shoulder to horizontal line and from there to armhole cutting line.
3. Lap the slash at the shoulder the amount of the decrease and tape.
4. Redraw shoulder seam and cutting lines.
5. Alter the side back the same as the side front pattern, matching shoulder seams.

D • For broad shoulders (princess style):

1. On the side front pattern at the armhole notch, draw a horizontal line, perpendicular to the grain line. From the center of the pattern section at the shoulder, draw a line parallel to the princess seam and intersect the first line.
2. Cut on the line from shoulder to horizontal line and from there to armhole cutting line.
3. Spread the slash at the shoulder the amount of the increase; tape.
4. Redraw shoulder seam and cutting lines.
5. Alter the side back the same as the side front pattern, matching shoulder seams.

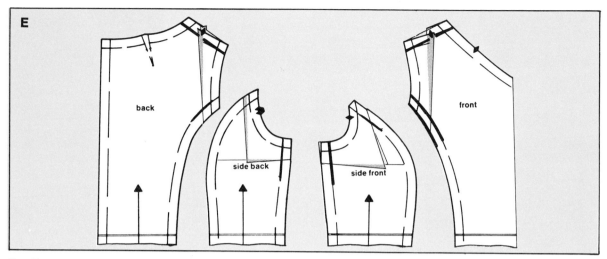

E • For narrow shoulders (modified princess style):

1. Lap and pin pattern fronts together along princess seam, seam lines coinciding.
2. Draw a horizontal line, perpendicular to the lengthwise grain line, from the underarm seam, just under the armhole, to the princess seam. Draw a vertical line, parallel to the front grain line from the shoulder to the horizontal line. Do not let the vertical line go through the armhole, but place it near the armhole.
3. Cut on the line from the shoulder to the horizontal line and from there to underarm seam's cutting line.
4. Lap the slash at the shoulder the full amount of the decrease; tape.
5. Remove pins and separate pattern sections. Add tissue and redraw shoulder and princess cutting and seam lines.
6. Alter the pattern back in the same way, matching shoulder seams.

F • For broad shoulders (modified princess style):

1. Lap and pin pattern fronts together along princess seam, seam lines coinciding.
2. Draw a horizontal line, perpendicular to the lengthwise grain line, from the underarm seam, just under the armhole, to the princess seam. Draw a vertical line parallel to the front grain line from the shoulder to the horizontal line. Do not let the vertical line go through the armhole, but place it near the armhole.
3. Cut on the line from the shoulder to the horizontal line and from there to the underarm seam's cutting line. Place tissue under the slash and tape the edge of the slash nearest center of pattern. Also tape lower edge of horizontal slash.
4. Spread slash at shoulder the full amount of the increase, letting the horizontal slash spread also. Tape remaining edges of slashes.
5. Unpin pattern sections, insert tissue where necessary and redraw shoulder and princess cutting and seam lines.
6. Alter back pattern sections in the same way, matching shoulder seams.

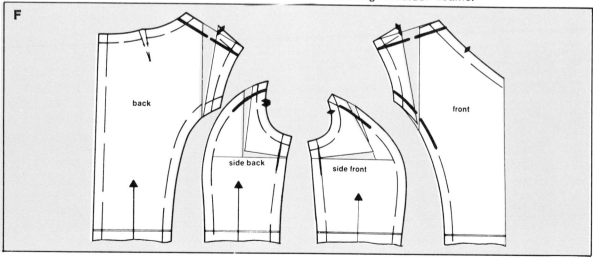

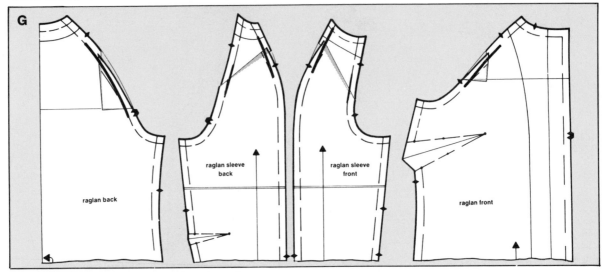

G • For narrow shoulders (raglan sleeve):

1. On a two-piece raglan-sleeve pattern, mark the midpoint of the shoulder seam between the neckline seam line and first notch. (On a one-piece raglan-sleeve pattern, mark the midpoint on the dart stitching line between the neckline seam line and point of dart.)
2. On the front pattern section, at the armhole seam above the lower notch, draw a horizontal line perpendicular to the grain line.
3. Lap and pin sleeve to armhole, above the notch, seam lines coinciding. Draw a vertical line from the midpoint mark at shoulder (step 1), parallel to the pattern front grain line, to the horizontal line (step 2).
4. Slash from the shoulder on the vertical line to the horizontal line, and from there to the cutting line of the armhole seam. Place tissue under the slash and tape the side of the vertical slash nearest the center of the pattern to the tissue. Also tape the lower edge of the vertical slash.

5. Lap the slash at the shoulder the full amount of the decrease and tape the remaining edges of the slashes.
6. Redraw the shoulder seam and cutting lines.
7. Remove pins and separate pattern sections. Redraw armhole and sleeve seams.
8. Alter the pattern back and sleeve in the same way, matching shoulder seams.

H • For broad shoulders (raglan sleeve):
Repeat steps 1, 2, 3 and 4 of alteration for narrow shoulders.
5. Spread the slash at the shoulder the full amount of the increase and tape the remaining edges of the slashes.
6. Redraw the shoulder seam and cutting lines.
7. Remove pins and separate pattern sections. Redraw armhole and sleeve seams.
8. Alter the pattern back and sleeve in the same way, matching shoulder seams.

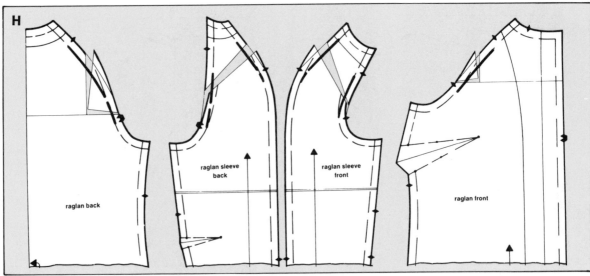

I • For square shoulders (plain style):

1. Draw a line about 2 inches from armhole parallel to grain line. Draw another line at right angle to grain line just under armhole. Mark front and back pattern pieces.
2. Cut along both lines.
3. Place tissue under pattern piece and tape inside edge of pattern to tissue.
4. Raise shoulder section the needed amount and tape to tissue.
5. Redraw shoulder and side seams.

J • For sloping shoulders (plain style):

1. Draw a line about 2 inches from armhole parallel to grain line. Draw another line at right angle to grain line just under armhole. Mark front and back pattern pieces.
2. Cut along both lines.
3. Lower shoulder needed amount.
4. Tape overlapped edges.
5. Redraw shoulder and side seams.

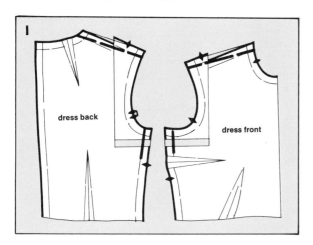

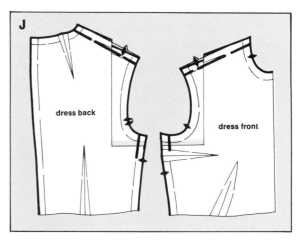

K • For square shoulders (princess style):

1. Lap and pin pattern fronts together along princess seams, seam lines coinciding.
2. Draw a horizontal line, perpendicular to the lengthwise grain line, from the underarm seam, just under the armhole to the princess seam. Draw a vertical line from the shoulder to intersect the horizontal line, positioned so that it does not pass through either the princess or armhole seams.
3. Cut on the vertical line from the shoulder to the horizontal line and from there through the underarm cutting line.
4. Place tissue under the slash and tape the body of the pattern to the tissue, leaving the cut-out armhole section free.
5. Raise the armhole section the full amount of the increase and tape in place.
6. Redraw the shoulder seam and cutting lines to form a straight line from armhole to neckline. Redraw side seam and cutting lines.
7. Remove pins and separate pattern sections. Add tissue and redraw shoulder and princess seam and cutting lines.
8. Alter pattern back sections in the same way.

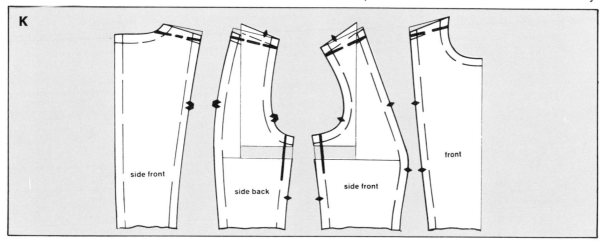

Alterations for Shoulder Variations (continued)

L • For sloping shoulders (princess style):

1. Lap and pin pattern fronts together along princess seams, seam lines coinciding.
2. Draw a horizontal line, perpendicular to the lengthwise grain line, from the underarm seam, just under the armhole to the princess seam. Draw a vertical line from the shoulder to intersect the horizontal line, positioned so that it does not pass through either the princess or armhole seams.
3. Cut on the vertical line from the shoulder to the horizontal line and from there through the underarm cutting line.
4. Lower the armhole section, overlapping the cut edges of the horizontal line but keeping the vertically cut edges abutted; tape in place.
5. Redraw the entire shoulder seam and cutting lines from neckline to armhole, adding tissue where needed.
6. Remove pins and separate pattern sections, and complete drawing of new shoulder seam and cutting lines.
7. Alter back pattern sections the same way.

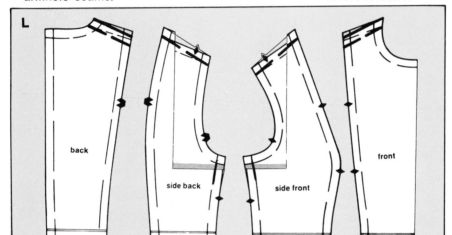

M • For square shoulders (modified princess style):

1. Lap and pin pattern fronts together along princess seam, seam lines coinciding.
2. Draw a horizontal line, perpendicular to the lengthwise grain line, from the underarm seam, just under the armhole to the princess seam. Draw a vertical line, parallel to the side-front grain line, from the shoulder to the horizontal line. Do not let the vertical line go through the armhole but place it near the armhole.
3. Cut on the line from the shoulder to the horizontal line and from there to the underarm seam's cutting line.
4. Place tissue under the slashes and tape the body of the pattern to the tissue, leaving the armhole section free.
5. Raise the armhole the needed amount at the shoulder, letting the edges of the horizontal slash separate and abutting the edges of the vertical slash; tape edges.
6. Redraw entire shoulder seam and cutting lines from neckline to armhole and redraw side seam and cutting lines.
7. Remove pins and separate pattern sections. Add tissue and redraw princess seam and cutting lines.
8. Alter pattern back in the same way, matching shoulder seams.

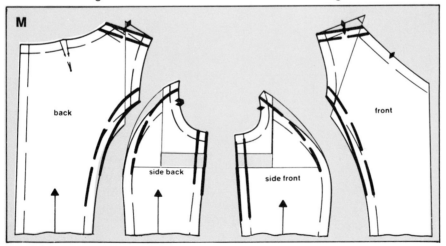

N • For sloping shoulders (modified princess style):

Repeat steps 1, 2 and 3 of alteration for square shoulders (modified princess style).

4. Lower the armhole section, overlapping the cut edges of the horizontal line, but keeping the vertically cut edges abutted; tape in place.
5. Redraw the entire shoulder seam and cutting lines from neckline to armhole, adding tissue where necessary.
6. Remove pins and separate pattern sections. Redraw new princess seam and cutting lines, adding tissue where needed.
7. Alter pattern back in the same way.

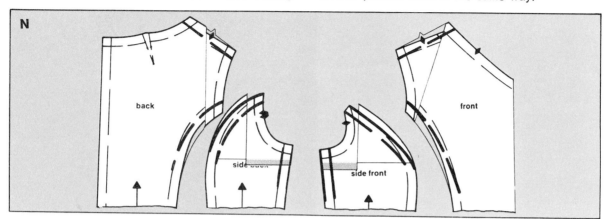

O • For square shoulders (raglan sleeve):

1. Mark shoulder point on sleeve front pattern.
2. Add tissue along shoulder and sleeve seam edges; tape in place.
3. On sleeve front pattern at the shoulder point, measure and mark the amount necessary to raise the shoulder point.
4. Redraw shoulder and sleeve seam and cutting lines from neckline through new shoulder point, tapering to the original pattern lines.
5. Make same change on the sleeve back pattern.

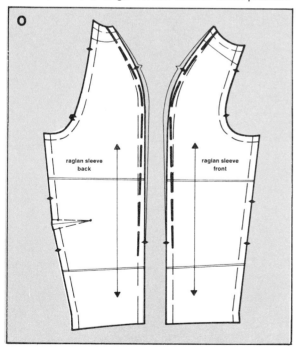

P • For sloping shoulders (raglan sleeve):

1. Mark shoulder point on sleeve front pattern.
2. At the shoulder point, measure and mark the amount necessary to lower the shoulder point.
3. Redraw shoulder and sleeve seam and cutting lines from neckline through the new shoulder point, tapering to the original pattern lines as illustrated.
4. Make the same change on the sleeve back pattern.

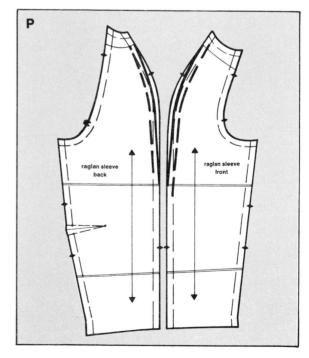

Alterations for Arm Variations

A • For a large upper arm (one-piece sleeve):

1. Trace the original sleeve cap from notch to notch on tissue paper.
2. Draw a line through center of sleeve from symbol at cap to lower edge and another line straight across cap from seam line to seam line.
3. Slash sleeve pattern on drawn lines and place tissue underneath.
4. Spread the vertical slash, adding the required extra width. Tape top of the sleeve cap seam lines together. This automatically laps the edges of the horizontal slash.
5. Redraw the sleeve cap to its original size by using the tracing you did in step 1.
6. Restore grain line.
7. Bodice front and back side seams must be altered so that sleeve fits with normal ease allowance. Add half the amount of the increased width of the sleeve to the side seam and taper to nothing at the waistline. Lower armhole notches in front and back bodice a corresponding distance.

B • For a thin arm (one-piece sleeve):

1. Draw a line parallel to the grain line from the symbol at top of sleeve cap to the wrist. On this line, make a tuck of the needed depth and tape in place.
2. On the front and back of the sleeve, raise the underarm seam one-half the amount taken up in the tuck.
3. Draw new seam and cutting lines at the top of the sleeve cap and below the notches.
4. On the front and back bodice patterns, take one-half the amount of the tuck in sleeve from the side seams at the underarm. Taper to nothing at the waistline. Draw new side seam lines, and raise the armhole seam in the same manner as you did the sleeve. Relocate armhole notches in front and back bodice, placing them the same distance from side seams as in original pattern.

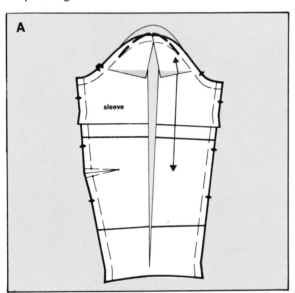

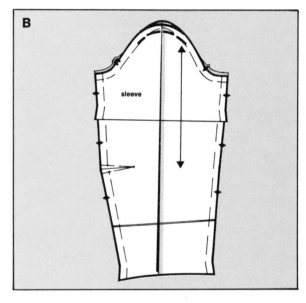

C • For large arm (one-piece sleeve):

This alteration increases the sleeve-cap seam length and therefore requires a change in the armhole.

1. Draw two horizontal lines 3 inches long, perpendicular to the lengthwise grain line; position one at each side of the sleeve, level with the sleeve-cap cutting line. At the inside end of each of these lines, draw vertical lines, parallel to the grain line, to the bottom of the sleeve pattern.
2. Slash on these lines and place tissue underneath, taping all cut edges of the center sleeve section to the tissue.
3. Spread each vertical slash at the top, one-half the increase. Tape in place.
4. Redraw seam and cutting lines at top of sleeve from notches to sleeve seam.
5. To alter the armhole of the back and front bodice, draw a vertical line parallel to the grain line from the armhole notch almost to waist line on both front and back patterns. Slash on these lines and place tissue underneath the slashes, taping the slashed edges nearest the center to the tissue.

(continued on following page)

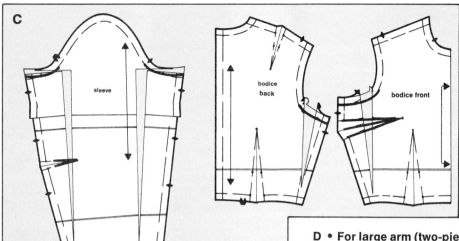

6. Spread the slashes at the armhole equally and the same width as the sleeve slashes were spread. Tape in place.
7. Redraw seam and cutting lines. Redraw darts.

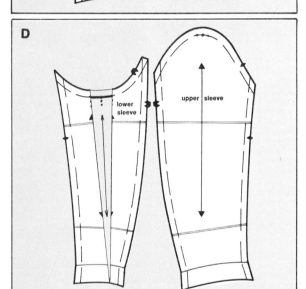

D • For large arm (two-piece sleeve):
1. At the underarm symbols on the under sleeve pattern, draw a line parallel to the grain line to the bottom of the sleeve.
2. Cut on this line from armhole to bottom of sleeve. Place tissue underneath slash.
3. Spread slash the amount of the increase and tape both edges to the tissue.
4. Redraw grain line in center of the tissue insertion. Also redraw seam and cutting lines and symbols at top of altered sleeve section.
5. Increase the armhole of the front and back patterns at the underarm seams to equal the sleeve increase.
6. To increase a two-piece sleeve more than 2 inches, apply half the increase to the upper sleeve and half to the under sleeve pattern sections. Refer to instructions for large upper arm (one-piece sleeve) opposite page.

E • For thin arm (two-piece sleeve):
1. Lap and pin the upper and under sleeve patterns at the front seam line.
2. On the upper sleeve, draw a line parallel to the grain line, from the symbol at the top of the sleeve cap to the bottom of the sleeve. Fold on this line to form a tuck one-half the width of the decrease. Tape the tuck.
3. Redraw seam and cutting lines at the sleeve cap and relocate the center symbol. Redraw the cutting line at the bottom of the sleeve.
4. On the under sleeve pattern, above the seam line at the underarm symbols, mark the location of the new armhole seam line the width of the folded tuck (one-half the total decrease). Redraw the new armhole seam and cutting lines from the mark, tapering to nothing at back and front notches.
5. Alter the back and front garment patterns, taking up one-half the total decrease from the underarm seams, and raise the armhole in the same manner as the sleeve. Relocate armhole notches to match sleeve.

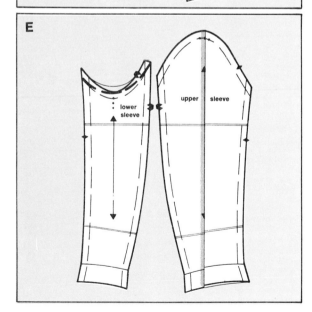

F • For a large upper arm (two-piece raglan sleeve):

1. Mark a line on the front and back sleeve patterns to indicate the position of the largest part of the arm; then measure out from each cutting line one-half the increase required; mark. Add tissue to sleeve edge if necessary.
2. Redraw new seam and cutting lines outside the original pattern lines, starting at the measured point and tapering to nothing at the shoulder notch. Again starting at the measured point and continuing to the bottom of the sleeve, mark new seam and cutting lines, keeping the amount of increase the same.
3. Alter front and back sleeve sections the same way.

G • For a thin upper arm (two-piece raglan sleeve):

1. Mark a line on the front and back sleeve patterns to indicate the position of the largest part of the upper arm; then measure in from each cutting line one-half the decrease required; mark.
2. Redraw new seam and cutting lines inside the original pattern lines, starting at the measured point and tapering to nothing at the shoulder notch. Again, starting at the measured point and continuing to the bottom of the sleeve, mark new seam and cutting lines, keeping the amount of decrease the same.
3. Alter front and back sleeve sections the same way.

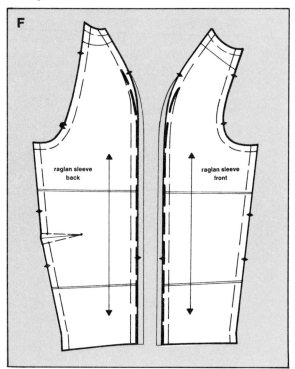

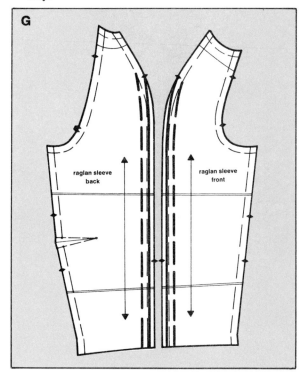

Chapter IX
reference charts

fabric, thread, needle, stitch length chart

FABRICS		THREAD		NEEDLES			STITCH LENGTH
The fabrics below can be of any fiber: cotton, linen, silk, wool, synthetic, rayon, blends. They are listed as examples of weight.		For any fabric except stretch	For wash and wear; stretch nylon, rayon, and polyester	Machine Type	Size	Hand Size	
Light-Weight	batiste jersey crepe lawn	mercerized size 70; "A" silk	Cotton-Covered Polyester Thread	Catalog 2020 (15x1)	11	9	15-20 stitches per inch
Medium-Weight	gingham pique linen wool crepe	mercerized size 60; "A" silk	3-ply nylon (if fabric is nylon)	Catalog 2020 (15x1)	14	7-9	12-15 stitches per inch
Medium-Heavy	sailcloth denim flannel suitings bonded wovens	mercerized size 50 or "heavy duty"	3-ply polyester (if fabric is polyester)	Catalog 2020 (15x1)	16	6	10-12 stitches per inch
Synthetic Knits	polyester doubleknit nylon tricot jersey bonded knits	Cotton-covered polyester thread 3-ply polyester thread 3-ply nylon thread "A" silk thread		Catalog 2045 (with yellow band) for Singer 640 *and 750 series.* Catalog 2021 for Singer machines not in 640 or 750 series (Size 11)		7-8	10-12 stitches per inch

your
measurements
chart

	Your body measurements	Minimum ease allowances		
		For Dresses	For Suit Jackets	For Coats
††To measure #1-7, stand at back, facing mirror. **1. Chest** (Take above bust and straight across back)				
†**2. Bust** (Take over fullest part of bust and straight across back)		3″	4½″ to 4¾″	5½″ to 6″
3. Bra Cup A, B, C, D, DD (Circle the letter that applies)				
4. Shoulder length (right)		NONE	¼″	⅜″
5. Shoulder to shoulder (back) (Take from armhole to armhole at shoulder seam)		¼″	⅜″ to ½″	½″ to ¾″
6. Back width (Take 3″ to 4″ below shoulder seam at back armhole)		¼″	½″	½″ to ¾″
†**7. Back waist length** (Take from neckline to waistline, center)		¼″	¼″ to ⅜″	½″
††To measure #8-10, stand in front, facing mirror. **8. Shoulder to apex of bust**		NONE	¼″	½″
9. Shoulder to waist, over apex		¼″	½″	¾″
10. Front chest (Take 3″ down from shoulder, from armhole to armhole)		¼″	¼″ to ⅜″	⅜″ to ¾″
††To measure #11, 12, 13, stand at side, facing mirror. †**11. Waistline** a. Entire		½″	3⅛″ to 4½″	4½″ to 6″
b. Side to side, back		¼″	2″	3″
c. Side to side, front		¼″	2″	3″
†**12. Hipline** a. Entire, 7″ from waistline		2″	3¼″ to 4½″	4½″ to 6″
b. Entire, 9″ from waistline		2″	3⅜″ to 4½″	5⅛″ to 6″
c. Side to side, back		1″	2″	3″
d. Side to side, front		1″	1⅜″	2⅛″
13. Arm a. Upper arm (around biceps at the fullest part of upper arm)		2″	2¾″	4″
b. Forearm (around fullest part below elbow)		1″	2½″	3½″
14. Sleeve length a. Entire (from edge of shoulder over bent elbow to desired length)		NONE	1″	1″
b. Shoulder to elbow (from center of sleeve cap at seam line to elbow)		NONE	½″	½″
15. Length a. Full (back of neck to hemline)		+ 2½″ hem	+ 2″ hem	+ 2½″ hem
b. Skirt (waistline to edge of skirt)		+ 2½″ hem	+ 2″ hem	+ 2½″ hem

BACK VIEW

FRONT VIEW

SIDE VIEW

†Transfer the above measurements to your Know Your Pattern Type and Size chart.
††Notes to person measuring.

know
your
figure
type

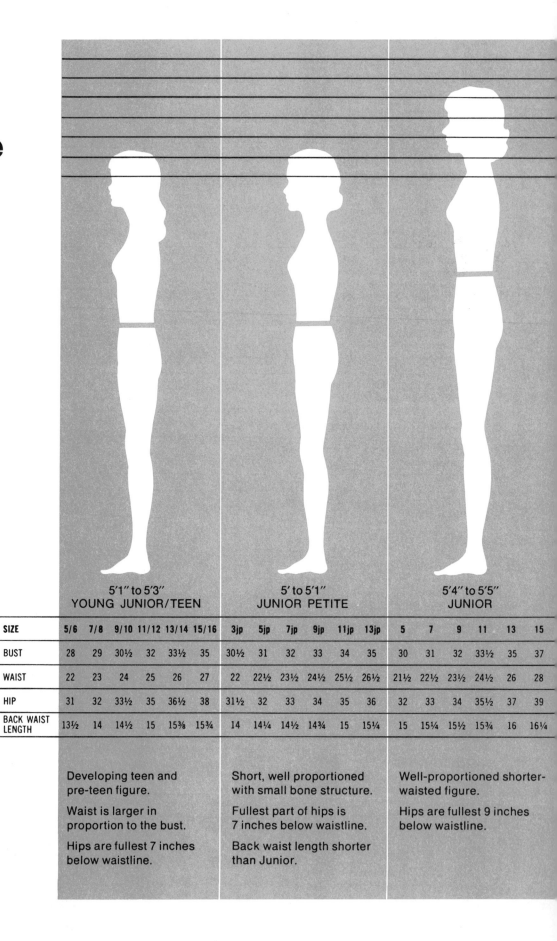

	5'1" to 5'3" YOUNG JUNIOR/TEEN						5' to 5'1" JUNIOR PETITE						5'4" to 5'5" JUNIOR					
SIZE	5/6	7/8	9/10	11/12	13/14	15/16	3jp	5jp	7jp	9jp	11jp	13jp	5	7	9	11	13	15
BUST	28	29	30½	32	33½	35	30½	31	32	33	34	35	30	31	32	33½	35	37
WAIST	22	23	24	25	26	27	22	22½	23½	24½	25½	26½	21½	22½	23½	24½	26	28
HIP	31	32	33½	35	36½	38	31½	32	33	34	35	36	32	33	34	35½	37	39
BACK WAIST LENGTH	13½	14	14½	15	15⅜	15¾	14	14¼	14½	14¾	15	15¼	15	15¼	15½	15¾	16	16¼

Developing teen and pre-teen figure.

Waist is larger in proportion to the bust.

Hips are fullest 7 inches below waistline.

Short, well proportioned with small bone structure.

Fullest part of hips is 7 inches below waistline.

Back waist length shorter than Junior.

Well-proportioned shorter-waisted figure.

Hips are fullest 9 inches below waistline.

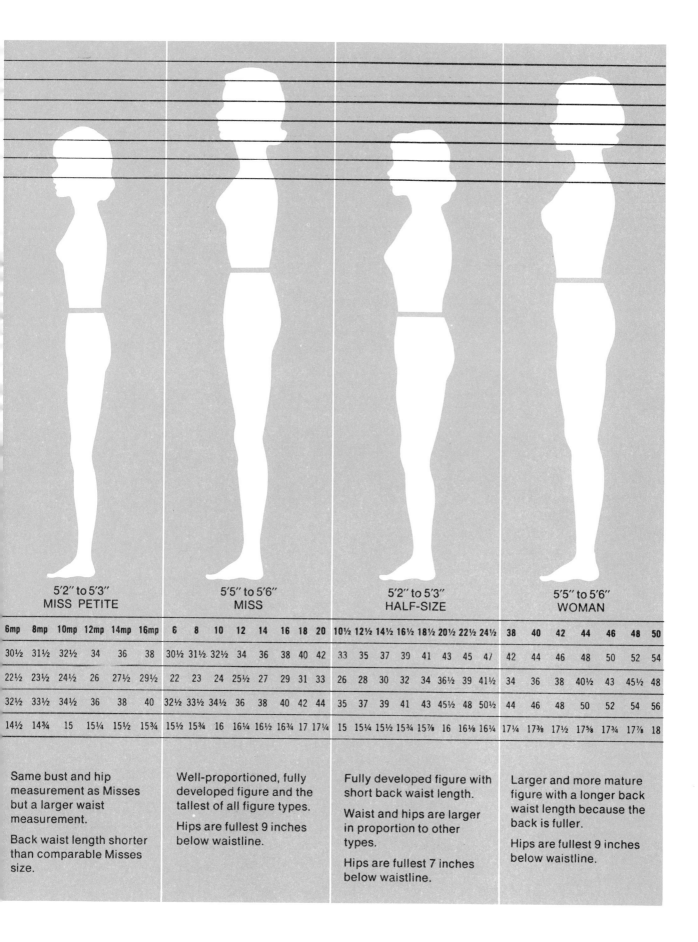

		MISS PETITE						MISS							HALF-SIZE								WOMAN					
6mp	8mp	10mp	12mp	14mp	16mp	6	8	10	12	14	16	18	20	10½	12½	14½	16½	18½	20½	22½	24½	38	40	42	44	46	48	50
30½	31½	32½	34	36	38	30½	31½	32½	34	36	38	40	42	33	35	37	39	41	43	45	47	42	44	46	48	50	52	54
22½	23½	24½	26	27½	29½	22	23	24	25½	27	29	31	33	26	28	30	32	34	36½	39	41½	34	36	38	40½	43	45½	48
32½	33½	34½	36	38	40	32½	33½	34½	36	38	40	42	44	35	37	39	41	43	45½	48	50½	44	46	48	50	52	54	56
14½	14¾	15	15¼	15½	15¾	15½	15¾	16	16¼	16½	16¾	17	17¼	15	15¼	15½	15¾	15⅞	16	16⅛	16¼	17¼	17⅜	17½	17⅝	17¾	17⅞	18

MISS PETITE — 5'2" to 5'3"

Same bust and hip measurement as Misses but a larger waist measurement.

Back waist length shorter than comparable Misses size.

MISS — 5'5" to 5'6"

Well-proportioned, fully developed figure and the tallest of all figure types.

Hips are fullest 9 inches below waistline.

HALF-SIZE — 5'2" to 5'3"

Fully developed figure with short back waist length.

Waist and hips are larger in proportion to other types.

Hips are fullest 7 inches below waistline.

WOMAN — 5'5" to 5'6"

Larger and more mature figure with a longer back waist length because the back is fuller.

Hips are fullest 9 inches below waistline.

know
your
fibers

FIBERS AND TRADE NAMES	ADVANTAGES AND SPECIAL FEATURES	USES	CARE
NATURAL **Wool**	Warm, resilient, will hold press, does not soil easily, durable, very versatile, easy to sew	Dresses, suits, coats, blankets, carpets, upholstery.	Dry-clean. Can shrink unless labeled hand washable. Must be protected from moths.
Cotton	Wrinkle resistant and absorbent, easy to sew, easily cared for, extremely durable, stands frequent laundering, easily ironed at high temperatures, inexpensive.	Dresses, suits, coats, blouses, slacks, house-hold fabrics, curtains, draperies, sheets, blankets.	Hand- or machine-wash. Machine-dry. May shrink if not pre-shrunk.
Linen	Cool, crisp, and comfort-able in warm weather; extremely durable. Retains beauty and luster through frequent hard laundering; wrinkles easily unless treated to resist wrinkles.	Women's and children's dresses and blouses; summer suiting, handker-chiefs, table linens, other household fabrics.	Hand- or machine-wash. Iron at high temperatures.
Silk	Beautiful, luxurious; comfortable to wear; strong; resilient. Naturally resistant to wrinkles and returns to shape readily; dyes well.	Light – and medium-weight clothing, accessories, upholstery and draperies.	Dry cleaning preferred. Careful hand laundry possible with some items. Protect from exposure to strong light. Can be attacked by moths.
MAN-MADE **Polyester** Dacron Fortrel Kodel Vycron Blue C Trevira	Resilient, crisp, strong, durable, stretch resistant; holds pleats and creases; resists wrinkles; dries quickly; can be blended with cotton, rayon and wool; doubleknits easy to sew.	Woven or knit: shirts, slacks, suits, blouses, dresses, lingerie, children's wear, uniforms, curtains, blankets, sheets, rugs, thread, major component of durable-press apparel.	Machine-washable, machine-dryable at low temperatures. Iron on low or synthetic setting.
Nylon Blue C Caprolan Celanese DuPont Enka Nytelle Qiana	Exceptionally strong, highly elastic, retains shape permanently, water and wind resistant, quick drying	Men's, women's and children's apparel, hosiery and socks, knitted shirts, swimwear, lingerie, sewing thread, laces, upholstery.	Machine-washable, machine-dryable at low temperatures. Iron at rayon or synthetic setting.

FIBERS AND TRADE NAMES	ADVANTAGES AND SPECIAL FEATURES	USES	CARE
MAN-MADE **Acrylic** Acrilan Creslan Zefran Zefrome	Fabrics can be crisp or springy, soft or luxurious, give warmth without weight, retain shape well.	Sweaters, slacks, skirts, dresses, suits, blankets, pile fabrics, carpets, draperies.	Machine-wash, machine-dry at low temperature; iron at rayon or synthetic setting.
Modacrylic Dynel Verel Aeress	Soft and resilient, resists wrinkles, can be processed to resemble fur in both appearance and warmth.	"Fake" fur coats, fluffy scatter rugs	Most are washable, but check bolt or hang tag for cleaning instructions.
Rayon Avril Coloray Nupron Zantrel	Soft, pliable, drapes well, takes dye well, absorbs moisture, can be finished to have drip-dry no-iron characteristics, can be blended with polyester, cotton, wool.	Light – and medium-weight clothing, drapery and upholstery fabrics, blankets, table linens, seam binding.	Launder carefully or dry-clean.
Acetate Acele Avisco Celanese Estran	Lustrous, soft, drapable; often woven into satins, taffetas, embossed with cotton and rayon.	Light – and medium-weight clothing, drapery and upholstery fabrics, backing for bonded fabrics.	Some acetate fabrics are washable, usually by hand. Check bolt or hang tag to see if dry cleaning is recommended.
Triacetate Arnel	Resists wrinkles, stretching and shrinking; holds pleats well. Absorbs little water, dries rapidly, more colorfast than acetate. Whites stay exceptionally white. Can be blended with cotton, rayon, polyester, nylon, silk and wool.	Suitings, sportswear, dresses, lingerie.	100% Arnel fabrics are completely washable, safe to iron at 425°F and wool-cotton setting.
Spandex Lycra Numa	Lighter and more durable than rubber elastic, can be made into finer threads than rubber.	Girdles, bras, bathing suits, sportswear and knits.	Hand- or machine-wash, drip-dry, do not use chlorine bleach.

coordinate your underlining and interfacing fabrics

FASHION FABRICS	DRESSMAKING-WEIGHT INTERFACINGS	TAILORING-WEIGHT INTERFACINGS	UNDERLININGS
Lightweight and medium-weight cottons and linens	Batiste, Veriform interfacing, lawn, all-bias nonwovens, SiBonne or Siri underliner	(These fashion fabrics are not suitable for tailored garments.)	Batiste, SiBonne or Siri underliner
Heavy-weight cottons and linens	Siri underliner, Veriform interfacing, all-bias nonwovens	Hair canvas, Bravo-Set interfacing	SiBonne or Siri underliner, hair canvas
Lightweight wools	Siri underliner, Veriform interfacing, all-bias nonwovens	Hair canvas, Bravo-Set or Sta-Shape interfacing	Unbleached muslin, China silk, acetate taffeta, SiBonne or Siri underliner
Medium- to heavy-weight wools	SiBonne or Siri underliner, Veriform interfacing, all-bias nonwovens	Hair canvas, Bravo or Sta-Shape interfacing	Unbleached muslin, acetate taffeta, hair canvas, Veriform interfacing, SiBonne or Siri underliner
Loosely woven fabrics and novelty weaves	SiBonne underliner, batiste, all-bias nonwovens	Hair canvas, Bravo or Sta-Shape interfacing	Acetate sheath, polyester sheath, batiste, SiBonne or Siri underliner
Knits	SiBonne underliner, batiste, all-bias nonwovens	Hair canvas, fusible canvas, Suit-Shape interfacing	Lightweight tricot, batiste, polyester sheath, acetate sheath, SiBonne or Siri underliner
Lightweight silks, rayons and crepes	Batiste, lawn, all bias nonwovens, SiBonne or Siri underliner	(These fashion fabrics are not suitable for tailored garments.)	Acetate sheath, SiBonne underliner
Polyester wovens	Batiste, all-bias nonwovens, Sibonne or Siri underliner	Hair canvas, Bravo-Set or Sta-Shape interfacing	Ciao underliner polyester sheath, SiBonne underliner
Leather— real and fake	(These fashion fabrics are not suitable for dress-weight garments.)	All-bias nonwovens, polyester nonwoven fleece, hair canvas	Unbleached muslin, Veriform interfacing, all-bias nonwovens, lightweight hair canvas
Fur— real and fake	(These fashion fabrics are not suitable for dress-weight garments.)	Hair canvas, thin felt, Veriform interfacing, cotton flannel, all-bias nonwovens, unbleached muslin	Cotton flannel, Siri underliner

pressing equipment

Iron—A combination steam and dry iron with a temperature control that indicates the proper heat setting for a wide variety of fashion fabrics.

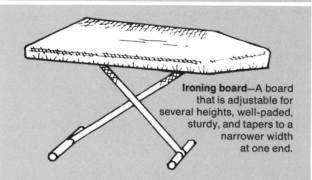

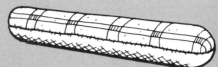

Seam roll—A long, cylindrical, firmly stuffed cushion used for pressing seams in small areas and in hard-to-reach areas such as the seams in sleeves. It prevents ridges from forming on the outside of the garment when the seams are pressed open.

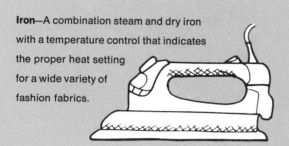

Ironing board—A board that is adjustable for several heights, well-paded, sturdy, and tapers to a narrower width at one end.

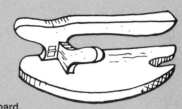

Tailor's board—A hardwood board used on top of the regular ironing board; it has a wide variety of shaped surfaces for pressing straight edges, curves, and points. The tailor's board can be used either padded or bare.

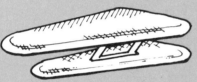

Sleeve board—A small ironing board that is used on top of a regular ironing board for pressing small areas of garments.

Pounding block or tailor's clapper—Used to flatten the edges of faced lapels and collars, hems, facings, and pleats on tailored garments made of bulky fabrics as they are steamed.

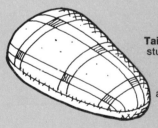

Tailor's ham—An oval, firmly stuffed cushion with rounded curves that simulate body curves, the tailor's ham is used for pressing areas that require shaping, such as darts and seams at the bustline, hips, and shoulders and for collars and lapels on tailored garments.

Velvet pressboard or needleboard—A board covered with fiber or wire needles used for pressing napped or pile fabrics without matting the surface.

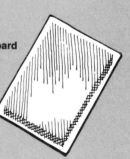

Press mitt—A padded mitten for pressing darts, the top of set-in sleeves, and curved seams where the contour and fit of the garment must be preserved. It is used either around the small end of the sleeve board or on the hand.

Press cloths—Placed between the fabric and the iron to prevent shine when the fabric is pressed, they can be used either wet or dry both with steam or dry irons. To press the full range of fabrics, three types are needed:
1. Chemically treated for pressing heavyweight fabrics.
2. Cheesecloth for pressing medium/lightweight fabrics.
3. Woven wool for top pressing.

index

NOTES

NOTES

NOTES